D1084295

Federalism: The Founders' Design

To the Memory of
James Madison
Staunch Guardian of the Founders' Design

Federalism
The Founders' Design

By Raoul Berger

University of Oklahoma Press : Norman and London

By Raoul Berger

Congress v. The Supreme Court (Cambridge, Mass., 1969)
Impeachment: The Constitutional Problems (Cambridge, Mass., 1973)
Executive Privilege: A Constitutional Myth (Cambridge, Mass., 1974)
Government by Judiciary: The Transformation of the Fourteenth Amendment (Cambridge, Mass., 1977)
Death Penalties: The Supreme Court's Obstacle Course (Cambridge, Mass., 1982)
Federalism: The Founders' Design (Norman, 1987)

Library of Congress Cataloging-in-Publication Data

Berger, Raoul, 1901–
    Federalism : the Founders' design.

    Bibliography: p.
    Includes index.
    1. Federal government—United States.   2. United
States—Constitutional law—Interpretation and
construction.   3. Judicial review—United States.
4. United States.   Supreme Court.   I. Title.
KF4600.B46   1987   342.73'042   86-40524
ISBN 0-8061-2059-2(alk. paper)   347.30242

The paper in this book meets the guidelines for permanence and durability of the Committee on Production Guidelines for Book Longevity of the Council on Library Resources, Inc.

Copyright © 1987 by the University of Oklahoma Press, Norman, Publishing Division of the University. Manufactured in the U.S.A. First edition.

Contents

Abbreviations

Berger	Raoul Berger, *Government by Judiciary: The Transformation of the Fourteenth Amendment* (1969)
Commager	Henry Steele Commager, *Documents of American History* (7th ed. 1963)
Corwin, *Commerce:*	Edward S. Corwin, *The Commerce Clause versus States Rights* (1936)
Corwin, *Twilight:*	Edward S. Corwin, *The Twilight of the Supreme Court* (1934)
Elliot	Jonathan Elliot, *Debates in the Several State Conventions on the Adoption of the Federal Constitution* (2d ed. 1836)
Farrand	Max Farrand, *The Records of the Federal Convention of 1787* (1911)
Federalist	*The Federalist* (Mod. Lib. ed. 1937)
McMaster & Stone	J. B. McMaster and F. Stone, *Pennsylvania and the Federal Constitution 1787* (1888)
Mason	Alpheus Thomas Mason, *The States Rights Debate: Antifederalism and the Constitution* (1964)
Murphy	William T. Murphy, *The Triumph of Nationalism: State Sovereignty, the Founding Fathers and the Making of the Constitution* (1967)

Poore	Ben P. Poore, *Federal and State Constitutions, Colonial Charters* (1877)
Story	Joseph Story, *Commentaries on the Constitution of the United States* (5th ed. 1905)
Wood	Gordon S. Wood, *The Creation of the American Republic 1776–1787* (1969)

Federalism: The Founders' Design

CHAPTER ONE

Introduction

Today the challenge of the Bicentennial Era is, as the Founding Fathers most commonly put it, to return to first principles.

—PAGE SMITH *

THE approaching second centennial of the Constitution invites fresh interest in a central feature—federalism, its distribution of powers between the federal government and the States. Long the subject of debate, the vast bulk of the voluminous literature has been written by political scientists, very little by legal scholars.[1] Since federalism is preeminently a constitutional issue, a lawyer, encouraged by Alpheus Thomas Mason's observation that "the States Rights debate must continue,"[2] may be indulged in scanning the sources anew. This study does not attempt a com-

* Page Smith, Dissenting Opinions 23 (1984).
[1] One of the rare books by lawyers is William T. Murphy's *The Triumph of Nationalism: State Sovereignty, the Founding Fathers, and the Making of the Constitution* (1967). "Relatively little attention has been given to the Framers' own view of federalism." Martin Diamond, "What the Framers Meant by Federalism," in *A Nation of States* 24, 25 (Robert A. Goldwin ed. 1961).
[2] Mason 194.

prehensive survey of the field, a task that would be redundant in light of detailed studies by others.[3] Instead it focuses on several problems that lie at the heart of the controversy. Nor does it consider the Supreme Court's course of adjudication, which in the case of the closely related "commerce" clause, led Edward Corwin to charge that its attitude had been "shot through with inconsistency," having competing doctrines at hand which enable it to go in either direction,[4] and leading in the result to "'a no-man's land' in which corporate enterprise was free to roam largely unchecked."[5] In consequence, he adopted as the motto of his "Commerce" monograph, "Back to the Constitution . . . the Constitution of George Washington, Alexander Hamilton, James Madison."[6] The Constitution as understood by

[3] E.g., Merrill Jensen, *The Articles of Confederation* (1940); Corwin, *Commerce;* Mason; Murphy.

[4] Corwin, *Commerce* 258, 167; Corwin, *Twilight* 117. "The precedents available to the Court as it faced the New Deal in the 1930s were rather varied, and not very consistent with each other." Christopher Wolfe, *The Rise of Modern Judicial Review* 170 (1986).

[5] Edward S. Corwin, "The Passing of Dual Federalism," 36 Va. L. Rev. 1, 22 (1950); see also Corwin, *Commerce* 152–153. "Instances have not been wanting where the concept of interstate commerce has been broadened to exclude state action, and narrowed to exclude Congressional action." Felix Frankfurter, *The Commerce Clause* 76 (1937).

[6] Corwin, *Commerce* ix. But Corwin qualifies his enthusiasm for the Constitution as envisioned by its Framers, saying "'*Back* to the Constitution'? The first requirement of the Constitution of a progressive society is that it keep pace with that society." Corwin, *Twilight* 184. What he desired was a Constitution more attuned to *his* predilections. See infra text accompanying note 8. Not long afterward, Justice Jackson, then Solicitor General, published an article entitled "Back to the Constitution," 25 A.B.A.J. 745 (1939), in which he compared the recent emergence of the constitutional text from beneath a laissez faire gloss to the rediscovery of an Old Master after the retouching brushwork of succeeding generations has been removed. Like Chief Justice Burger and Justices Frankfurter and Douglas, infra, note 7, I claim the right to look at the Constitution itself, stripped of judicial encrustations, as the index of constitutional law.

the Founders has long been my beacon, so I heartily join in Corwin's invocation of Charles Warren's statement, "However the Court may interpret the Constitution, it is still the Constitution which is the law, and not the decision of the Court."[7]

Corwin, however, unhesitatingly avowed "a sympathetic interest in the larger features of the New Deal" and sought to "link up the constitutional principles upon which the New Deal's validity would seem to depend . . . to the more congenial trends of our constitutional law and theory in the past."[8] No comparable espousal of States' Rights prompted this study; indeed, they were for long associated in my mind with Southern condonation of lynchings, with official oppression of blacks, and with demagogues who duped their constituents. My interest arose, rather, out of sheer intellectual curiosity, and my conclusions not infrequently are at war with my predilections. For the task of the historian, as Ranke enjoined, is to tell it as it was, no matter how far current thinking has departed from that of the Founders.

A field that has been so often and sedulously plowed leaves few if any new facts to be gleaned; instead controversy revolves around interpretation of the available facts.

---

[7] Corwin, *Commerce* xi. Chief Justice Burger "categorically" rejected the "thesis that what the Court said lately controls over the Constitution." Coleman v. Alabama, 399 U.S. 1, 22–23 (1970). Justice Douglas wrote that a judge "remembers above all that it is the Constitution which he swore to support and defend, not the gloss which his predecessors may have put upon it." William O. Douglas, "Stare Decisis," 49 Colum. L. Rev. 735, 736 (1949). Justice Frankfurter stated that "the ultimate touchstone of constitutionality is the Constitution itself and not what we have said about it." Graves v. O'Keefe, 306 U.S. 466, 491–492 (1939), concurring opinion. They had been anticipated by Justice Daniel in The License Cases, 46 U.S. (5 How.) 504, 612 (1847): "Nor will I abide by the decisions of judges, believed by me to be invasions of the great *lex legum*. I, too, have been sworn to observe and maintain the Constitution."

[8] Corwin, *Twilight* xxvii.

One who pores over the sources afresh may not shrink from avowing his own conclusions forthrightly. In fact, a scholar falls short who is content to launch yet another "interpretation," leaving the reader adrift on a sea of conflicting opinions.[9] Nor may he ignore a body of contrary opinions even though that may conduce to a polemical tone.[10] The "rigorous criticism," said physicist J. W. N. Sullivan, "the complete lack of indulgence, that is shown by the scientific world, is one of its most agreeable characteristics. Its one simple but devastating criterion [is] 'Is it true?'"[11] Very rarely, however, may one hope in sifting historical data to find "truth." "If we really want truth," Charles McIlwain observed, "we may be compelled to be satisfied with somewhat less than absolute demonstration."[12] Judges and lawyers long have been content to settle controversies on the preponderance of the evidence.[13] On a number of key issues the preponderance seems to be overwhelming, and it may conduce to still fur-

[9] Recently a critic complained that a researcher "state[d] all sides of a dispute without taking a stand. Very fair, to be sure, but ultimately unsatisfactory." Howard Gardner, "Book Review," New York Times, Book Review Section, July 22, 1984, at 3, 27.

[10] Charles H. McIlwain, *The High Court of Parliament and Its Supremacy* ix (1910). McIlwain explained that during the course of his study, "he came to the conclusion that the weight of contemporary evidence was against some views held by men whom I have always looked up to. . . . As these divergences . . . concerned things which are the very marrow of the subject under discussion, this has unavoidably given to certain parts of the book a polemical cast, and might lead one to think that it was written from the beginning merely to bolster up a preconceived theory. Such is not the case." Id. Before I began this study, I had a very foggy idea of the terrain covered by federalism and the commerce clause, etc.

[11] J. W. N. Sullivan, *The Limitations of Science* 173–174 (1949).

[12] Charles H. McIlwain, *The American Revolution: A Constitutional Interpretation* 64 (1923).

[13] As Judge Bruce S. Jenkins wrote: "In the pragmatic world of 'fact' the court passes judgment on the probable. Dispute resolution demands rational decision, not perfect knowledge." New York Times, May 11, 1984, A–1, A–17.

ther futile controversy to pile fact upon fact. My resort to cumulative detail at the risk of tedium[14] is intended to afford the reader a basis for comparing my inferences with his own evaluation of the facts. In other cases, e.g., the impact of the commerce clause upon federalism, the evidence, though not overwhelming, still seems to be compelling, as the reader may judge for himself. I do not expect those who start from a desired result as the "touchstone of constitutionality"[15] to be influenced by facts showing that in revising the Founders' design for federalism, the Supreme Court has usurped power the people reserved to themselves. Instead, this study is directed at those who, with Herbert Storing, do "not adopt the current cant that the fundamental law is shapeless stuff to be formed at will by future generations."[16]

At the threshold we are met by the question, why should we, at a remove of 200 years, look to the Founders for guidance; why should a nation of 220 million souls spread from ocean to ocean feel bound by an instrument fashioned for

[14] Reviewing my *Government by Judiciary,* Lord Beloff, an Oxford emeritus professor, said, "Berger is obliged to document his argument exhaustively because he is writing against what has become a rather widespread belief, namely that the Supreme Court was intended to be and is entitled to act as a continuing constitutional convention." M. Beloff, "Arbiters of American Destiny," London Times, Higher Education Supplement, April 7, 1978.

[15] Gerald Lynch regards Brown v. Board of Education, 347 U.S. 483 (1954), as "the touchstone of constitutional theory." Lynch, "Book Review," 63 Cornell L. Rev. 1091, 1099 (1978). See also Robert Cover, "Book Review," *New Republic,* January 14, 1978, at 26, 27.

Michael Perry observed of "the seminal case of *Brown* and its progeny . . . the legislative history of the fourteenth amendment clearly discloses that the Framers did not mean for the amendment to have any effect on segregated schooling." M. Perry, "Interpretivism, Freedom of Expression and Equal Protection," 42 Ohio. St. L. J. 261, 292 (1981). For documentation see Berger 117–133 (1977); R. Berger, "The Fourteenth Amendment: Light From the Fifteenth," 74 Nw. U.L. Rev. 311, 326–330 (1979).

[16] 1 Herbert Storing, *The Complete Anti-Federalist* 3 (1981).

the governance of three million people sparsely scattered along the East Coast? Why, an instrumentalist has asked, should the Founders rule us from their graves?[17] We are not, of course, "bound" by the Founders; rather the issue is who may revise the Constitution—the people by amendment or the judges,[18] who are unelected, unaccountable, and virtually irremovable. Activists long to have the Court keep the Constitution "in tune with the times," but they furnish no constitutional warrant for judicial revision.[19] Current endorsement of such revision in the context of federalism is reflected in Martin Shapiro's acceptance of the fact that "Many of the constitutional provisions that were designed by the originators of our federalism to insure its successful operation have been modified or abandoned or reduced to facades."[20] Alluding to the recent *Usery* case,[21] wherein the Court for the moment resuscitated the State sovereignty doctrine, Archibald Cox stated that though it "is almost

[17] Arthur S. Miller, "Book Review," Washington Post, November 13, 1977, $E (Book World) at 5, 8. Society, Edmund Burke observed, is a "partnership not only between those who are living, but between those who are dead, and those who are to be born." E. Burke, *Reflections on the Revolution in France* 245 (Harvard Classics, 1909).

[18] So the issue was framed by Willard Hurst in 1954. W. Hurst, "Discussion," in *Supreme Court and Supreme Law* 75 (Edmond Cahn ed. 1954).

[19] Justice Black dismissed "rhapsodical strains, about the duty of this Court to keep the Constitution in tune with the times. The idea is that the Constitution must be changed from time to time and that this Court is charged with a duty to make those changes. . . . The Constitution makers knew the need for change and provided for it" by the amendment process. Griswold v. Connectitcut, 381 U.S. 479, 522 (1965), dissenting opinion. For a withering indictment of judicial activist commentary, see Judge Robert Bork, Foreword, Gary McDowell, *The Constitution and Contemporary Constitutional Theory* (1985).

[20] Martin Shapiro, "American Federalism," 359, 362, in *Constitutional Government in America* (R. Collins ed. 1981).

[21] National League of Cities v. Usery, 426 U.S. 833 (1976).

surely consistent with the original conception of the federal union and might not have surprised any constitutional scholar prior to the 1930s, it is thoroughly inconsistent with the constitutional trends and decisions of the past forty years."[22] Such utterances suggest that the Constitution changes with shifting fashions. As a practical matter, are we "better off being bound by the dead hand of the past than being subject to the whims of willful judges trying to make the Constitution live"[23]—often in spite of the people's will?[24] More basic is the fact that after intense debate the Constitution was ratified by the people and immediately accepted as the document that would rule their destiny.[25] It remains their "civil religion."[26] No such referendum has legitimated the unwritten Constitution so dear to the revisionists.

The scope of judicial review is itself the subject of vigor-

[22] Archibald Cox, "Federalism and Individual rights under the Burger Court," 73 Nw. U.L. Rev. 1, 22 (1978). Judge Story wrote; "The policy of one age may ill suit the policy or wishes of another. The Constitution is not to be subject to such fluctuations. It is to have a fixed, uniform, permanent construction." Story §426 at 326.

[23] Mark Tushnet, "Following the Rule Laid Down: A Critique of Interpretivism and Neutral Principles," 96 Harv. L. Rev. 781, 787 (1983). He considers the argument for the "dead hand" "fairly powerful."

[24] The "most significant decisions of [the Warren] Court overturned legislation that substantial local and probably national majorities supported both in theory . . . and in practice." Mark Tushnet, "Book Review," 57 Tex. L. Rev. 1295 (1979).

[25] "[O]nce the Constitution was ratified . . . virtually everyone in America accepted it immediately as the document controlling his destiny." John H. Ely, "Constitutional Interpretation: Its Allure and Impossibility," 53 Ind. L.J. 399, 409 (1978).

[26] Paul Brest acknowledges that "the written Constitution lies at the core of the American 'civil religion.' Not only judges and other public officials, but the citizenry at large, habitually invoke the Constitution." P. Brest, "The Misconceived Quest for the Original Understanding," 60 B.U. L. Rev. 204, 234 (1980).

ous ongoing debate,[27] and it is essential to brush in some background if the role of the Founders' "original intention" is to be intelligible to the unschooled reader. The view here taken, characterized as "interpretivism," "intentionalism," or "originalism"—judges are confined to the four corners of the Constitution as explained by the Founders—is, wrote Thomas Grey, himself a revisionist, "of great power and compelling simplicity . . . deeply rooted in our history and in our shared principles of political legitimacy. It has equally deep roots in our Constitution."[28]

Fearful of the greedy lust for ever more power,[29] the Founders resorted to a written Constitution in order, Chief Justice Marshall stated, to "define and limit" the power they delegated,[30] reflected in Jefferson's urgent admonition to

[27] For an assessment of the debate see Randall Bridwell, "The Scope of Judicial Review: A Dirge for the Theorists of Majority Rule?", 31 S. C. L. Rev. 617 (1980); William Gangi, "Judicial Expansionism: An Evaluation of the Ongoing Debate," 8 Ohio N. U.L. Rev. 1 (1981); Perry, supra note 15 at 285, note 100.

[28] Thomas Grey, "Do We Have an Unwritten Constitution?", 27 Stan. L. Rev. 703, 705 (1975). Philip Kurland considers that its opposite—noninterpretivism—"makes nonsense of the concept of a written Constitution." P. Kurland, "Curia Regis: Some Comments on the Divine Right of Kings and Courts 'To Say What the Law Is,'" 23 Ariz. L. Rev. 581, 582 (1981). He calls it "deconstruction."

[29] Long before Lord Acton, Thomas Burke, a delegate from North Carolina to the Continental Congress, wrote to Governor Richard Caswell on March 11, 1777, "Power of all kinds has an irresistible propensity to increase a desire for itself . . . this is a passion which grows in proportion as it is gratified. . . . [T]he delusive intoxication which power naturally imposes on the human mind . . inevitably lead[s] to an abuse & competition of power, & is in my humble opinion the proper subject of vigilance & jealousy." 6 *Letters of Delegates to Congress, 1774–1789* 427 (P. Smith ed. 1980). Alpheus Mason noted that "America was steeped in this distrustful philosophy long before it found embodiment in the Articles of Confederation and the Constitution." Mason, supra note 2 at 8. See also Bernard Bailyn, *The Ideological Origins of the American People* 56, 57 (1967).

[30] Marbury v. Madison, 5 U.S. (1 Cranch) 137, 176 (1803).

bind the delegates "down from mischief by the chains of the
Constitution."[31] If it was to serve its purpose, the Constitution had to be "fixed," unalterable save by amendment,[32] the
more so because it expressed the *consent* of the people,[33]
who chose "to be governed," in the words of a prominent
Founder, James Iredell, "under such and such principles.
They have not chosen to be governed or promised to submit

[31] 4 Elliot 543.

[32] In his Farewell Address, Washington said that the Constitution,
"until changed by an explicit and authentic act of the whole people, is
sacredly obligatory on all." 35 G. Washington, *Writings* 224 (J. Fitzpatrick
ed. 1940). That had been earlier stated in the Federalist No. 78 at 509. See
also infra note 47.

Justice William Paterson, a framer, declared that the "Constitution is
certain and fixed . . . and can be revoked or altered only by the authority
that made it." Van Horne's Lessee v. Dorrance, 2 U.S. (2 Dall.) 304, 308
(C.C.D. Pa. 1795). In Marbury v. Madison, 5 U.S. (1 Cranch) 137, 177
(1803), Chief Justice Marshall stated that if the Constitution is not "un-
changeable by ordinary means . . . then written constitutions are absurd
attempts, on the part of the people, to limit a power, in its own nature
illimitable."

The Court repeatedly reaffirmed that view: "If in the future further
powers seemed necessary they should be granted by the people in the
manner they had provided for amending" the Constitution. Kansas v.
Colorado, 206 U.S. 46, 90 (1907). "Nothing new can be put into the Constitution except through the amendatory process. Nothing old can be
taken out without the same process." Ullman v. United States, 350 U.S.
422, 428 (1958). See also Philip Kurland, *Watergate and the Constitution* 7
(1978); infra Chapter 9 note 41.

[33] Hamilton wrote, "The fabric of American empire ought to rest on
the solid basis of THE CONSENT OF THE PEOPLE." Federalist No.
22 at 141. That was an age-old English tradition. In 1464–1470 Sir John
Fortescue wrote: "Neither can a king who is head of the body politic
change the laws thereof, nor take from the people what is theirs by right,
against their consents. For he is appointed to protect his subjects in their
lives, properties, and laws, for this very end and purpose he has the delegation of power from the people." Quoted Hippolyte A. Taine, *History of
English Literature* 154, 156 note 1 (1965). "[O]nly in America had public
consent as the basis of government attained its greatest perfection." Wood
612.

upon any other."[34] Judicial "abandonment" or revision
of the federalism the Founders designed subverts that
consent.[35]

No activist has cited constitutional authorization for judicial revision of the Constitution. That would have been,
Michael Perry justly observes, "a remarkable delegation for
politicians to grant an institution like the Supreme Court,
given the electorate's long-standing commitment to policy
making . . . by those accountable unlike the Court, to the
electorate,"[36] and particularly because, Hamilton assured
the Ratifiers, the judiciary was "next to nothing."[37] It would
also have been an unexplained departure from the long judicial tradition excluding judges from law making,[38] reiterated
by Justice James Wilson in his 1791 Lectures: the judge "will
remember that his duty and his business is, not to make the
law, but to interpret and apply it."[39] It had been proposd in

[34] 2 G. J. McRee, *Life and Correspondence of James Iredell* 146 (1958). "It
may be admitted," wrote Justice Story, "that a power given for one purpose cannot be perverted to purposes wholly opposite, or besides its legitimate scope." 2 Story, §1081, at 30.

[35] Roger Sherman stated: "The greatest security that a people can have
for the enjoyment of their rights and liberties, is that no laws can be made
to bind them . . . without their consent by representatives of their own
choosing. "H. Storing, "The 'Other' Federalist Papers," 6 Pol. Sci. Reviewer 215, 227 (1976).

[36] Michael Perry, *The Constitution, the Courts, and Human Rights* 20
(1982). Perry considers that "the principle of electorally accountable
policymaking is axiomatic; it is judicial review, not the principle, that requires justification." Id. at 9.

[37] Federalist No. 78 at 504.

[38] Francis Bacon counseled judges "to remember that their office is to
interpret the law, and not to make it." F. Bacon, *Selected Writings* 138
(Mod. Lib. ed. 1955). Blackstone condemned "arbitrary judges" whose decisions are "regulated only by their own opinions, and not by any fundamental principles of law," which "judges are bound to observe." 1 William
Blackstone, *Commentaries on the Laws of England* 269 (1765–1769).

[39] James Wilson, *Works* 502 (R. McCloskey ed. 1967). "We are to construe," said Story, "and not to frame the instrument." 1 Story, §424, at

the Convention that the Justices should participate in the legislative process by assisting the President in exercising the veto power. But that was rejected,[40] Edward Corwin summarized, on the ground that "the power of *making* ought to be kept distinct from that of *expounding* [i.e., construing] the law."[41]

Two other factors fed into this dichotomy. The Founders had a "profound fear of judicial independence and discretion,"[42] given colorful utterance by the Tory Chief Justice Hutchinson of Massachusetts: "The *Judge* should never be the *Legislator*. Because then the Will of the Judge would be the Law, and this tends to a State of Slavery."[43] Then there was the fact that judges, often unsympathetic to colonial as-

---

324. In a landmark assertion of judicial review, Justice Tucker said the court is "to expound what the law is." Kamper v. Hawkins, 1 Va. Cas. 20, 78 (Gen. Ct. 1793).

Chief Justice Taney stated, "It is the province of a Court to expound the law, not to make it." Luther v. Borden, 48 U.S. (7 How.) 1, 41, (1849). Minor v. Happersett, 88 U.S. (21 Wall.) 162, 178 (1874), per Chief Justice Waite: "Our province is to decide what the law is, not to declare what it should be."

[40] James Wilson explained that "laws may be . . . unwise, may be dangerous . . . and yet not so unconstitutional as to justify the judges in refusing to give them effect." Elbridge Gerry and Nathaniel Gorham objected that policy making was not for judges. 2 Farrand 73; 1 Farrand 97–98, 108.

[41] Edward S. Corwin, *The Doctrine of Judicial Review* 42 (1914). In Wayman v. Southard, 23 U.S. (10 Wheat.) 1, 47 (1825), Chief Justice Marshall stated, "The difference between the departments undoubtedly is that the legislature makes, the executive executes, and the judiciary construes the laws."

[42] Wood 298, 304.

[43] Morton Horwitz, "The Emergence of an Instrumental Conception of American Law 1780–1820," in 5 *Perspectives in American History* 287, 292 (1971). Hutcheson echoed Montesquieu, who was to be the oracle of the several conventions and who had written that if judges were to be the legislators, the "life and liberty of the subject would be exposed to arbitrary control." 1 Charles de Montesquieu, *The Spirit of the Laws,* book 11, chapter 6 at 181 (English trans., Philadelphia, 1802).

pirations, were saddled on the colonists by the Crown, so
that Justice Wilson did not find it surprising in 1791 that
judges "were objects of aversion and distrust."[44] To give the
last word on policy to judges, therefore, would not only
have geen a "remarkable delegation," it would have required
a repudiation of established tradition in the interest of a de-
tested judiciary. Instead, as Hamilton assured the Ratifiers,
judicial authority was confined to "certain cases *particularly
specified*. The expression of those cases marks the *precise limits* beyond which the federal courts cannot extend their jurisdiction."[45] Consequently, jurisdiction of cases "arising
under" the Constitution impliedly excludes cases that do
not arise thereunder.[46] Similarly, the Article V provision for
amendment by the people according to prescribed procedure precludes amendment by the Court.[47] Even the legislature, darling of the Founders, cannot change the Constitution, for as Madison said, "It would be a novel and
dangerous doctrine that a Legislature could change the
Constitution under which it held its existence."[48] Its at-

[44] 1 Wilson, supra note 39 at 292.

[45] Federalist No. 83 at 541 (emphasis added).

[46] This rule of construction—the unmentioned is excluded—is frequently met in the constitutional records; Wilson, in John B. McMaster
and Frederick D. Stone, *Pennsylvania and the Federal Constitution* 254
(1888); Iredell in North Carolina, 4 Elliot 220; C. C. Pinckney told the
South Carolina House of Representatives that "by delegating express
powers we certainly reserve to ourselves any power and right not mentioned." 3 Farrand 256; see also infra Chapter 4, text accompanying notes
8 and 9.

[47] Madison adverted to amendment as the "mode preferred by the
Convention" for making "alterations." Federalist No. 43 at 286. In the
Massachusetts Convention, Dr. Jarvis said that "we shall have under this
article [V] an adequate instrument for all purposes of political reforma-
tion." 2 Elliot 116. In Pennsylvania, Wilson observed that the Pennsylvania
Constitution "cannot be amended by any other mode than that which it
directs." 2 Elliot 457. See also supra note 32, and infra Chapter 9, note 41.

[48] 2 Farrand 92.

tempt to do so by enlarging the "original jurisdiction" of the Court was rejected in *Marbury v. Madison.*[49] The revisionists' extravagant rationalizations of such judicial alteration have never been iterated by the Court. Instead, as Robert Bork commented, "The Supreme Court regularly insists that its results . . . do not spring from the mere will of the Justices . . . but are supported, indeed compelled, by a proper understanding of the Constitution. . . . Value choices are attributed to the Founding Fathers, not to the Court."[50]

For a "proper understanding" of federalism, nowhere mentioned in the Constitution, we must look to the explanations of the Founders, what is characterized as the "original intention."[51] That canon of construction is centuries old, as the Court itself has pointed out, saying, "The inten-

[49] 5 U.S. (1 Cranch) 137, 177 (1803). Writing to W. C. Nicholas about the Louisiana purchase, President Jefferson said, "I had rather ask for an enlargement of power from the nation where it is found necessary, than to assume it by a power of construction which would make our power boundless." 4 Dumas Malone, *Jefferson and His Time* 318 (1970). He was persuaded by influential Senators to swallow his convictions lest ratification of the purchase be jeopardized.

[50] Robert Bork, "Neutral Principles and Some First Amendment Problems," 47 Ind. L.J. 1, 3–4 (1971). Judge Learned Hand noted that judges "wrap up their veto in a protective veil of adjectives such as 'arbitrary' . . . 'inherently,' 'fundamental,' or 'essential,' whose office usually, though quite innocently, is to disguise what they are doing, and impute to it a derivation far more impressive than their personal preferences, which are all that in fact lie behind their decision." L. Hand, *The Bill of Rights* 70 (1962). In his Apology, Socrates said that a judge "has sworn that he will judge according to the laws, and not according to his own pleasure." 2 *Harvard Classics* 22 (1909).

[51] If, wrote Madison, "the sense in which the Constitution was accepted and ratified by the Nation . . be not the guide in expounding the Constitution, there can be no security for a . . . faithful exercise of its powers." 9 James Madison, *The Writings of James Madison* 191 (G. Hunt ed. 1900–1910). He expanded on this in a letter to Andrew Stevenson, March 25, 1826:

tion of the lawmaker is the law," rising even above the text.[52] On the heels of the convention, Justice James Wilson, who had been a leading framer and Ratifier, said, "The first and governing maxim in the interpretation of a statute is, to discover the meaning of those, who made it."[53] Justice Joseph Story reiterated that "The first and fundamental rule in the interpretation of *all* instruments is, to construe them according to the sense of the terms and *the intention of the parties*."[54] Very early the Court declared that construction "must necessarily depend on the words of the constitution; the meaning and *intention of the convention which framed* and proposed it for adoption and ratification to the conventions . . . in the several states . . . to which this court has always

---

I cannot but highly approve the industry with which you have searched for a key to the sense of the Constitution, where alone the true one can be found; in the proceedings of the Convention, the contemporary expositions, and above all in the ratifying Conventions of the States. If the instrument be interpreted by criticisms which lose sight of the intention of the parties to it, in the fascinating pursuit of objects of public advantage or conveniency, the purest motives can be no security against innovations materially changing the features of the Government.

3 Farrand 473, 474.

For other Madison citations to the original understanding, see 3 Farrand 450, 464, 534; cf. id. 550. For Washington's appeal to the Journals of the Convention, see id. 371; and see infra text accompanying note 63; Raoul Berger, "Original Intention in Historical Perspective," 54 Geo. Wash. L. Rev. 101 (1986).

[52] Hawaii v. Mankichi, 190 U.S. 197, 212 (1903). *Mankichi* borrowed from Matthew Bacon, *A New Abridgement of the Laws of England,* "Statute" I(5) (3d ed. 1768): "Such construction ought to be put upon a statute, as may best answer the Intention which the Makers of it had in view." Id. See Berger, supra note 51.

[53] 1 Wilson, supra note 39 at 75.

[54] 1 Story, §400 at 305. That was accepted learning at the adoption of the Constitution. Rutherford wrote that "the end, which interpretation aims at, is to find out what was the intention of the writer, to clear up the meaning of his words." Thomas Rutherforth, *Institutes of Natural Law* 309 (1754–1756).

resorted in construing the constitution."⁵⁵ "Of course," Justice Holmes later wrote, "the purpose of written instruments is to express some intention or state of mind of those who write them, and it is desirable to make that purpose effective."⁵⁶ That is the essence of communication; it begins with the speaker who alone is entitled to say what *he* meant. No listener or reader may insist in the teeth of the speaker's own explanation that he meant exactly the opposite. Even Humpty Dumpty stopped short of maintaining that he could decide what Alice meant.⁵⁷ In fine, the Court, said Jacobus TenBroek, "has insisted, with almost uninterrupted regularity, that the end of constitutional construction is the discovery of the intention of those persons who formulated the instrument."⁵⁸ That insistence found fresh iteration only the day before yesterday.⁵⁹

Against this, activists argue that over the years words change their meaning. But that does not authorize us to saddle the Founders with *our* meaning.⁶⁰ To change the

---

⁵⁵ Rhode Island v. Massachusetts, 37 U.S. (12 Pet.) 657, 721 (1938). See also Cawley v. United States, 272 F. 2d 443, 445 (2d Cir. 1959) per Judge Learned Hand.

⁵⁶ O. W. Holmes, *Collected Legal Papers* 206 (1920).

⁵⁷ "When I use a word," Humpty Dumpty said, "it means just what *I* choose it to mean." Lewis Carroll, *Through the Looking Glass* 163 (Norton ed. 1971).

⁵⁸ Jacobus tenBroek, "Use by the Supreme Court of Extrinsic Aids in Constitutional Construction: The Intent Theory of Constitutional Construction," 27 Calif. L. Rev. 399 (1939).

⁵⁹ Cf. Immigration & Naturalization Service v. Chadha, 103 S. Ct. 2764 (1983); Marsh v. Chambers, 103 S. Ct. 3330, 3334 (1983). Henry Monaghan insists that "any theory of constitutional interpretation which renders unimportant or irrelevant questions as to original intent, *so far as that intent can be fairly discerned,* is not, given our tradition, politically or intellectually defensible." Henry Monaghan, "The Constitution Goes to Harvard," 13 Harv. C.R.-C.L.L. Rev. 117, 124 (1978).

⁶⁰ Paul Brest observed: "Suppose that the Constitution provided that some acts were to be performed "bi-weekly." At the time of the framing

meaning the words had for the Founders is to revise the provisions of the Constitution. If, declared Chief Justice Taney, "we are at liberty to give old words new meanings . . . there is no power which may not, by this mode of construction, be conferred on the general government and denied to the states,"[61] even if it spells a radical shift in the constitutional balance of power. In this, he echoed Madison: if "the sense in which the Constitution was accepted and ratified by the Nation . . . be not the guide in expounding it, there can be no security . . . for a faithful exercise of its powers."[62] And it was shared by the Reconstruction framers. In January, 1872 a unanimous Senate Judiciary Committee Report, signed by Senators who had voted for the Fourteenth Amendment, stated: "A construction which would give the phrase . . . a meaning differing from the sense in which it was understood and employed by the people when they adopted the Constitution, would be as unconstitutional as a departure from the plain and express language of the Constitution."[63] In sum, it is established learning that what the Constitution

---

of the Constitution, this meant only "once every two weeks"; but modern dictionaries bowing to pervasive misuse, now report "twice a week" (i.e., semi-weekly). To construe the definition now to mean "semi-weekly" would certainly be a change of meaning (and an improper one at that)." Paul Brest, *Processes of Constitutional Decision Making: Cases and Materials* 146 note 38 (1975).

[61] The Passenger Cases, 48 U.S. (7 How.) 238, 478 (1849) dissenting opinion.

[62] 9 Madison, supra note 51 at 191.

[63] S. Rep. No. 21, 42d Cong. 2d Sess. (1872), reprinted in Alfred Avins, *The Reconstruction Amendments Debates* 571 (1967). This was likewise the view of an eminent contemporary, Chief Justice Thomas Cooley: a court "which should allow a change in public sentiment to influence it in giving construction to a written constitution not warranted by the intention of its founders, would be justly charged with reckless disregard of official oath and public duty." Thomas Cooley, *Constitutional Limitations* 54 (1868).

meant when it left the hands of the Founders it means to-day.[64] The activists' attack on the original intention tacitly acknowledges that it precludes the changes they sought from the Court.[65]

In seeking that meaning we should be ever mindful of the admonition in five pre-1787 State constitutions to require from our magistrates a "constant observance" of "the fundamental principles of the Constitution."[66] A search for the "original intention" is faithful to "the rule of law," a central tenet of our democratic system.[67] That rule, Philip Kurland reminds us, postulates that "we are all to be governed by the same preestablished rules and not by the whim of those charged with executing those rules."[68] It was a common as-

---

[64] Cooley wrote, "A constitution is not to be made to mean one thing at one time, and another at some subsequent time when the circumstances may have changed as perhaps to make a different rule in the case seem desirable." Cooley, supra note 63 at 54. "The constitution is a written instrument. As such its meaning does not alter. That which it meant when adopted, it means now." South Carolina v. United States, 199 U.S. 437, 448 (1905). See also Hawke v. Smith, 253 U.S. 221, 227 (1920).

[65] For example, Paul Brest challenges the assumption "that judges . . . were bound by the text or original understanding of the Constitution"— this notwithstanding they are sworn to support it. Brest, supra note 65 at 224. Chief Justice Marshall asked, however, "Why does a judge swear to discharge his duties agreeably to the Constitution . . . if that Constitution forms no rule for his government?" Marbury v. Madison, 5 U.S. (1 Cranch) 137, 180 (1803). But Robert Cover tells us that the Constitution is of no moment because "we" have decided to "entrust" judges with forming an "ideology" by which legislation can be measured. Cover, supra note 15.

[66] See infra Chapter 9 note 39.

[67] All Englishmen and colonials adhered to the rule of law as a basic principle. Samuel E. Morison, *The Oxford History of the American People* 171 (1965).

[68] Philip Kurland, "Curia Regis: Some Comments on the Divine Right of Kings and Courts 'To Say What the Law Is'," 23 Ariz. L. Rev. 581, 582 (1981).

sumption of the Founders that those who govern must do so "in accordance with a known, settled, standing law."[69] They wanted no personal justice administered after the fashion of the Caliph Haroun-al-Rashid, under the shade of a tree, no conjuring of rules from a crystal ball, but rather the administration of known laws with an absolute minimum of discretion. That is what is meant by "a government of laws and not of men."

A word of explanation about what may seem a concatenation of unrelated matters; they have a common thread—their effect on State sovereignty. If the nation was established first and the States were its creation, the argument for State sovereignty is greatly weakened. If, on the other hand, the sovereign States preceded the nation, what was the effect of the Constitution to be on State sovereignty, the subject of Chapter 2? It has been argued that the Tenth Amendment was not meant to be consequential in preserving the reserved domain of the States, and that the "necessary and proper," "supremacy," and "general welfare" clauses were designed to enlarge the sphere of the federal government. The "commerce" clause is immediately relevant because the great mass of cases involving federalism arose under that clause; and finally, it is necessary to examine the impact of the Fourteenth Amendment on the Founders' design.

[69] Benjamin F. Wright, *Consensus and Continuity, 1776–1787,* at 9 (1958).

CHAPTER TWO

Nation or Sovereign States: Which Came First?

WHETHER the States were independent sovereignties before the adoption of the Constitution has long
been a subject of controversy.[1] The issue is fundamental to
States' Rights claims and therefore deserves close attention.
In sorting out the facts, it should be borne in mind that as
the debate progressed from the floor of the Convention to

[1] See Claude Van Tyne, "Sovereignty in the American Revolution: A
Historical Study," 12 Am. Hist. Rev. 529 (1907); Charles Lofgren, "The
Origins of the Tenth Amendment: History, Sovereignty, and the Problem
of Constitutional Intention," in *Constitutional Government in America*,
331, 352 note 34 (R. Collins ed. 1981). Van Tyne lists a formidable array of
commentators who consider that the Continental Congress, rather than
the States, was sovereign. Chief of these was Justice Joseph Story, who
numbers Richard Morris among his adherents. Richard Morris, "'We the
People of the United States': The Bicentennial of a People's Revolution,"
82 Am. Hist. Rev. 1 (1977). Among contemporary authorities who go the
other way are Edward S. Corwin, "The Passing of Dual Federalism, 36 Va.
L. Rev. 1, 3 (1950): "The *structural* features of our Federal System still remain what they always have been. . . . As in all federations, the union of
several autonomous political entities or 'States' for common purposes."
Max Beloff, *The American Federal Government* 15–16 (1959); S. E. Morison
and H. S. Commager, *The Growth of the American Republic* 287 (1950);
Richard A. Posner, "Toward an Economic Theory of Federal Jurisdiction," in Symposium on Federalism, 6 Harv. J. of Law & Public Policy 41
(1982); Robert Rutland, *The Ordeal of the Constitution: The Anti-Federalist
Ratification Struggle of 1787–1788*, at 4 (1965).

the arguments the Federalist addressed to the Ratifiers and then to the several Ratification Conventions, a given speaker may have changed his mind.

The authority perhaps most often cited for the separation from Great Britain as a united nation is James Wilson. In the Federal Convention he denied that "when the Colonies became independent of G. Britain, they became independent also of each other. He read the declaration of independence, observing thereon that the *United* Colonies were declared to be free & independent States; and inferring that they were independent, not *Individually* but *Unitedly.*"[2] Hamilton concurred. But, wrote Justice Story, although the colonies "owed a common allegiance" to the Crown, "they had no direct political connection with each other. Each was independent of all the others; each, in a limited sense, was sovereign within its territory. There was neither alliance nor confederacy between them."[3] In the Albany Congress of 1754, "eight of the thirteen colonies had made an attempt to agree on a plan of union for common defense" against the French and Indians, Samuel Eliot Morison recounts, but "Not one colonial assembly ratified the Plan. Every one refused to give up any part of the exclusive taxing power, even to a representative body."[4] In fact, the relations of the colonies "with one another were often unfriendly . . . as a result of rival

[2] 1 Farrand 324. Notwithstanding, Wilson said, "I don't agree that the Genl. Govt. will swallow up the state. . . . I think they must be preserved, they must be continued—our country is too extensive for a single Govt." Id. at 330. In stating that Wilson "could not admit the doctrine that when the colonies became independent of Great Britain, they became independent also of each other," William Murphy overlooks that in the Pennsylvania Convention Wilson changed his mind. Murphy 47. See infra, text accompanying note 57.

[3] 1 Story, §177 at 128. See also infra text accompanying note 16.

[4] Samuel E. Morison, *The Oxford History of the American People* 161 (1965).

land claims. Actual warfare had been prevented only by the external power of Britain."[5] The colonies were also separated by different origins and traditions,[6] and above all, by distance.

The taming of the continent's vast distances by modern technology makes it difficult today to appreciate how the primeval wilderness appeared to the colonists. Men were oppressed by the immensity of the land mass. What distance meant may be inferred from Hamilton: "several of the states, particularly New Hampshire, Connecticut and New Jersey, thought it would be difficult to send a great number of delegates *from the extremes* of the continent to the national government"[7] in Philadelphia. Of the even more distant Georgia and Carolina, it was said that "a delegate to the Congress . . . obliged to travel 700 or 800 miles . . . could scarcely have entered upon the duties of his appointment, before the year would be past."[8] When William Houston was sent from Georgia to the Continental Congress in 1785, he "thought of himself as leaving his 'country' to go to 'a strange land amongst Strangers.'"[9] Madison, who had adventured from Virginia to Princeton in New Jersey, said, "Of the affairs of Georgia I know as little as of those of Kamskatska."[10] Distance and parochialism bred suspicion. Pierce Butler asked in the Convention, "Will a man throw afloat his property & confide it to a govt. a thousand miles *distant?*" In South Carolina James Lincoln declaimed that adoption of the

[5] Merrill Jensen, *The Articles of Confederation* 117 (1940).

[6] Id. 117–118, 124.

[7] 2 Elliot 273–274 (emphasis added).

[8] John B. McMaster and Frederick D. Stone, *Pennsylvania and the Federal Constitution* 291 (1888).

[9] Carl van Doren, *The Great Rehearsal: The Story of the Making and Ratifying of the Constitution of the United States* 45 (1948).

[10] Id. 15.

Constitution meant the surrender of self-government "into the hands of a set of men who live one thousand miles distant from you."[11]

Before considering Wilson's deduction from the Declaration of Independence, it will be illuminating to examine the immediately preceding Resolution profferred by Richard Henry Lee in the Continental Congress, which was voted on July 2, 1776: "That these United Colonies are . . . free and independent States. That a plan of confederation be prepared and transmitted to the respective Colonies for their consideration and approbation."[12] Mark that the "United Colonies" were not declared to be a "United States," but instead "independent States," a result dictated by the instructions delegates had received from their States.[13] During

[11] 1 Farrand 173; 4 Elliot 313.

[12] Commager 100.

[13] Lee's resolution was compelled by the intense devotion of the States to their independence, a sentiment that found powerful expression in the Pennsylvania Constitution of 1776. The Declaration of Rights stated, "Whereas it is absolutely necessary for the welfare and safety of the inhabitants of said colonies, that they be henceforth free and independent States." 2 Poore 1540. For a similar declaration in the Massachusetts Constitution of 1780, before ratification of the Articles of Confederation, see infra, text accompanying note 80.

"We have seen," wrote Merrill Jensen, "how most of the states, in the instructions permitting their delegates in Congress to vote for independence and for a confederation, reserved to themselves the complete control of their internal affairs and particularly of their 'internal police.'" Jensen, supra note 5 at 119. As late as 1787, "None of the delegates had been empowered to strike at the core of a state supremacy. . . . Uproot state sovereignty? No." Mason 28. The sturdy insistence by the colonies on independent entities found expression in the instructions by North Carolina to the delegates to the Continental Congress to unite "in declaring Independency and forming foreign alliances, reserving to this Colony the sole and exclusive right of forming a Constitution and laws for this Colony." So too, Rhode Island cautioned its delegates to secure "its present established Form and all the powers of Government, so far as relates to its internal Police and Conduct of our own Affairs, civil and reli-

the debate it was stressed by leading figures that the colonies were "as yet perfectly independent of each other."[14] That such independence was recognized is evidenced by Lee's recommendation that "a plan of confederation" be submitted for approval by "the respective Colonies," a recommendation that flowered in the Articles of Confederation. Two days later, on July 4, Lee's Resolution was followed by the Declaration of Independence. Jefferson's original title for the Declaration was "A Declaration by the *Representatives of the United States* of America, in General Congress assembled." On July 19 an act of Congress changed it to "The unanimous Declaration of the *thirteen united States of America.*" The change from "Representatives of the United States" to "the thirteen United States" demonstrated unreadiness to forge a nation and a will to preserve the sovereignty of the States, as is confirmed by the fact that the signatories subscribed separately on behalf of each of the individual States.[15]

Justice Samuel Chase, who had been a member of the Continental Congress, declared in *Ware v. Hylton* (1796):

> I consider this a declaration, not that the united colonies jointly, in a collective capacity, were independent states, &c. but that each of them was a sovereign and independent state, that is, that each of them had a right to govern itself by its own au-

---

gious." Jensen, supra note 5 at 102. A similar instruction issued from Virginia: "the power of forming government for, and the regulations of the internal concerns of each colony, be left to the respective colonial legislatures." Murphy 17.

For comment on the instructions, see van Tyne, supra note 1 at 530, 531–532.

[14] Van Tyne, supra note 1 at 537; John Witherspoon, president of Princeton College, stated, "Every Colony is a distinct person." Jensen, supra note 5 at 143.

[15] Saul Padover, *Jefferson* 61 (1942); Commager 100, 102 (emphasis added).

thority and its own laws, without any control from any other power upon earth.[16]

These facts, to my mind, disprove Story's contention that the Declaration "was emphatically the act of the whole *people* of the united colonies."[17] The people acted severally, through the medium of their individual colonies, just as the later ratification of the Constitution was not by the people of the entire Union but by the people of the individual States.[18] Even less do the facts support Story's quotation of Charles C. Pinckney's statement that the "separate independence and individual sovereignty of the several States were *never thought of* by the enlightened band of patriots who framed this declaration."[19] Independent State sovereignty remained the object of the "patriots'" jealous regard throughout the framing of the Articles of Confederation, the Constitutional Convention, the Federalist, and the various Ratification Conventions, as will now appear.

When the Continental Congress agreed on November 15, 1777 to recommend the Articles of Confederation to the States,[20] it made the independent sovereignty of the States

[16] 3 U.S. (3 Dall.) 199, 224 (1796). See Iredell, infra text accompanying notes 124 and 125.

[17] 1 Story, §211 at 154.

[18] Article VII recites, "Done in Convention by the Unanimous Consent of the States present," and is signed on behalf of each of the individual States. Commager 145. In No. 39 of the Federalist at 247, Madison wrote, "Each State in ratifying the Constitution, is considered as a sovereign body, independent of all the others." And, "[A]ssent and ratification is to be given by the people, not as individuals composing one entire nation, but as composing the distinct and independent States to which they respectively belong. It is to be the assent and ratification of the several States." Id. at 246.

[19] 1 Story, §212 at 155 (emphasis added). In the Virginia Ratification Convention, Madison reiterated that the parties to the Constitution are "The people—but not the people as composing one great body, but the people as composing thirteen States." 3 Elliot 94.

[20] 1 Story, §224 at 164.

emphatically plain. Reciting that the members acted as the "delegates of the States affixed to our Names," they provided by Article II that "Each state retains its sovereignty, freedom and independence, and every Power . . . which is not by this confederation expressly delegated . . . to the United States, in Congress assembled."[21] In logical sequence, Article III provided that "The said states hereby *severally enter into a firm league of friendship* with each other for their common defence."[22] The drafters recited that they acted "in the name and in behalf of our *respective* constituents," not the collective "people" of the whole United States, and proceeded to sign "On the part & behalf of the State of New Hampshire," and in like fashion for each of the twelve other States.[23] This responded to an instruction by Congress in November, 1777 to its committee to draft a circular letter "requesting the States respectively to authorize their delegates to subscribe [to the Articles] in behalf of the State."[24]

The continued leading role of the States is exemplified by the Article IX provision that for the management of "the general affairs of the united states" during a recess of the Congress, it should appoint a committee "to be denominated 'a Committee of the States,' and to consist of one delegate from each state."[25] Article V provided that "Each state shall maintain [pay] its own delegates in a meeting of the states,"[26] marking them as State delegates rather than as

[21] Commager III; see also supra note 13.
[22] Commager III. In the Federal Convention, Edmund Randolph said, "Originally our confederation was founded on the weakness of each state to repel a foreign enemy." 1 Farrand 262. And Paterson said, "When independent societies confederate for mutual defence." 1 Farrand 259. Luther Martin remarked that "The federal government they formed, to defend the whole agst. foreign nations, in case of war." Id. 341.
[23] Commager 115, 116.
[24] 1 Story, §224 at 164.
[25] Commager 114.
[26] Id. 112.

members of a national Congress. The reference to a "meeting of the states" reflects the primary meaning of "congress" before the Founders employed it to designate the national legislature, namely, a "conference for the discussion or settlement of some question; *spec.* (in politics) a formal meeting of envoys, deputies or plenipotentiaries, representing sovereign states." The Continental Congresses of 1774–1776 "were properly congresses in [this] sense."[27] So it was understood by John Adams, that indefatigable organizer of the Continental Congress, who wrote in 1787 that the Confederation was "only a diplomatic assembly."[28] Claude van Tyne observed that Congress "was never forgetful that the member was there in the capacity of a diplomat from a foreign state."[29] Justifiably, Merrill Jensen concludes that "the delegates to the first Continental Congress came as ambassadors of twelve distinct nations."[30] No one, Martin Diamond states, "regarded the Articles as having created any sort of *government* at all, weak or otherwise. . . . The word government never appears in that document . . . it was . . . a

[27] *Oxford Universal Dictionary,* "Congress," subheads 6 and 7 (3d ed. 1955). Use of the term for a meeting is assigned to 1678. Parliament, Burke explained "was 'not a *congress* of ambassadors from different and hostile interests' but a deliberative assembly of a single nation." Stephen R. Graubard, *Burke, Disraeli and Churchill* 49 (1961). The word Congress "first came into use" in this sense "in the seventeenth century. . . . The adoption of the name Congress for the national legislative body in the United States . . . was simply a development from this usage; for the continental congresses . . . were, as inter-state representative deliberative bodies, analogous to international congresses." 6 *Encyclopaedia Britannica* 253 (14th ed. 1929).

[28] J. N. Rakove, *The Beginnings of National Politics* 383 (1979). Rakove considers that "before 1787 proponents of the conflicting doctrines of popular and legislative sovereignty could agree on at least one point: sovereignty was clearly not an attribute of Congress." Id. at 384.

[29] Van Tyne, supra note 1 at 542.

[30] Jensen, supra note 5 at 56.

league not a government."[31] What does clearly appear is that the delegates, deputized to act on behalf of the several States, were bent on keeping the reins of government in the States' hands. For the "Thirteen States were not yet ready to grant a federal legislature what they had refused to an imperial Parliament, or to surrender the substance of sovereignty for the shadow of union."[32]

This independent sovereignty, writ large on the face of the Articles of Confederation, was plainly recognized in the Treaty of Peace with Great Britain of September 3, 1783. By Article I, Britain "acknowledges the said United States, viz. [that is to say] New Hampshire, Massachusetts," and so down the roster, to be "sovereign and independent States," and further provides by Article V that British subjects were to be free to go to "any of the thirteen United States,"[33] signifying that Britain was treating with thirteen sovereign States,[34] not with one "unitary" nation.

Usually, Herbert Storing wrote, the Federalists "conceded the historical and legal priority of the states."[35] Certainly that was the decided sentiment in the Convention. On June 30, Gunning Bedford stated, "That all the states at present are equally sovereign and independent, has been asserted from every quarter of this house."[36] Early on, Charles

[31] Martin Diamond, "What the Framers Meant by Federalism," in *A Nation of States* 21 (R. A. Goldwin ed. 1961).

[32] Morison and Commager, supra note 1 at 258.

[33] Commager 117, 119.

[34] In the Convention, Roger Sherman considered that "our Treaties wd. be void if we change the nature of our Confederacy—they are all formed with the US of NH,M. &c." 1 Farrand 350. During the ratification process in South Carolina, Rawlins Lowndes stated, "The treaty of peace expressly agreed to acknowledge us as free, sovereign, and independent States." Cecelia Kenyon, *The Antifederalists* 178 (1966).

[35] Herbert Storing, "The 'Other' Federalist Papers: A Preliminary Sketch," 6 Pol. Sci. Rev. 215, 220 (1976); see also Murphy 148.

[36] 1 Farrand 500.

Pinckney "laid before the House . . . the draught of a federal government to be agreed upon between the free and independent States of America."[37] William Paterson said, "We are met as the deputies of 13 independent, sovereign states, for federal purposes."[38] Oliver Ellsworth observed that "in the hour of common danger" we "associated as free and independent states."[39] Referring to the "old confederation," Jonathan Dayton said, "We, as distinct societies, entered into the compact."[40] Luther Martin declared, "At the separation from the British Empire, the people of America preferred the Establishment of themselves into thirteen separate sovereignties instead of incorporating themselves into one."[41] Roger Sherman urged election of Senators by State legislatures "in order to preserve the state sovereignty."[42] The sense of the Convention emerges from Washington's letter transmitting the Constitution to Congress, drafted by the Committee on style pursuant to the Convention's instructions[43]: "it is obviously impracticable in the federal Government of these States, to secure *all* Rights of independent Sovereignty to each. . . . Individuals entering into a society *must give up a Share* of Liberty to preserve the rest."[44] The surrender of a "share" of "independent sovereignty" posits a preexisting sovereignty.

Remarks to the contrary are scarce. In addition to Wilson's above-quoted statement—he was to swing 180 degrees—Rufus King asserted that "The States were not 'sovereigns' in the sense contended by some. They did not possess the

[37] Id. 16.
[38] Id. 182. David Brearley was of the same opinion. Id. 181.
[39] Id. 475.
[40] Id. 497.
[41] Id. 340–341.
[42] Id. 204.
[43] 2 Farrand 556–557, 583.
[44] Id. 584 (emphasis added).

peculiar features of sovereignty. They could not make war, nor peace."[45] But he himself noticed that "If the States therefore retained some portion of their sovereignty, they had certainly divested themselves of essential portions of it."[46] True it is that the States had delegated several powers requiring united action to the Continental Congress, but they had taken the precaution of expressly reserving undelegated powers to themselves. Elbridge Gerry too "urged that we never were independent States, were not such now, & never could be even on the principles of the Confederation." At the same time he noted, however, that "The States & the advocates for them were intoxicated with the idea of their sovereignty."[47] And he "thought the community not yet ripe for stripping the states of their powers."[48] Commenting on the proposed congressional negative on State legislation, he said "such a power as this may enslave the States. Such an idea will never be acceded to."[49] These remarks recognize the existence of sovereign States.

Madison's frequently relied-upon utterance deserves more extended notice. According to his own notes, he

> agreed with Docr. Johnson, that the *mixed* nature of the Govt. ought to be kept in view; but thought too much stress was laid on the rank of the States as political societies. There was a gradation, he observed from the smallest corporation, with the most limited powers, to the largest empire with the most perfect sovereignty. He pointed out the *limitations on the sovereignty* of the States as now confederated. . . . Under the proposed Govt. the [power of the States] will be *much further reduced.*[50]

The notes of Richard Yates represent Madison as saying,

[45] 1 Farrand 323.
[46] Id. 324.
[47] Id. 467.
[48] Murphy 123.
[49] 1 Farrand 165.
[50] Id. 463–464 (emphasis added).

"Some contend that states are sovereign, when in fact they are only political societies. . . . The states *never possessed* the essential rights of sovereignty. These were always vested in congress."[51] In later life, Madison severely reprehended Yates, stating his version "is incredible, when it is recollected that the *second* of the Articles of Confederation emphatically declares 'that each State *retains* its *sovereignty* freedom & independence and every power &c. which is not expressly delegated to the U.S. in Congress assembled.'"[52] As a former member of the Continental Congress, Madison was little likely to overlook that reservation. Earlier in the Convention he had in fact noted that "the Union was a federal one among sovereign States."[53] But if it be assumed that Yates' notes truly reflected Madison's utterance in the Convention, Madison, like other members, felt free to change his mind,[54] and for this we must look to his subsequent statements in the Federalist and the Virginia Ratification Convention.

Preexisting State sovereignty was confirmed by Hamilton in No. 15 of the Federalist: "the concurrence of thirteen distinct sovereign wills is requisite, under the Confederation."[55] In No. 39, Madison assured the Ratifiers that "Each

[51] Id. 471. Luther Martin read Article 2 of the Articles of Confederation to the Convention on the heels of Madison's remark. Id. 468.

[52] 3 Farrand 522.

[53] 1 Farrand 37.

[54] Early in the Convention, John Rutledge counseled his colleagues to speak out forthrightly and not to suppose themselves "precluded by having frankly disclosed their opinions from afterwards changing them." Id. 65. Gouverneur Morris said his "opinion had been changed by the arguments used in this discussion." 2 Farrand 68. Madison remarked that few "did not change in the progress of discussions the opinions on important points which they carried into the Convention." 3 Farrand 455. For his admission of change on an important point—the proposed congressional negative on State legislation, see 3 Farrand 523.

[55] The Federalist at 94. And he said in No. 31 at 192, "The State governments, by their original constitutions, are invested with complete sovereignty."

State, in ratifying the Constitution, is considered to be a sovereign body, independent of all others."[56] In No. 40, Madison asked if the States would "be regarded as distinct and independent sovereigns?" and answered, "They are so regarded by the Constitution proposed."[57]

Ratifiers in the State conventions likewise recognized pre-existing State sovereignty. In Pennsylvania, Wilson, departing from his earlier remarks, referred to a country "composed of thirteen distinct and independent States," it being the task of the Federal Convention to frame a government for "thirteen independent and sovereign states."[58] His colleague, Chief Justice Thomas McKean, stated that "This system proposes a union of thirteen sovereign and independent States."[59] In Massachusetts, Bowdoin referred to "the several States" as "distinct sovereignties";[60] and Cabot assured the delegates that "the sovereignty of the individual states" was represented in the Senate. [61] In Connecticut, Oliver Ellsworth stated, "This Constitution does not attempt to coerce sovereign bodies, states, in their political capacities."[62] In New York, Livingston said, "we have thirteen distinct governments."[63] One of the foremost Federalists, James Iredell, referred in North Carolina to "thirteen governments confederated, upon a republican principle."[64] As Herbert

[56] Id. at 247.

[57] Id. at 253.

[58] McMaster & Stone 219, 218. As Justice Wilson, he later said, "in relation to the present Constitution, she [Virginia] still retains her sovereignty and independence as a State, except in the instances of express delegation to the federal government." Ware v. Hylton, 3 U.S. (3 Dall.) 199, 281 (1796).

[59] McMaster & Stone 272.

[60] 2 Elliot 129.

[61] Murphy 326.

[62] 2 Elliot 197.

[63] Id. 385.

[64] Mason 163.

Storing observed, "it is striking how widely the Federalists adopted the view of the Union as a coming together of sovereign states."[65] Subsequently, Chief Justice Marshall, who had been a member of the Virginia Ratification Convention, stated in *Gibbons v. Ogden* (1824) that prior to the adoption of the Constitution, the States "were sovereign, were completely independent, and were connected with each other only by a league."[66] Viewed against this background, the early remarks of Madison and Wilson indicate, to borrow from Robert Rutland, that the "Federalists had undoubtedly underestimated the attachment of citizens to their states,"[67] and when that fact dawned on them, they bowed before the wind.

It fell to Joseph Story to mount a vigorous attack on the independent state view, which continues to find favor with respected scholars.[68] Prior to the Declaration of Independence, he wrote: "none of the colonies were, or pretended to be, sovereign states, in the sense in which the term 'sovereign' is sometimes applied to states. . . . By 'sovereignty' in its largest sense is meant supreme, absolute, uncontrollable power."[69] The colonies, however, were "subjected, to the British Crown."[70] In the period before adoption of the Articles of Confederation, Story argues, Congress exercised "the powers of a general government, whose acts were bind-

[65] Storing, supra note 35 at 222.

[66] 22 U.S. (9 Wheat.) 1, 187 (1824). Justice Story would depreciate the force of this statement: "It is manifest that [Marshall] uses the term 'sovereign' in a very restricted sense. Under the confederation there were many [self-imposed] limitations upon the powers of the States." 1 Story, §215 at 158, note. Marshall's reference to a "league" of "completely independent" States is not so easily disposed of.

[67] Rutland, supra note 1 at 31. For evidence of such attachments, see infra Chapter 3, text accompanying notes 7–11, 17–24.

[68] E.g., Morris, supra note 1 at 12.

[69] 1 Story, §207 at 149.

[70] Id. §210 at 152.

ing on all the States." And though "they constantly admitted the States to be 'sovereign and independent communities,' yet it must be obvious that the terms were used in the subordinate and limited sense . . . since a majority of the States could by their public acts in Congress control and bind the minority."[71] What was "obvious" to Story was not apparent to the Founders. For example, Rhode Island declared its independence of Great Britain on May 4, 1776, substituted "*the authority of the governor* and Company of Rhode Island . . . for that of the King," and instructed its delegates "to cooperate with those of other colonies in *promoting confederation*."[72] Virginia also declared its independence from Great Britain on May 15, 1776, instructed its delegates to move that "the United Colonies were . . . 'independent States,'" and assented to "a confederation of all the colonies."[73] Story himself notes that on June 11, 1776, Congress resolved that there be prepared "the form of a confederation *to be entered into* between these colonies,"[74] thereby testifying that no central government existed as yet, and that steps had to be taken for its formation.

How could a nation have been called into existence when some of the colonies were not prepared to cut the umbilical cord that bound them to Britain? Story notes that the government formed by New Hampshire in December, 1775

was manifestly intended to be temporary, "during (as they said) the unhappy and unnatural contest with Great Britain." New

[71] Id. §215 at 158.

[72] Jensen, supra note 5 at 102 (emphasis added). Van Tyne instances negotiations by several States with France to borrow money, obtain arms and naval supplies. Nine States fitted out their own navies; state armies were filled by drafts, though Congress appealed for a stop to "this ruinous rivalry." Van Tyne, supra note 1 at 540–541.

[73] Jensen, supra note 5 at 103. For a similar action by North Carolina, see id. 102; for Pennsylvania and Maryland, see Murphy 16–17.

[74] 1 Story, §222 at 163; see also infra text accompanying notes 82 and 86.

Jersey too established a frame of government on the 2d of July, 1776; but it was expressly declared that it should be void upon a reconciliation with Great Britain. And South Carolina, in March 1776, adopted a constitution of government but this was, in like manner, "established until an accommodation between Great Britain and America could be obtained."[75]

Van Tyne adds that "as late as October in 1775, reconciliation is a common sentiment. . . . Even as late as January 15, 1776, Samuel Adams could not head off a motion to explain to the people that reconciliation was the desire of Congress." Still later, in February, 1776, James Wilson argued that many steps taken by Congress "could not be accounted for if their aim was an independent empire."[76] The depth of such perceptions was underlined by the New York Constitution of 1777:

> Whereas the many tyrannical and oppressive usurpations of the King and Parliament . . . on the rights and liberties of the people of the American colonies had reduced them to the necessity of introducing a government by congresses and committees, *as temporary expedients,* to exist no longer than the grievances of the people should remain without redress.[77]

Continued hope of maintaining or restoring British ties was incompatible with an intention to establish a new nation. No State, moreover, could declare independence on behalf of another.[78]

In truth, Story's reliance on abstract analysis of "sover-

[75] 1 Story, §211 at 154.
[76] Van Tyne, supra note 1 at 533.
[77] 2 Poore 1328–1329 (emphasis added).
[78] "Members of the Continental Congress recognized that independence could not be declared until the congressional delegates were authorized by their respective states to declare it, and that 'if the delegates of any particular colony had no power to declare such colony independent . . . others could not declare it for them, the colonies being as yet perfectly independent of each other.'" Murphy, supra note 13 at 16.

eignty" does not reflect the thinking of the Founders. "Whatever the limitations," Gordon Wood concluded,

> the Confederation may have placed in fact on the individual sovereignty of the states [by their own consent], few believed that their union in any theoretical sense contravened that sovereignty. As Vattel, whom many Americans read, had written in his *Law of Nations*, "several sovereign and independent states may unite themselves together by a perpetual confederacy without each in particular ceasing to be a perfect state. . . . The deliberations in common will offer no violence to the sovereignty of each member." It was this kind of confederation that the Revolutionaries intended to make in 1776, a "league of friendship."[79]

That is further evidenced by the Massachusetts Constitution of 1780, adopted while ratification of the Articles of Confederation was still in process; Article IV provided:

> The people of this commonwealth have the sole and exclusive right of governing themselves as a free, sovereign and independent State, and do, and forever hereafter shall, exercise and enjoy every power, jurisdiction, and right which is not, or may not hereafter be, by them expressly delegated to the United States of America in Congress assembled.[80]

Next Story asks, "[I]n what manner did the colonies become a nation, and in what manner did Congress become possessed of this national power?" His answer, in part, is that the Congress of 1775 "assumed at once . . . the exercise of some of the highest functions of sovereignty," such as "measures for national defence and resistance," and that these measures "could in no other manner be justified or accounted for, than upon the supposition that a national union for national purposes already existed."[81] At this junc-

[79] Wood 354–355.
[80] Article IV, 1 Poore 958.
[81] 1 Story, §§213 and 214 at 156–157. That was not the view of John Adams, a leading organizer of the Confederation. On February 4, 1777, he

ture, it should be remembered, the Congress was merely a conference of delegates from the colonies, assembled to consider a joint defense against Britain. Sitting and working together, the delegates from the thirteen colonies—who as early as June 12, 1776, proposed preparation of "the form of a confederation *to be entered into* between these colonies,"[82] and who agreed to the Articles of Confederation on November 15, 1777[83] (which were not ratified until March, 1781) assumed that they were empowered to authorize the necessary "confederated" acts pending ratification of the proposed Articles. Far removed from their constituents, forced to act on their own, the delegates acted *ex necessitate,* taking measures in the common cause. In Story's own words, "The people, relying on the wisdom and patriotism of Congress silently acquiesced in whatever authority *they assumed*."[84] Well-nigh insuperable difficulties of communication left no alternative.

Story's theory of spontaneous generation[85] collapses on his own recital of events preceding the Articles of Confederation. The Committee appointed in November, 1777 to draft "a circular letter, *requesting* the States respectively *to authorize* their delegates in Congress to subscribe [to the Articles] in behalf of the State," wrote "that to form a permanent union, accommodated to the opinions and wishes of the delegates of so many States . . . was found to be a

---

wrote, "Although we were not confederated the same principles of equity and reason should govern us as if we were united by a confederation." 6 *Letters of Delegates to Congress* 218 (P. Smith ed. 1980).

[82] 1 Story, §222 at 163 (emphasis added).

[83] Id. §224 at 164.

[84] Id. §217 at 161 (emphasis added). In November, 1830, Madison wrote that prior to ratification of the Articles of Confederation by Maryland in 1781, "the power of Congress was measured by the exigencies of war, and derived its sanction from the acquiescence of the States." 3 Farrand 483, 487.

[85] He claimed that "the union was 'spontaneously formed by the people of the United Colonies.'" Morris, supra note 1 at 12.

work in which nothing but time and reflection . . . could mature and accomplish." It adjured the States to rise "superior to local attachments" in the interest of "the general confederacy."[86] This "strong and eloquent appeal" carried "very slowly . . . to the minds of the local legislatures,"[87] Story remarks, and what "strikes us with most force is the unceasing jealousy and watchfulness everywhere betrayed in respect to the powers to be *confided* to the general government." He explains that the protracted struggle with the Crown, "the inconveniences of the restrictive legislation of the parent country" had "naturally led to a general feeling of resistance to all external authority," even to "dread of any legislation not exclusively originating in their domestic assemblies."[88] In the upshot, the Congress of the Articles, he considered, "in peace was possessed of but a delusive and shadowy sovereignty, with little more than the empty pageantry of office."[89]

In spite of all this—which speaks too plainly to require further exegesis—the delegates, on Story's reasoning, by their cooperation for defense had brought into being the very central nation that they well knew could only be erected by their States, and this despite Story's own emphasis upon the "real difficulties attendant" upon "adoption of the Articles of Confederation and perpetual union between the United States"—"even in times when the necessity of it was

[86] 1 Story, §§224–225 at 164–165 (emphasis added). "If the instructions to Congress meant anything," wrote van Tyne, "the delegates came together unauthorized by the people to act as a national government." Van Tyne, supra note 1 at 532.

[87] 1 Story, §225 at 165.

[88] Id. §224 at 173.

[89] Id. §245 at 174. Yet Story stated that the colonies "at the moment of their separation . . . were under the dominion of a superior controlling national government whose powers were vested and exercised by the general Congress with the consent of the people of all the States." Id. §214 at 157.

forced upon the minds of men not only by the common dangers . . . and by common efforts of defence."[90]

John Jay, Secretary of Foreign Affairs to the Continental Congress, better understood the state of affairs. In 1786 he considered "the thirteen independent sovereign states as having, by express delegation of power, formed and vested in Congress a perfect though limited sovereignty for the general and national purposes specified in the Confederation."[91] Were the inferences from the delegates' conduct given the effect Story attributes to them, they would yet have to yield to the limited national sovereignty expressly delineated by the Articles of Confederation. A draft by John Dickinson, submitted on July 12, 1776,[92] looking to a central government of great power, was speedily curtailed in favor of a compact between sovereign States, delegating "strictly limited powers."[93] The subject was debated until November 15, 1777, when the Articles were adopted by Congress;[94] and they were "ratified by all the States, except Delaware and Maryland, in 1778; by Delaware in 1779, and by Maryland . . . [in] 1781."[95] The delegates were therefore well aware of the circumscribed limits of their power, which they themselves had forged from July, 1776 on. It would therefore be a violent presumption that they had exceeded those limits *sub silentio*.[96]

Acknowledging that prior to the promulgation of the

[90] Id. §220 at 163.
[91] Murphy 37.
[92] 1 Story, §223 at 164.
[93] Murphy 28, 17–20.
[94] 1 Story, §224 at 164.
[95] Id. §225 at 165.
[96] Speaking of the Congresses of 1775 and 1776, Story said, "[T]he language of their [the delegates] commissions generally were sufficiently broad to embrace the right to pass measures of a national character and obligation." Id., §213 at 156.

Declaration of Independence, "some of the States had previously formed incipient governments themselves," Story explains that "it was done *in compliance* with the recommendations of Congress."[97] *Compliance* suggests submission, but that distorts the facts. As troops from the colonies gathered around Boston for its defense in 1775, Massachusetts informed the Congress that "the establishment of civil government was necessary to control the military gathering around Boston. What should be done?" It suggested that "Congress should take over . . . supervision and regulation" of the troops.[98] Since it was the New England colonies that began the war, the other colonies being dragged into the struggle, the Massachusetts Congress was reluctant "'to assume the reins of civil government' on its own authority and perhaps thereby to disrupt the unity of the Colonies." Therefore in May, 1775 it applied to the Continental Congress for the "most explicit advice, respecting the taking and exercising the powers of civil government."[99] In October, 1775 New Hampshire appealed to Congress for advice and was told to "call a full and free representation of the people, and that the representatives, *if they think it necessary,* establish such a form of government, as in their judgment will best produce the happiness of the people."[100] "Dissatisfied with the moderate piecemeal advice given to the individual colonies . . . the Whig radicals moved the Congress toward a general and decisive 'Recommendation to the People of all the States to institute Governments' [May 10, 1776]—a recommendation that would in effect drag the reluctant colonies into independence."[101] Certainly the Continental Con-

[97] Id., §211 at 153 (emphasis added).
[98] Jensen, supra note 5 at 80–81.
[99] Wood 130.
[100] Jensen, supra note 5 at 96 (emphasis added); Van Tyne, supra note 1 at 536.
[101] Wood 131.

gress entertained no illusions that its "Recommendation" issued from a sovereign who could require "compliance," for it recited that "whereas doubts have arisen whether this congress are invested with sufficient power and authority to *deliberate* and *determine* on so important a subject as *the necessity* of erecting and constituting a new form of government and internal police, to the exclusion of all foreign jurisdiction, dominion and control whatever."[102] Confronted by an agonizing decision whether to sever links with the mother country, to resist it by force of arms, it was quite natural that the individual colonies should solicit the collective wisdom of the thirteen delegations gathered in solemn conclave.

The recommendation that issued on May 15, 1776 urged the State "assemblies and conventions, 'where no Government . . . hath been hitherto established, to adopt such Government as shall, in the Opinion of the Representatives of the People [of the particular State] best conduce to the happiness and Safety of their Constituents in particular, and America in General."[103] No reference is here made to the safety of the "United Colonies" but to an amorphous "America," whereas the State's right of self-government is expressly recognized. "Recommendations" made pursuant to requests for "advice" are not the equivalent of "commands," which neither the colonies nor the States felt themselves bound to follow.[104] All this hardly adds up to a union "spontaneously formed by the people of the United Colonies,"[105] let alone that the final agreement only set up a

[102] 2 Poore 1329 (quoted in New York Constitution of 1777) (emphasis added).

[103] Morris, supra note 1 at 13.

[104] Jensen properly observes that "these requests for 'advice' were not dictated by . . . any recognition of its authority, but by motives of political expediency." Jensen, supra note 5 at 96 note 66.

[105] Supra note 85.

"league" and was signed on behalf of the individual States.[106] To my mind, the evidence does not support Richard Morris' summation:

> A review of the historical evidence makes abundantly clear . . . the process whereby the United States was created by the people in collectivity rather than by the individual states. . . . [T]he separate states, exercising a limited or internal sovereignty, may rightly be considered a creation of the Continental Congress which preceded them and brought them into being.[107]

The Story argument received fresh impetus from some ill-considered dicta of Justice George Sutherland in the

[106] Morris, however, reads such events as showing the "Congress filled the continuing power vacuum by assuming the initiative in establishing revolutionary governments in the colonies and ultimately transforming them into states." Morris, supra note 1 at 8, 12.

[107] Morris, supra note 1 at 14. See Madison, supra note 18. Jack Rakove shares Morris' conclusion and cites Samuel Beer for a similar endorsement. Rakove, supra note 28 at 173–174. Apparently Walter Berns considers that "the Union preceded the States." Berns, "Teaching the Founding of the United States," 13 Teaching Pol. Sci. 5, 7 (1985). As Rakove notes, however, "there could be little doubt that the states were a more appropriate repository for sovereignty than was the union: they elected and instructed the members of Congress, and their consent was indispensably necessary for the ratification of confederation." Id. 172. No such consent was required for the colonists' formation of States. "With the exception of a few ultranational Federalists, all the participants in the dispute over the Constitution's ratification . . . had regarded the Articles as a compact among the States as independent sovereigns, and the Confederation Congress as the agent, not the superior of the states." Jefferson Powell, "The Original Understanding of Original Intent," 98 Harv. L. Rev. 885, 928– 929 (1985).
The facts, in my judgment, confirm Jensen's view that at the time of independence, "sovereignty of the people . . . was understood to be the people organized as states, not the people organized in a nation known as the 'United States.'" Jensen, supra note 5 at 165. See also infra, text accompanying note 124. Sidney Hook observed that "What makes a thing true is not who says it, but the evidence for it." Sidney Hook, *Philosophy and Public Policy* 121 (1980). Having long pondered on the evidence herein set forth, I am content to let it speak for itself.

Curtiss-Wright case,[108] to which the Court lent further credit
in *United States v. Pink.*[109] Sutherland asserted that

> Since the states severally never possessed international powers,
> such powers could not have been carved from the mass of state
> powers but obviously were transmitted to the United States
> from some other source. . . . [T]he powers of external sover-
> eignty passed from the Crown not to the colonies severally, but
> to the colonies in their collective and corporate capacity as the
> United States. . . . Sovereignty is never held in suspense. . . .
> When, therefore, the external sovereignty of Great Britain in
> respect of the colonies ceased, it immediately passed to the
> Union. (See Penhallow v. Doane, 3 Dall. 54,80–81).[110]

Sovereignty did not pass to Congress from the Crown but
was an expressly partial grant from the States. Article IX of
the Articles of Confederation provided that "The united
states in Congress assembled shall have the sole and exclusive right of determining on peace and war . . . entering
into treaties and alliances."[111] This express grant alone undermines Sutherland's view that these powers were derived
from "some other source" than the States.

For the Founders the *people* were the sovereign. Power
flowed from them, not from the Crown to fill a vacuum.[112]
So, James Iredell said in North Carolina, "It is necessary to
particularize the powers intended *to be given* in the Constitution, as having no existence before."[113] "The people,"
Madison stated in the Convention, "were in fact the fountain of all power,"[114] Seven early State constitutions express-

[108] United States v. Curtiss-Wright Export Corp., 299 U.S. 304 (1936).
[109] 315 U.S. 202, 229 (1942).
[110] 299 U.S. at 316–317.
[111] Commager 113.
[112] Compare supra text accompanying note 72.
[113] 4 Elliot 179.
[114] 2 Farrand 476. For similar remarks by George Mason, James Iredell,
and others, see Raoul Berger, *Congress v. The Supreme Court* 173 note 199,
and pp. 174–175 (1977). See also Wood 329, 362–363, 371–372, 382–383.

ly declared that all power originates or derives from the people.[115] Wilson told the Pennsylvania Ratifiers that "the supreme power . . . *resides* in the PEOPLE, as the fountain of government. . . . They can distribute one portion to . . . State governments" and "another proportion to the government of the United States."[116]

Sutherland's reference to *Penhallow v. Doane* cites only to Justice Paterson's opinion. Paterson, however, had stated in the Convention, "The idea of a national government, as contradistinguished from a federal one, never entered into the minds of any of [the States]. . . . A confederacy supposes sovereignty in the members composing it." And he said, "We are met here as the deputies of 13 independent states."[117] It is true, as he stated in *Penhallow*, that the Continental Congress exercised the "rights and powers of war," and that the "States individually did not."[118] But, by Article IX the States had delegated the power to the Congress. As Justice Chase said in a cognate case, the very fact of such delegation by the States attests that the States must have "rightfully possessed" it.[119] In fact, the States kept the ultimate war-making decision in their own hands; Article IX provides that Congress "shall never engage in a war . . . nor appoint a commander in chief of the army or navy, unless nine states assent to the same."[120] War could only be made with the assent of the *States.*

[115] Georgia (1777), 4th whereas clause, 1 Poore 378; Maryland (1776), Declaration of Rights, Article I, 1 Poore 817; Massachusetts (1780), Declaration of Rights, Article IV, 1 Poore 958; New Hampshire (1784), Article VIII, 2 Poore 1281; North Carolina (1776), Declaration of Rights, Article I, 2 Poore 1409; Pennsylvania (1776), Declaration of Rights, Article IV, 2 Poore 1541; Virginia (1777), Bill of Rights, sec. 2, 2 Poore 1900.

[116] McMaster & Stone 316, 302.

[117] 1 Farrand 178, 182.

[118] 3 U.S. 80–81.

[119] Ware v. Hylton, 3 U.S. (3 Dall.) 199, 231 (1796).

[120] Commager 114–115.

That the States had the war-making power *ab initio* is illustrated by a resolution of the Congress on November 4, 1775:

> That the town of Charleston ought to be defended . . . and that the convention or council of safety of the colony of South Carolina, ought to pursue such measures, as to them shall seem most efficacious for that purpose, and that they proceed immediately to erect such fortifications and batteries in or near Charleston, as will best conduce to promote its security, the expence to be paid by said Colony.[121]

This was of a piece with the earlier recommendation of July 18, 1775 that the colonies lacking revolutionary committees "set them up to direct *their* defenses."[122] Other testimony that each of the colonies was thought to possess its own war-making power is furnished by the July 12, 1776 draft of the Articles of Confederation: "The said Colonies unite themselves . . . and hereby *severally enter* into a firm League of Friendship . . . binding the said Colonies *to assist one another* against all Force offered to or attacks made upon them."[123]

Justice Iredell, whose opinion in *Penhallow* went unnoticed by Sutherland, understood all this full well. Each province, he pointed out, had "composed a body politic," in no wise "connected with each other, than as being subject to the same common sovereign."[124] If Congress, he continued, "previous to the articles of confederation, possessed any authority, it was an authority . . . derived from the people of each province. . . . This authority was conveyed by each body politic separately, and not by all the people in

---

[121] 3 *Journal of the Continental Congress* 326 (1775).
[121] Morris, supra note 1 at 13 (emphasis added).
[123] 5 *Journal of the Continental Congress* 546–547 (1776) (emphasis added).
[124] 3 U.S. at 90.

the several provinces or States jointly."[125] And he concluded that the war-making authority "was not possessed by Congress unless given by all the States."[126] In this view he was joined by Justice William Cushing,[127] and both were abundantly confirmed by the specific grants of war and treaty powers to Congress in the Articles of Confederation. It is one of the curiosa of the Court's adjudications that *Curtiss-Wright* should have been based on one opinion in *Penhallow*, without mention of Iredell's and Cushing's views to the contrary, to say nothing of the historical data that buttressed their views.

In sum, the colonies, having severed their common allegiance to Great Britain, were sovereign and independent of each other. Lee's resolution of July 2, 1776, attests such independence, and it is confirmed by the Declaration of Independence signed on behalf of the thirteen separate States. That independence was explicitly safeguarded in the Articles of Confederation, which merely set up a "league," and it was further recognized in the peace treaty with Britain, signed on behalf of the thirteen individual States.

What was the impact of the Constitution on such State sovereignty? Did it "consolidate" the States into one sovereign, or did it erect a system which came to be known as "dual federalism?"

[125] Id. at 92–94.
[126] Id. at 95.
[127] Id. at 117. Cushing later referred to "a principle which is believed to be undeniable, that several States which composed the Union, so far at least as regarded their municipal regulation, became entitled, from the time when they declared themselves independent, to all the rights and powers of sovereign States." He also notes that "the constitution of New Jersey was formed previous to the general declaration of independence." McIlvaine v. Coxe, 8 U.S. (4 Cranch) 209, 212 (1808).

CHAPTER THREE

National Supremacy or Dual Sovereignty

I do not think that a credible case for federalism can be made today . . . without a credible theory about the federalism that is embedded in the Constitution. The issue of federalism will invariably raise for us the question of what is meant by fidelity to a regime of law and fidelity to the Constitution.

—PAUL BATOR*

AFTER an extended survey of the sources, William Murphy concluded that "The Convention thus had before it a clear-cut choice between two systems . . . a national system of virtually unlimited power armed with a complete and absolute supremacy over the states," and "a confederation in which the central authority had enforceable supremacy only in sharply limited areas, with the states retaining their sovereignty in all others." In his opinion, "the convention rejected the continuation of a system based on state sovereignty and decided in favor of a system based on national supremacy. It was a decision which was never changed."[1] Apparently Alpheus Mason also considers that

---

*Paul Bator, "Some Thoughts on Applied Federalism," in Symposium on Federalism, 6 Harv. J. of Law & Pub. Pol. 51, 58 (1982).

[1] Murphy 147, 148. "And because it was recognized that the Consti-

"national supremacy" was the order of the day until the advent of Chief Justice Taney, at which time the Court "switch[ed] from the doctrine of national supremacy to that of dual federalism."[2] But Madison, as will appear, explained the proposed system in terms of dual sovereignty, and that view held the boards[3] until the emergence of the "reconstructed" Court.[4]

A recent article by Martin Shapiro opens, "Any discussion of federalism in a legal context must begin with the absurdity of federalism as a legal concept. . . . The key feature of the nation state," he wrote, "was the rejection of the medieval system of multiple . . . feudal obligations and its replacement by a single political authority."[5] It is true that

tution was fatal to the sovereignty of the states, [the Convention] bypassed the state governments and went directly to the people for ratification of the great transition. There was no misunderstanding as to the effect that the Constitution would have upon state sovereignty, for in the campaign for ratification one of the principal bases of opposition to the Constitution was that it would destroy the sovereignty of the states." Id. 410. Murphy takes no account of assurances to the contrary in the Federalist and the several Ratification Conventions.

[2] Mason 189; cf. id. 52.

[3] "From the Taney Court through the heyday of the 'Four Horsemen' in the 1930's, the [Tenth] Amendment was associated with 'Dual Federalism.'" Charles A. Lofgren, "The Origins of the Tenth Amendment: History, Sovereignty, and the Problem of Constitutional Intention," in *Constitutional Government in America* 331 (R. Collins ed. 1981).

[4] So described by Justice Frankfurter in Graves v. New York *ex rel.* O'Keefe, 306 U.S. 466,487 (1939).

[5] Martin Shapiro, "American Federalism" in *Constitutional Government in America* 359 (R. Collins ed. 1981).

Gordon Wood notes that the doctrine of indivisible sovereignty "was the single most important abstraction of politics in the entire Revolutionary era. Every new institution and new idea sooner or later had to be reconciled with this powerfully persuasive assumption that there could be but one . . . supreme authority in every state to which all other authorities must be ultimately subordinate." Wood 345. See also supra, Chapter 2 text accompanying note 79.

dual sovereignty was deemed by some to be a solecism. Gouverneur Morris asserted in the Federal Convention that "in all communities there must be one supreme power, and one only," and Hamilton declared that "Two sovereignties cannot co-exist within the same limits."[6] But the intense attachment of the Founders to the sovereignty and independence of their States compelled theory to bend to political necessity. "State attachments, and State importance," said Morris, "have been the bane of this country."[7] Midway in the Convention, Washington wrote, "independent sovereignty is so ardently contended for . . . the local views of each State . . . will not yield to a more enlarged scale of politicks."[8] The fact was, as John Dickinson, a Federalist stalwart, perceived, "We cannot abolish the States and consolidate them into one Govt.—Indeed if we could I shd. be agt. it."[9] Ellsworth and George Mason expressed similar sentiments;[10] Hamilton, a proponent of a very strong central

[6] 1 Farrand 34, 258.

[7] Id. 530.

[8] 3 Farrand 51. George Read said, "Too much attachment is betrayed to the State Governments." 1 Farrand 136. In the Virginia Ratification Convention Madison said, "The people will be attached to their state legislatures from a thousand causes . . . that scale will preponderate." 3 Elliot 258. So Hamilton averred in the Federalist No. 17 at 103, and in the New York Ratification Convention, 2 Elliot 304. As late as 1836, John Quincy Adams referred to "State Sovereignties [as] feudal baronies, tenacious of their own liberty, impatient of a superior, and disdainful of a paramount Sovereign, even in the Democracy of the nation." A. Mason, "The Nature of Our Federal Union Reconsidered," 65 Pol. Sci. Q. 502, 508 (1950).

[9] 1 Farrand 159. Iredell agreed that if the proposed Constitution tended to "annihilation of the state govenment . . . it ought to excite . . . resentment and execration." 4 Elliot 53. See also Roger Sherman, 1 Farrand 350.

[10] Ellsworth remarked, "We know that the people of the states are strongly attached to their own constitutions." 1 Farrand 414. For Mason, see id. 155. Sherman "never would agree to abolish the State Governments, or render them absolutely insignificant. They were as necessary as

government, recognized that such a sweeping proposal would "shock the public opinion."[11]

Theory had to yield to political realities,[12] as Hamilton frankly recognized in Federalist No. 34: "To argue upon abstract principle that this coordinate authority [over revenue] cannot exist, is to set up supposition and theory against fact and reality."[13] In the New York Ratification Convention he met the indivisible sovereignty theory head on: "That two supreme powers cannot act together is false. They are inconsistent only when they are aimed . . . at one indivisible object."[14] But it was Wilson who triumphed over "indivisibility" by a bold takeover: conceding that ultimate authority must be centered somewhere, he proceeded from the widely accepted axiom that power resided in the people; they could distribute it to their several agents as they thought best.[15]

---

the Genl. Govt. and he would be equally careful to preserve them." 1 Farrand 340. Repeatedly the delegates insisted that the States must be preserved. Ellsworth "urged the necessity of maintaining the existence & agency of the States," id. 406, being joined by Dr. William Johnson and Hugh Williamson, who added that "The happiness of the people depended on it." Id. 407. Similar remarks were made by Madison, id. 499–500; Wilson, id. 495; Baldwin, 3 Farrand 169; and Hamilton, 2 Elliot 353.

[11] 1 Farrand 287. Symptomatic of Federalist awareness of such public opinion is Ellsworth's motion "to expunge the word *national,* in the first resolve, and to place in the room of it, *government of the United States—* which was agreed to, *nem con.*" 1 Farrand 344.

[12] The "conservatives were political realists and had to compromise with the political reality of actual state sovereignty." Merrill Jensen, *The Articles of Confederation* 245 (1940). See infra notes 64, 101.

[13] Federalist No. 34. at 203. In No. 23 at 146, Hamilton wrote, "Let us not attempt to reconcile contradictions, but firmly embrace a rational alternative."

[14] 2 Elliot 355–356.

[15] Supra, Chapter 2, text accompanying notes 115–116. Wilson observed that "all Government originates from the People," a maxim "widely accepted by almost every one." Wood 330; see also Wood 530.

Instead of denying the indivisibility of sovereignty, he relocated it in the people. Without this conception, Wilson declared, "we shall never be able to understand the principle on which this system was constructed."[16] Because the Founders' insistence on preservation of local self-government is central to the constitutional balance of power, I may be indulged for setting forth additional evidence.

The drumfire of Antifederalist charges that the proposed Constitution would create a "consolidation" as differentiated from a union of thirteen independent republics[17] forced the Federalists vigorously to disclaim such aims. Replying to such charges in the Pennsylvania Ratification Convention, Wilson said if that meant a system that "puts the thirteen United States into one, that the general government will destroy the government of the States, I will admit that such a government would not suit the people of America."[18] In North Carolina, William Davie, a delegate to the Federal Convention, said that were the Constitution to produce a consolidation, it would be "an insuperable objection";[19] and his colleague, Iredell, even more forcefully said that consolidation "ought to excite . . . resentment and execration," adding that the Convention was "averse to consolidation."[20] Wilson assured Pennsylvanians that the framers' "anxiety to preserve the State governments unimpaired . . . was their favorite object."[21] "With respect to converting the confedera-

[16] Wood 530.
[17] For a few representative examples see *The Antifederalists* 71, III, 169, 202, 239 (Cecelia M. Kenyon ed. 1966). The antifederalists believed that "the Constitution established a consolidation of previously independent states into one" wherein "the states, once sovereign, would retain only a shadow of their former power." Jackson T. Main, *The Antifederalist Critics of the Constitution* 120 (1961).
[18] McMaster & Stone 390.
[19] 4 Elliot 58.
[20] Id. 53, 133.
[21] McMaster & Stone 265.

tion to a complete consolidation," Madison told the Virginia Convention, "no such consequence will follow from the Constitution."[22] He had stated in Philadelphia, "I mean, however, to preserve the state rights with the same care, as I would trials by jury,"[23] so dear to the hearts of the Founders. "One gentleman alone (Col. Hamilton)," Dr. William Johnson stated in the Convention, "boldy and decisively contended for an abolition of the State Govts."[24] And Madison later wrote, "Certain it is that no more than two or three members of the Body, and they rather theoretically than practically were in favor of an unlimited Govt. founded on a consolidation of the States."[25]

Allied to solicitude for preservation of the States were assurances that they would only *surrender a portion* of their sovereignty to the federal government while *retaining* a considerable portion. Thus Dickinson was "for a strong national Govt. but for leaving the States a considerable agency in the System," a view repeated by General C. C. Pinckney.[26] "Whatever power may be necessary for the Natl. Govt.," said Mason, "a certain portion must necessarily be left in the States," observing later, "The United States will have a qualified sovereignty only. The individual States will retain a part of the Sovereignty."[27] Such sentiments were reiterated in the Federalist; Hamilton wrote in No. 9 that the Constitution "leaves in their possession certain exclusive and very important portions of sovereign power." He repeated in No.

[22] 3 Elliot 34.
[23] 1 Farrand 499, 500. See also James Varnum and John Brooks in Massachusetts, 2 Elliot 78, 79.
[24] 1 Farrand 355.
[25] 3 Farrand 473–474. In McCulloch v. Maryland, 17 U.S. (4 Wheat.) 315, 402 (1819), Chief Justice Marshall stated, "No political dreamer was ever wild enough to think of breaking down the lines which separate the states, and of compounding the American people in one common mass."
[26] 1 Farrand 136, 137.
[27] Id. 155; 2 Farrand 347.

32 that "the State governments would clearly retain all the rights of sovereignty which they before had, and which were not by that act, exclusively delegated to the United States."[28] "In the new government as in the old," Madison wrote in No. 40, "the general powers are limited . . . the States, in all unenumerated cases, are left in the enjoyment of their sovereign and independent jurisdiction."[29] James Bowdoin said in the Massachusetts Ratification Convention that each State would be "giving up a portion of its sovereignty, and thereby better to secure the remainder of it."[30] In forwarding the Constitution to the Governor of Connecticut, Sherman and Ellsworth explained that the granted "powers extend only to matters respecting the common interests of the union, and are specially defined, so that the particular states retain their sovereignty in all other matters."[31]

Although Gunning Bedford expostulated that "there was no middle way between a perfect consolidation and a mere confederacy,"[32] the preponderant opinion was, in Ellsworth's words, that the general government must be *partly federal and partly national.*"[33] "The truth was," said Madison in the Virginia Convention, the Constitution was "not completely consolidated, nor is it entirely federal" but "of a mixed nature."[34] Had the people believed that the Constitution

[28] Federalist No. 9 at 52; No. 32 at 194.

[29] Federalist No. 40 at 255.

[30] 2 Elliot 129. In Pennsylvania, Wilson said the "general government will take from the state governments their power in some particulars." Id. 443.

[31] 3 Farrand 99.

[32] 1 Farrand 490.

[33] Id 474.

[34] 3 Elliot 94. The delegates "accepted a mixed form, a new system combining nationalism and federalism," Benjamin F. Wright, *Consensus and Continuity, 1776–1781,* at 34 (1958).

would "'reduce the [States] to little more than geographical subdivisions of the national domain . . . it would never have been ratified."[35] In sum, as John Dickinson wrote on behalf of the Constitution, a United America required government "by a combination of republics, each retaining all the rights of supreme sovereignty, except such as ought to be contributed to the union."[36]

Today some might regard the anti-Federalist attachment to State sovereignty as already outmoded and irrational in the face of the generally conceded need in certain areas for united action on a national scale. But it was deeply rooted in human nature and the colonial experience, and it had a rational basis. Edmund Burke noted that "to be attached to the subdivision, to love the little platoon we belong to in society, is the first principle (the germ as it were) of public affection."[37] Hamilton explained in the New York Ratification Convention that "The early connections we have formed, the habits and prejudices in which we have been bred, fix our affections so strongly, that no future objects of

---

The term "federalism" originally connoted a league of confederated States in contrast to a *national* unitary sovereign. Martin Diamond, "What the Framers Meant by Federalism," in *A Nation of States* 24, 26–27 (R. A. Goldwin ed. 1961). "The politically sagacious supporters of the Constitution realized that to campaign for its ratification as 'Nationalists' might arouse the fears of many people. They shrewdly pre-empted for themselves the label Federalists, simultaneously placating popular opinion and leaving to the opponents of the Constitution the negative style of Anti-federalists." Murphy 268. For a more mordant view, see Jensen, supra note 12, at 245.

[35] Lofgren, supra note 3 at 349.

[36] 3 Farrand 304. In Federalist No. 39 at 247, Madison wrote, "Each State in ratifying the Constitution is considered as a sovereign body, independent of all others. . . . In this relation, then, the new Constitution will . . . be a *federal,* and not a *national* constitution."

[37] Edmund Burke, *Reflections on the Revolution in France* 195 (Harvard Classics 1909).

association can easily eradicate them."[38] Madison likewise recognized this "natural attachment."[39] Consequently, Judge Pendleton felt called upon to assure the Virginia Ratifiers that "Our dearest rights—life, liberty, and property—as Virginians, are still in the hands of our state legislature."[40] Some sixty years later Nathaniel Hawthorne, seeking to account for Southern sentiment during the Civil War, observed, "We inevitably limit to our own State, or at farthest, to our own little section, that sentiment of physical love for the soil."[41]

Convinced that the distant British government had oppressed them, the colonists were little minded to put their trust in a remote federal government. It will be recalled that Pierce Butler and James Lincoln feared to trust their fortunes to a government a thousand miles distant.[42] Most Americans had a "deeply rooted distrust of central power,"[43]

[38] 2 Elliot 266, 354.

[39] Federalist No. 46 at 305. Madison wrote in 1788 that "'a spirit of *locality*' permeated American politics." Wood 195.

[40] Murphy 359. In the Convention Ellsworth said, "What he wanted was domestic happiness. The Natl. Govt. could not descend to the local objects on which this depended. . . . He turned his eyes therefore for the preservation of his rights to the State Govts." 1 Farrand 492. In Federalist No. 17 at 102–103, Hamilton observed, "upon the same principle that a man is more attached to his family than to his neighborhood, to his neighborhood than to the community at large, the people of each state would be apt to feel a stronger bias towards their local governments than towards the government of the nation."

[41] Henry James, "Hawthorne," reprinted in Edmund Wilson, *The Shock of Recognition* 427, 561 (1943). Hawthorne remarked on "The anomaly of two allegiances, of which that of the State comes nearest home to a man's feelings, and includes the altar and hearth, while the General Government claims his devotion only to an airy mode of law, and has no symbol but a flag." Id. 560.

[42] Supra Chapter 2, text accompanying note 11.

[43] "The danger of the Union's falling to pieces, however great, meant little in the face of most Americans' deeply rooted distrust of power." Wood 464. See also Mason 8.

and as Benjamin Wright noted, the antifederalists "distrusted the new system because it would be remote and not so immediately subject to control."[44] Then there was the "great objection," recognized by Madison, that "the Genl. Govt. could not extend its care to all the minute objects which fall within the cognizance of the local jurisdictions."[45] To this may be added the conviction that "those closest to the matter to be dealt with best knew what ought to be done."[46] Local government, it was felt, would be more responsive to and controllable by the people; it "could be kept under closer observation."[47] The antifederalists were convinced that "a remote, impersonal government could scarcely be democratic in tone."[48] A critic of antifederalism, Cecelia Kenyon, acknowledged that "there was a healthy toughness in the Anti-Federalist insistence on the importance of local interests";[49] and over the years diverse Justices have underscored that view.[50] The antifederalists may have been "men

[44]Wright, supra note 34 at 55.

[45]1 Farrand 357; see Ellsworth, *supra* note 40. Hamilton adverted to the "Difficulty of judging of local circumstances." 1 Farrand 305.

[46]A perceptive British student of American constitutional history, Lord Max Beloff, wrote: "In an age when government's functions were very limited, and among a people who were convinced that those closest to the matters to be dealt with best knew what ought to be done, the internal powers of the state governments and of local governments which had been preserved from imperial encroachments were unlikely to be impinged upon by the Constitution-makers." M. Beloff, *The American Federal Government* 15–16 (1959).

[47]Cecelia M. Kenyon, ed. *The Antifederalists* lxxxvi (1966).

[48]Robert A. Rutland, *The Ordeal of the Constitution: The Antifederalists and the Ratification Struggle of 1787–1788* 313 (1965).

[49]Cecelia M. Kenyon, "Men of Little Faith: The Anti-Federalists on the Nature of Representative Government," 12 Wm. & Mary Q., 3d Series, 3, 9 (1966). "Our traditional forms of democracy are jeopardized by the tendency to remove decisions on public policy and its application from the localities and states to Washington." Leonard D. White, *The States and the Nation* 5 (1953).

[50]In Powell v. Texas, 392 U.S. 514, 547 (1968), Justices Black and Harlan

of little faith" in the bright future the Federalists painted, but they had solid reasons for clinging to their accustomed way, and their arguments, as Herbert Storing noted, have echoed through history.[51]

Given such deep-seated devotion to local self-government, it would be wrong to assume that the Founders were satisfied to exchange the kernel for the husk. What they sought was to preserve an independent, "inviolable" sphere of action,[52] underscored by repeated assurances that the federal sphere was limited. Implicit in Hamilton's "two supreme powers" is the existence of two independent spheres of government, as he himself explained in the New York Ratification Convention: "The laws of the United States are supreme, as to all their proper constitutional objects; the laws of the states are supreme in the same way."[53] He fleshed this out: "the states have certain independent powers, in which their laws are supreme; for example, in making and executing laws concerning the punishment of certain crimes, such as murder, theft, etc. the states cannot be controlled."[54] There too Robert Livingston said, "We have thirteen dis-

---

observed that throughout "the Nation remembered that it could be more tranquil and orderly if it functioned on the principle that the local communities should control their own peculiar affairs under their own local rules." Justice Powell shared their sentiment: "This Court has emphasized the importance in a democratic society of preserving local control of local matters." City of Rome v. United States, 446 U.S. 156, 201 note 12 (1980).

[51] 1 Herbert Storing, *The Complete Anti-Federalist* 6, 72 (1981).

[52] Infra, text accompanying note 63.

[53] 2 Elliot 355. Marshall also said: "In America the powers of sovereignty are divided between the government of the Union, and those of the States. They are each sovereign with respect to the objects committed to it, and neither sovereign with respect to the objects committed to the other." McCulloch v. Maryland, 17 U.S. (4 Wheat.) 316, 410 (1819).

[54] 2 Elliot 362. Is it conceivable that one year later, the Founders, without explanation, took such control away by outlawing "cruel and unusual punishments"? See Raoul Berger, *Death Penalties: The Supreme Court's Obstacle Course* (1982).

tinct governments . . . the states, and the United States, have distinct objects. They are both supreme. As to national objects the latter is supreme; as to internal and domestic objects, the former."[55] The general government and the States, Roger Sherman opined, "ought to have separate and distinct jurisdictions."[56] In the Connecticut Ratification Convention, Ellsworth stressed that each "has its province; their limits may be distinguished." And he said in the Federal Convention that the United States "are sovereign on one side of the line dividing the jurisdiction, the States on the other."[57] In Virginia, Judge Edmund Pendleton, the Nestor of the Ratification Convention, explained that "The two governments act in different manners, and for different purposes, the general government in great national concerns, in which we are interested in common with other members of the Union; the state legislature in our mere local concerns. . . . They can no more clash than two parallel lines can meet."[58]

Within each sphere, it needs emphasis, the respective governments were to enjoy *exclusive* jurisdiction. So, with respect to the States, Hamilton said that the Constitution "leaves in their possession certain exclusive and very important portions of sovereign power,"[59] to which Marshall later

[55] 2 Elliot 385.
[56] 1 Farrand 150.
[57] 2 Elliot 195; 2 Farrand 349. When Mason 50, says "notwithstanding these *apparent* disclaimers, the Convention had provided for national supremacy," he seemingly is unaware that the people are entitled to rely on such representations, and that to repudiate them would, as Justice Story wrote, constitute a fraud upon the people. Infra, Chapter 5, text accompanying note 7.
[58] Wood 529.
[59] Federalist No. 9 at 52. Francis Corbin assured the Virginia Ratification Covention that "the internal administration of government is left to the state legislatures, who exclusively retain such powers as will give the states the advantages of small republics." 3 Elliot 107. Kent wrote, "the

referred as "that immense mass of legislation which embraces everything within the territory of a State, not surrendered to the general government."[60] The obverse also was
stated by Marshall: "The sovereignty of Congress, though
limited to specified objects, is plenary as to *those* objects."[61]
Hamilton assured the Ratifiers in Federalist No. 32 that

> the State governments would clearly retain all the rights of sov-
> ereignty which they before had, and which were not *exclusively*
> delegated to the United States. This exclusive delegation, or
> rather alienation, of State sovereignty, would only exist in three
> cases: where the Constitution in express terms granted ex-
> clusive authority to the Union; where it granted in one instance
> an authority to the Union, and in another prohibited the States
> from exercising the like authority; and where it granted an au-
> thority to the Union, to which a similar authority in the States
> would be absolutely and totally *contradictory* and *repugnant.*[62]

In this Hamilton and Madison were in complete accord.
Madison stated in Federalist No. 39 that the jurisdiction of
the proposed government "extends to certain enumerated
objects only, and leaves to the States a residuary and *inviolable* sovereignty *over all other objects,*" adding in No. 40
that the Constitution regards the States "as distinct and independent sovereigns."[63] As Justice Story, that arch-nationalist,

---

principal rights and duties which flow from our civil and domestic relations, fall within the control . . . of the state governments." 2 Mark de. W.
Howe, *Justice Oliver Wendell Holmes: The Shaping Years* 30 (1963).
    [60] Gibbons v. Ogden, 22 U.S. (9 Wheat.) 1, 203 (1824).
    [61] Id. at 197 (emphasis added).
    [62] Federalist No. 32 at 194.
    [63] Id. 249, 253 (emphasis added). Herbert Storing considers that
"there was no substantial difference between Hamilton and Madison on
the subject of federalism, or the relation of the nation and states at the
time of the Founding." H. Storing, "The Problem of Big Government,"
in *A Nation of States* 65, 69, note 9 (R. A. Goldwin ed. 1961). Shortly after
the Convention, Abraham Baldwin, a delegate, recounted, "pretty unanimous agreement" that the jurisdiction "of each State shd. be left intire &

stated in *Martin v. Hunter's Lessee*, "[I]t is perfectly clear that the sovereign powers vested in State governments . . . remained unaltered and unimpaired except so far as they were granted to the government of the United States."[64] Consequently dual federalism, envisioning two exclusive jurisdictions, was embodied in the Constitution. And although it contemplated a federal government supreme within its sphere, it was a sphere limited and defined. "National supremacy" can mean no more.

The creation of two separate spheres poses the more difficult question: where did the Founders draw the line? Shapiro maintains that "neither the Marshall nor Taney Courts could find the neat boundaries that would have avoided the absurdity of two-sovereignty federalism," and asserts that "this absurdity cannot be bridged by constructing precise functional boundaries between the two sovereigns that will allow each to operate unhindered in its own sphere."[65] The label "absurdity" must not obliterate what Chief Justice Marshall described as "that immense mass of legislation . . . not surrendered to the general government."[66] If the tortuous judicial course under the commerce clause has, "from the point of view of drawing boundaries between sovereigns," resulted in "vapid judicial posturings,"[67] the diffi-

---

preserved as inviolate as possible with . . . preservg the Union with firmness." 3 Farrand 168–169.

[64] 14 U.S. (1 Wheat.) 304, 325 (1810). Herbert Wechsler perceived thirty years ago that "Federalism was the means and price of formation of the Union." The Founders "preserved the states as separate sources of authority and organs of administration—a point on which they hardly had a choice." H. Wechsler, "The Political Safeguards of Federalism: The Role of the States in the Composition and Selection of the National Government," 54 Colum. L. Rev. 543 (1954).

[65] Shapiro, supra note 5 at 360, 367.

[66] Gibbons v. Ogden, 22 U.S. (9 Wheat.) 1, 203 (1824).

[67] Shapiro, supra note 5 at 360.

culty may inhere not so much in the "absurdity" of dual sovereignty as in the Court's employment of the commerce clause as a shuttlecock that has been the toy of shifting majorities on the Bench.[68]

Shapiro's emphasis on "neat," "precise" boundaries was anticipated by Alpheus Mason, who suggests that dual federalism contemplated "a precise constitutional line defining their respective jurisdictions," whereas "no precise line has been drawn delimiting national power in the interests of the States."[69] The Framers, said Wilson in the Pennsylvania Convention, did not pretend "that the line is drawn with mathematical precision; the inaccuracy of language must to a certain degree prevent the accomplishment of such a desire." But, he stressed, "the powers are as minutely enumerated and defined as was possible";[70] the care with which the Framers proceeded is illustrated by numerous examples.[71] It does not follow that because "precise" boundaries were not drawn that there are *no* boundaries. After 1937, Shapiro recounts, the Court, responding to "economic realities" recognized that "no boundary between inter and intra state

[68] Supra Chapter 1, text accompanying notes 4 and 5.

[69] Mason 189, 4. "National power could be interpreted as indefinite in relation to state power. No precise line dividing the two spheres had been drawn." Id. 50.

[70] McMaster & Stone, 344. "This Constitution deserves approbation" because of "the *accuracy* with which the *line is drawn* between the powers of the *general government* and those of the *particular state governments*." Id. 343.

[71] Infra Chapter 4, text accompanying notes 68–77. The records confirm Chief Justice Taney: "Every word apears to have been weighed with the utmost deliberation, and its force and effect to have been fully understood." Holmes v. Jennison, 39 U.S. (14 Pet.) 540, 571 (1840). E.g., Gouverneur Morris' motion to strike the words "'enforce treaties' as being superfluous since treaties were to be 'laws' was unanimously approved." 2 Farrand 389–390.

commerce can be drawn," whereby "the interstate commerce clause is *deleted* from the Constitution." [72] Not so fast. The Court is not empowered to "delete" a clause from the Constitution, nor does difficulty of drawing the line constitute the authorization. The law is replete with imprecise boundaries. Difficulty in drawing the line at twilight between day and night will not prevent a court from distinguishing between bright day and blackest night. [73] Let us begin by distinguishing functions undoubtedly local— janitoring for a village school, transportation between points in a town—from transactions that undeniably cross State lines. We may not wash our hands of the task of tracing the boundary if only because Madison assured the Ratifiers that the federal "jurisdiction extends to certain objects only, and leaves to the States a residuary and *inviolable* sovereignty over all other objects." [74] Invasions of the residuary authorities," Hamilton wrote in Federalist No. 33, would "be merely acts of usurpation." [75] In the New York Convention he emphasized that "This balance between the national and State governments . . . is of the utmost importance. It forms a double security for the people." [76] In these circumstances any intelligible boundary is better than none; like Ellsworth we should prefer "doing half the good we could, rather than do nothing at all," [77] particularly when such

[72] Shapiro, supra note 5 at 361 (emphasis added).
[73] Chief Justice Marshall stated in Brown v. Maryland, 25 U.S. (12 Wheat.) 419, 440 (1827), that although "the intervening colors between white and black, approach so nearly as to perplex the understanding, as colors perplex the vision in making distinction between them. Yet the distinction exists, and must be marked as the cases arise."
[74] Federalist No. 39 at 249 (emphasis added).
[75] Id. No. 33 at 202.
[76] 2 Elliot 257.
[77] 1 Farrand 469.

"usurpation" would endow the federal government with un-limited power. For the Founders' harping insistence that *federal powers were limited* counsels against a construction favoring illimitable power.

Madison wrote in No. 40 that "the general powers are limited; and that the States, in all unenumerated cases, are left in enjoyment of their sovereign and independent juris-diction." He reiterated in the Virginia Convention that the federal government had power over "defined and limited objects beyond which it cannot extend its jurisdiction."[78] There Henry Lee rejected Patrick Henry's attribution of "infinitude to powers clearly limited and defined, for certain designated purposes."[79] Governor Johnson likewise assured the North Carolina Convention that "The powers of Con-gress [to whom the vast bulk of powers was given] are all circumscribed, defined and clearly laid down. So far they may go, but no farther."[80] In the Pennsylvania Convention, Wilson stated that the federal powers were not "unlimited and undefined"; and his colleague, Chief Justice McKean, rejected the argument that "the powers are so vaguely ex-pressed, so indefinite and extensive in their nature, that they may be stretched to every act of legislation."[81] Very early Chief Justice Marshall declared that a written constitution was designed to define and limit power.[82] Resort was had to

[78] 3 Elliot 95.

[79] Id. at 406.

[80] 4 Elliot 64. Writing to Jefferson after the Convention, Madison re-ferred to "the limited powers of the federal government and the jealousy of the subordinate governments." Mason 173.

[81] McMaster & Stone 329, 276.

[82] "The powers of the legislature are defined and limited; and that those limits may not be mistaken or forgotten, the Constitution is writ-ten." Marbury v. Madison, 5 U.S. (1 Cranch) 137, 176 (1803). "The theory of our government . . . is opposed to the deposit of unlimited power any-where." Loan Ass'n v. Topeka, 87 U.S. (20 Wall.) 655, 663 (1874).

a "limited constitution," said Jefferson, "to bind" our delegates "down from mischief."[83] Any construction which unbinds those chains subverts the entire constitutional scheme and constitutes a fraud on the Ratifiers.[84]

The *enumeration* of specific powers was deemed adequately to demark such limits; what was not enumerated was not given. At the outset Resolution No. 6 of the Virginia Plan, introduced by Randolph, authorized Congress to "legislate in all cases to which the separate States are incompetent."[85] Charles Pinckney and John Rutledge "objected to the vagueness of the term *incompetent*" and asked for "an exact enumeration of the powers comprehended by this definition." Whereupon Randolph "disclaimed any intention to give indefinite powers to the national Legislature, declaring that he was entirely opposed to such an inroad on the State jurisdictions."[86] In due course the desired enumeration took shape. In keeping with the Latin maxim *espressio unius exclusio alterius,* Wilson told the Pennsylvania Convention that "everything not expressly mentioned will be presumed to be purposely omitted."[87] The great importance attached to the enumeration is illustrated by Henry Lee's statement in the Virginia Convention: "When a question arises with respect to the legality of any power" the question will be "*Is it enumerated in the Constitution?* . . . It is otherwise arbitrary and unconstitutional."[88] There too

[83] 4 Elliot 543.

[84] Infra Chapter 5, text accompanying note 64.

[85] 1 Farrand 21.

[86] Id. 53.

[87] McMaster & Stone 254. In North Carolina, Iredell stated, "The powers of the government are particularly enumerated and defined: they can claim no other but such as are so enumerated." 4 Elliot 220.

[88] 3 Elliot 186 (emphasis added). Iredell said of the related supremacy clause, "the question . . will always be, whether Congress had exceeded its authority." 4 Elliot 179.

Marshall stated that if Congress were "to make a law not warranted by any of the powers enumerated," the judges would declare it void.[89]

For the moment let us postpone inquiry whether "enumeration" of power over "commerce," for example, furnishes a useful guide, and consider William Murphy's remarkable statement that "there is nothing in the records of the convention to indicate that the convention intended that Congress should have less power after enumeration than was contemplated under the former general grant. The sum of one hundred is no less when ten is listed ten times than when the full sum is set forth in one figure."[90] The problem arises, however, when it is urged that the general term *exceeds* the 100 to which the enumerated powers add up. That argument is refuted by the materials above set forth. And as Madison said in No. 41, "For what purpose could the enumeration of particulars be inserted, if these and all others were meant to be included in the preceding general power?" Such an idea, he added, "is an absurdity."[91] To find "vagueness" where the Framers considered that they had "clearly" and "accurately" defined their objectives, suggests that the interpreter seeks to effectuate goals they did not contemplate and would have rejected.

Another guide to construction is the great solicitude the Founders exhibited to safeguard the "internal," "local" affairs of the individual States. Although Washington, for example, desired to strengthen the federal power to deal with "the general concerns of the country," having experienced its impotence as commander-in-chief, he recognized in 1786 that "local policies and interests . . . should be attended to

[89] 3 Elliot 553.

[90] Murphy 199.

[91] Federalist No. 41 at 269. Randolph spoke to the same effect in the Virginia Convention: "[I]f its powers were to be general, an enumeration would be needless." 3 Elliot 464. See also Story, infra Chapter 4, note 31.

by the states."[92] Those who consider the "police power" to be a Taney concoction[93] overlook the States' anxiety to preserve their "internal police." The 1776 Pennsylvania Constitution provided that the people of the State had the "exclusive . . . right of . . . regulating the internal police."[94] Rhode Island took similar action in 1776.[95] In the Federal Convention, Randolph was against "intermeddling with their [States'] police";[96] and Wilson stated that the preservation of the States' "internal good police depends on their existence in full vigor," and that a "general government" could not "be adequate to the government of the whole without this distinction."[97] Williamson said that the States "ought to possess independent powers in cases purely local, and applying to their internal policy."[98] And the Committee of Eleven recommended to the Convention that the provision for the general welfare should not interfere with the States "in matters which respect only their internal police."[99]

Such views, it may be thought, did not represent the consensus of the Convention because when Sherman twice pro-

[92] Murphy 58.

[93] Edward S. Corwin, "The Passing of Dual Federalism," 36 Va. L. Rev. 1, 15 (1950). Felix Frankfurter, *The Commerce Clause* 27 (1937), notes that "In *Gibbons v. Ogden* there begins to emerge a source of authority for state legislation characterized as designed 'to act directly on its system of police.'"

[94] Declaration of Rights, Article III, 2 Poore 1541.

[95] "The Rhode Island delegates were instructed to cooperate with those of other colonies in promoting confederation . . . taking care however to secure to Rhode Island 'in the strongest and most perfect Manner . . . all the Powers of Government so far as relates to its internal Police and Conduct of our own Affairs, civil and religious." Jensen, supra note 12, at 102.

[96] 2 Farrand 26.

[97] 1 Farrand 157.

[98] Id. 171. Similar sentiments were expressed by Charles Pinckney, id. 404.

[99] 2 Farrand 367.

posed that the federal government may not "interfere with the Government of the individual States in any matters of internal police which respect the Govt. of such States only, and wherein the General welfare of the United States is not concerned," he was voted down.[100] But when the Framers emerged from the secrecy of the Convention and were exposed to the sharp winds of public opinion, they reversed course.[101] In Federalist No. 17, Hamilton dismissed the "slender allurements" that "regulation of the mere domestic police of a State" might have for federal officialdom.[102] He told the New York Convention that "were the laws of the Union to new-model the internal police in any State," that would be objectionable.[103] Judge Pendleton assured the Virginia Convention that the Constitution "does not interfere with the local, particular affairs of the State."[104] In North Carolina Iredell said, "With the mere local concerns of a

[100] Id. 25, 630. In the first instance, Gouverneur Morris objected that "internal police" might be understood to include "paper money & other tricks by which citizens of other States might be affected." Id. 26. On the second occasion, Madison said, "Begin wth these special provisos, and every State will insist on them, for their boundaries, experts &c." Id. 630. These votes illustrate Madison's observation, "No one acquainted with the proceedings of deliberative bodies can have failed to notice the uncertainty of inferences drawn from a record of naked votes." 3 Farrand 520. See also Jensen, supra note 12.

[101] "As has often been noted, if that record [of the Convention] had come to light at the time of the ratification debates, the Constitution would never have been passed." Garry Wills, *Cincinnatus: George Washington and the Enlightenment* 157 (1984). "[W]ithout Madison's concession to rampant state loyalties, there may not have been any Constitution of 1787." A. J. Mason, "The Nature of Our Federal Union Reconsidered," 65 Pol. Sci. Q. 502. 519 (1950).

[102] Federalist No. 17 at 101.

[103] 2 Elliot 267. See Gary Wills, *The Federalist Papers by Alexander Hamilton, James Madison and John Jay* xiv (1982); story, infra Chapter 6, text accompanying note 99.

[104] 3 Elliot 40.

State, Congress are to have nothing to do."[105] William Davie, who had been a delegate to the Federal Convention, stated in North Carolina, "There is not one instance of a power given to the United States, whereby the internal policy or administration of the state is affected."[106] General Heath told the New York Convention that "the states have a right, and they will regulate their own internal affairs as to themselves appears proper."[107] Similar statements were made by Nicholas and Corbin in Virginia.[108] When Sherman returned to Connecticut to campaign for adoption of the

[105] Mason 124.

[106] 4 Elliot 160. At times the Court apparently has not grasped the meaning of the reserved police power. Thus it was said in Gulf C. &. S.F.R. Co. v. Hefley, 158 U.S. 98,104 (1895), that the laws "though resting upon the police powers of the State . . . must yield whenever Congress, in the exercise of powers granted to it legislates upon the precise subject matter, for that power, like all other reserved powers of the States, is subordinate to those in terms conferred . . . upon the nation." Powers that were "reserved" to the States were not "conferred . . . upon the nation." Compare McDermott v. Wisconsin, infra Chapter 6, text accompanying notes 101–102.

[107] 2 Elliot 115.

[108] 3 Elliot 14, 108; see also Henry Lee, id. 182; James Monroe, id. 214. As Madison stated, the States "have the care of all local interests—those familiar domestic objects, for which men have the strongest predilection. The general government, on the contrary, has the preservation of the aggregate interest of the Union—objects which, being less familiar, and more remote from men's notice, have a less powerful influence on their minds. . . . [T]he powers in the general government are those which will be exercised mostly in the time of war, while those of the state governments will be exercised in time of peace." Id. 257–259. See also William in New York. 2 Elliot 241.

David Engdahl observes of "matters which had traditionally been considered appropriate for the 'police power' of the states—e.g. matter of public health, safety and morals. None of the enumerated federal powers by its terms places these matters within the circle of enumerated federal concerns, and some straightforward attempts by Congress to deal with them were consequently held invalid." D. Engdahl, *Constitutional Powers: Federal and State in a Nutshell* 44 (1974).

Constitution, he wrote, "The powers vested in the federal government are clearly defined, so that each state will retain its sovereignty in what concerns its own internal government," a statement Herbert Storing considers a "rather typical description of the Constitution."[109] Such was the basis of ratification.[110] If there is conflict between the utterances of the Framers and the assurances made to the Ratifiers, the latter must prevail because it is they who gave effect to what,

[109] Herbert Storing, "The 'Other' Federalist Papers: A Preliminary Sketch," 6 Pol. Sci. Rev. 215, 222 (1976). See also supra note 59. New York v. Miln, 36 U.S. (1 Pet.) 102, 139 (1837), therefore, was richly justified in concluding "that all those powers which relate to merely municipal legislation, or what may, perhaps, more properly be called *internal police,* are not thus surrendered or restrained; and that, consequently, in relation to these, the authority of a State is complete, unqualified and exclusive." See also the License Cases, 46 U.S. (5 How.) 504, 574, 578 (1847). Justice McLean stated: "A State regulates its domestic commerce . . . and acts upon all internal matters which relate to its moral and political welfare. Over these subjects the Federal government has no power." Id. at 588. Subsequently, Justice Harlan stated that "there is a power, sometimes called the police power, which has never been surrendered by the States, in virtue of which they may, within certain limits, control everything within their respective territories, and upon the proper exercise of which, under some circumstances, may depend the public health, the public morals, or the public safety, is conceded in all the cases." New Orleans Gas Co. v. Louisiana Light Co., 115 U.S. 650, 661 (1885).

In light of the foregoing, I dissent from Corwin's rejection of the thought "that the police powers of the State constitute a reserve of *exclusive* powers, with the result that any subject-matter which falls within their jurisdiction is, *for that reason,* outside the delegated powers of the United States." Corwin, *Commerce* 125. For if it was an "exclusive," not surrendered, State power, it was not delegated to the federal government. See also infra, Chapter 5, text accompanying notes 2, 3.

[110] Apparently Corwin did not appreciate the weight that attaches to representations to the Ratifiers for the purpose of swaying their votes. For he wrote, "The Convention being over, Madison adopted a different tone, in advocating, both in the Virginia Ratification Convention and in the Federalist, the adoption of the Constitution," quoting his remarks that "The powers of the general government relate to external objects, and are but few," and his reference to the States' "residuary and inviolable

prior to ratification, was merely a document in blank, and presumably they were influenced by the assurances made to them.

We come now to the nub of the issue: what did the Founders consider to be "internal"? Wilson said:

> It was easy to discern a proper and satisfactory principle. . . . Whatever object of government *is confined* in its operation and effect, *within the bounds* of a particular state, should be considered as belonging to the government of that state; whatever object of government extends, in its operation or effects, *beyond the bounds* of a particular state, should be considered as belonging to the government of the United States.[111]

"Whenever an object occurs," he said, "to the direction of which no state is competent [e.g., war, treaties], the management of it must, of necessity, belong to the United States."[112] Anticipating Madison's Federalist No. 45, Sherman stated in the Convention:

> The objects of the Union . . . were few: 1. defence agst. foreign danger. 2. agst. internal disputes & a resort to force. 3. Treaties with foreign nations. 4. regulating commerce & drawing revenue from it. These and perhaps a few lesser objects alone rendered a Confederation of the States necessary. All other matters civil and criminal would be much better in the hands of the States.[113]

Closely paralleling Sherman, Madison wrote in No. 45 that:

> The powers delegated in the proposed constitution to the federal government are few and defined. Those which are to remain in the State governments are numerous and indefinite.

---

sovereignty over all other subjects." Corwin, *Commerce* 119–120. Madison was no ideologue; he realized that to secure adoption he had to accept safeguards for State sovereignty. Supra note 101; text accompanying note 63; notes 12, 64.

[111] 2 Elliot 424.
[112] Mason 12.
[113] 1 Farrand 133.

The former will be exercised principally on *external objects* as war, peace, negotiations and foreign commerce. . . . The powers reserved to the States will extend to all objects which, in the course of affairs, concern the lives, liberties and properties of the people; and the *internal* order, improvement and prosperity of the State.[114]

That there was great apprehension on this score is evidenced by Madison's repeated assurances in the Virginia Convention. Thus he said, "the powers of the federal government are enumerated; it can only operate in certain cases; it has legislative power on defined and limited objects, beyond which it cannot extend its jurisdiction."[115] Later he stressed, "The powers of the general government relate to external objects, and are but few," adding reassuringly, they "are *not so much an augmentation of powers* in the general government, as a change rendered necessary for the purpose of giving efficacy to those which were vested in it before,"[116] for example, replacing the Continental Congress' requisitions on the States for purposes of conducting the war—frequently not honored—by a power of direct taxation.

Wilson stated in the Convention that "the powers of peace, war, treaties, coinage and regulating of *commerce* ought to reside" in the general government. And he repeated that "War, Commerce and Revenue were the great objects of the Genl. Government. All of them are connected with money"[117]—not morals or social welfare. In the New

---

[114] Federalist No. 45 at 303 (emphasis added). In the Virginia Convention, Madison repeated, "The powers of the general government relate to external objects, and are but few, but the powers in the State relate to those great objects which immediately concern the prosperity of the people." 3 Elliot 259.

[115] 3 Elliot 95.

[116] Id. 259 (emphasis added).

[117] 1 Farrand 413; 2 Farrand 275 (emphasis added). Earlier he had said, "All the principal powers of the Natl. Legislature had some relation to money." 2 Farrand 233.

York Convention, Hamilton said, "The great leading objects of federal government . . . are to maintain domestic peace, and provide for the common defence" which comprehends "the regulation of commerce,—that is, the whole system of foreign intercourse—the support of armies and navies." The States, he continued, have no "concern with regulation of commerce, the procuring alliances or forming treaties of peace. . . . Their objects are merely civil and domestic."[118] John Jay put the matter more succinctly, distinguishing between "matters of a private nature which require minute and local information" and federal jurisdiction over "the interests of the states in relation to each other, and in relation to foreign powers."[119] For as said by Abraham Baldwin, there were things the States could not "determine or enforce," such as "Treaties with foreign Nations, War & Armies . . . necessy [sic] to be ceded by the individual States" to the general government.[120]

"It seemed inconceivable" to Madison and Hamilton (and very probably to most of the Founders) "that a central authority could or would want to descend to enforcement

[118] 2 Elliot 350.
[119] Id. 283. Jay referred to the State's "interest in its trade, its agriculture, its manufacturers." Id.
[120] 3 Farrand 168, 169. The "essential object" of the Constitution, Lord Beloff wrote, "was transparently clear. It was that the states should be as one with regard to the outside world, but separate and independent in their internal concerns. The powers expressly granted to the Federal Government were essentially the powers of war and peace; and the precise allocation of functions between the Federal Government and the States was largely determined by considerations arising out of this primary criterion. For the Federal Government adequately to represent the States abroad it must be able to tax directly, to enforce its own laws and the execution of its treaty obligations, to regulate inter-state commerce, and to have the full treaty making power; the States must be deprived only of those powers that could encroach upon this monopoly." Beloff, supra note 46 at 16.

of local laws.[121] In the Convention Mason said that the
"General government could not know how to make laws for
every part—such as respect *agriculture*."[122] And Hamilton
wrote in Federalist No. 17 that "the supervision of agriculture and of other concerns of a similar nature . . . which are
proper to be provided for by local legislation, can never be
desirable cares of a general jurisdiction," including in the
local province "the ordinary administration of criminal and
civil justice."[123] That education was likewise deemed a local
matter may be inferred from the Convention's rejection of
power to "establish a University."[124] Sherman explained this
was because "it was thought sufficient that this power should
be exercised by the States in their separate capacities."[125]
With good reason, therefore, did Samuel Eliot Morison and
Henry Steele Commager write:

> To the States belong, not by virtue of the Federal Constitution
> but of their own sovereign power, the control of municipal and

[121] Wills, supra note 103 at xiv. See Hamilton, supra text accompanying
note 103. In the Convention, Ellsworth said, "The Natl. Govt. could not
descend to the local objects." 1 Farrand 492.

[122] 1 Farrand 160.

[123] Federalist No. 17 at 102–103. In the New York Ratification Convention, Hamilton repeated, "the states have certain independent powers, in
which their laws are supreme; for example, in making and executing laws
concerning the punishment of certain crimes, such as murder, theft, the
states cannot be controlled." 2 Elliot 362.

[124] 2 Farrand 616.

[125] 3 Farrand 362. In his last annual message Washington proposed a national university, but Harry Jaffa comments, "Washington's platonic
wisdom was turned aside by his countrymen." H. V. Jaffa, "The Case for a
Stronger National Government," in *A Nation of States,* supra note 63 at
107, 120. "Platonic wisdom" could not overcome the Convention's rejection of a national university. In his message of December 2, 1806, President Jefferson said of a federal institution to foster sciences, "I suppose an
amendment to the Constitution, by consent of the States, necessary, because the objects now recommended are not among those enumerated in
the Constitution, and to which it permits the public money to be appropriated." 4 Elliot 349.

local government, factory and labor legislation, . . . statutory development and judicial administration of civil and criminal law . . . the control of education, and the general 'police power' over the health, safety, and welfare of the people.[126]

A State's regulation of its schools, hospitals, jails, and the like ordinarily has no "effect" beyond its borders, and under Wilson's principle it remains the domain of the State. Once, therefore, a particular function is identified as "local" as understood by the Founders—e.g., "agriculture"—it is protected by the State's "exclusive" jurisdiction of such matters.[127] Were the Constitution to grant to the federal government a specific power over "agriculture," that, of course, would override the State's power.[128] But State constitutions "must yield" to the Federal Constitution, said Iredell, "only in those cases where power is given by it,"[129] a

---

[126] S. E. Morison and H. S. Commager, *The Growth of the American Republic* 287 (4th ed. 1952). To the States, the Court declared in Lane County v. Oregon, 74 U.S. (7 Wall.) 71, 76 (1868), "nearly the whole charge of interior regulation is committed or left." See Story, infra Chapter 6, text accompanying note 99.

[127] Supra text accompanying notes 122, 123.

[128] Corwin argues, "To say that the National Government has not a specifically delegated power to regulate agriculture is one thing; to say that it may never so excise any of its delegated powers to regulate agriculture . . . is quite another thing, *unless and until it is shown that the regulation of agriculture is exclusively appropriated to powers not delegated* to the National Government." Corwin, *Commerce* 243. Hamilton, a broad constructionist, excluded agriculture from the national jurisdiction, supra text accompanying note 123, a view expressed by Mason in the Convention, id. at note 117, and by John Jay in New York, supra note 119. No ardent Federalist objected to these expressions, and no contrary opinion was uttered in the several conventions.

[129] 4 Elliot 179. But, "If Congress under pretence of executing one power, should in fact usurp another," Iredell assured the North Carolina Convention, "they will violate the Constitution." Id. As Justice Daniel said in the License Cases, 46 U.S. (5 How.) 504, 613 (1847), "Every power delegated to the Federal government must be expounded in coincidence with a perfect right in the States to all they have not delegated."

proposition implicit in Marshall's statement in *McCulloch v. Maryland*, "the government of the Union, though limited in its powers, is supreme within its sphere."[130] For the supremacy clause provides that the "Constitution and laws of the United States . . . *in pursuance thereof* . . . shall be the supreme law of the land." That, I submit, is what "plenary" federal power and "national supremacy" mean, no more.[131] The problem whether a facially *amorphous* provision such as commerce overrides a *plainly* internal power is hereinafter discussed. At the very least, the Founders' emphasis, again and again, upon "limited" federal powers, upon preservation of the States' jurisdiction over "internal," "local" matters that operate only within a State's borders, counsels against an over-generous construction of federal powers.[132] That approach is buttressed by the Tenth Amendment, and it was that of Lincoln. On the eve of the Civil War, he referred in his First Inaugural Address, March 4, 1861, to a proposed amendment that "has passed the House, to the effect that the Federal Government shall never interfere with the domestic institutions of the State," and considered "such a provision is now to be implied constitutional law."[133]

[130] McCulloch v. Maryland, 17 U.S. (4 Wheat.) 316, 405 (1819) (emphasis added).

[131] For detailed discussion of the supremacy clause,, see infra Chapter 4, text accompanying notes 87–104.

[132] See infra Chapter 6, text accompanying notes 136–168. "We sometimes forget that the original thirteen states were in existence before the Constitution was enacted. . . . The issue is not for us . . . simply whether it would be better to have more or less centralization of government, unless we are prepared to alter the Constitution in the most fundamental way imaginable." Richard Posner, "Toward an Economic Theory of Federal Jurisdiction," 6 Harv. J. of L. & Pub. Pol. 41 (1982).

[133] *The Jeffersonian and Hamiltonian Tradition in American Politics* 18 (Albert Fried ed. 1968). See also infra Chapter 7, note 1.

CHAPTER FOUR

The Tenth Amendment, the "Necessary and Proper" and "Supremacy" Clauses

THE TENTH AMENDMENT

THE Tenth Amendment provides:

> The powers *not delegated* to the United States by the Constitution, nor prohibited by it to the States, are reserved to the States respectively, or to the people.

It is the fashion to belittle the Amendment as inconsequential, "redundant," a "constitutional tranquilizer, and empty declaration."[1] Such views derive from Chief Justice Stone's dictum in *United States v. Darby:*

> The amendment states but a *truism* that all is retained which has not been surrendered. There is nothing in the history of its adoption to suggest that it was more than *declaratory* of the relationship between the national and state governments as it had been established by the Constitution before the Amendment or that its purpose was other than to allay the fears that the new national government might seek to exercise powers not granted, and that the states might not be able to exercise fully their reserved power.[2]

[1] Felix Frankfurter, *The Commerce Clause* 40 (1937); Mason 190, 5.

[2] 312 U.S. 100, 124 (1941) (emphasis added). That issue arose early in our history. Frankfurter wrote that counsel had urged the Court in *Gibbons v. Ogden* to read the Tenth Amendment "as a generating principle

One may surmise that Stone was troubled by the possible argument that the Amendment cut into *delegated* national powers, for he inquired of Charles Beard, "Have you found . . . any indication that the framers of the [Tenth Amendment] intended the reserve powers of the States to constitute a limitation on the *powers* of Congress?"[3] If such powers were granted to the United States, they were not, of course, reserved to the States. Long ago Justice Story observed: It could not have been the intention of the framers of this amendment to give effect as an abridgement of any of the powers *granted* under the Constitution. . . . Its sole design is to exclude any interpretation, by which *other* powers should be assumed *beyond* those that are granted."[4]

The opponents of the Constitution "had conjured up the image of a national colossus, destined to swallow or destroy the defenseless states."[5] State control of internal functions, as we have seen, was dear to the hearts of the Founders. It will be recalled that the Pennsylvania Constitution of 1776 provided that the people of the State had "the sole, exclusive and inherent right of governing and regulating the internal police of the same."[6] Rhode Island also acted in 1776 to secure "in the strongest and most perfect Manner . . . all the Powers of the Government, so far as it relates to its internal Police and the conduct of our own affairs."[7] Article IV of the 1780 Massachusetts Constitution provided that its

of restriction upon the affirmative *grants* of national power," but that Marshall rejected it "as an active principle of limitation." Frankfurter, supra note 1 at 40. Granted powers are outside the reservation of powers "not delegated." See Story, infra text accompanying note 4.

[3] Mason 190.

[4] 2 Story, §1908 at 653 (emphasis added).

[5] A. T. Mason, "The Bill of Rights: An Almost Forgotten Appendage," in *The Future of Our Liberties* 39, 47 (S. E. Halperin ed. 1982).

[6] Declaration of Rights, Article III, 2 Poore 1541.

[7] See supra Chapter 3 note 95.

people "have the sole and exclusive right of governing themselves . . . and enjoy every power . . . which is not . . . by them expressly delegated to the United States."[8] Explicit confirmation of such reservations was embodied in Article II of the Articles of Confederation: "Each state retains its sovereignty . . . and every Power . . . which is not by this confederation expressly delegated to the United States."[9] The Founders were repeatedly assured by Wilson, Hamilton, and Madison, and by Marshall in the Virginia Convention, that no such provision was required in the Constitution.[10] In short, the Federalists maintained that the government would "have only the powers expressly delegated to it . . . and that all other powers would be reserved to the States."[11]

But they could "not overcome widespread suspicion";[12] there was pervasive distrust of power,[13] which time and again was pointedly expressed. Typical was Patrick Henry in the Virginia Convention: "What do they tell us? That our rights are reserved. Why not say so?"[14] Mason asked, "If they are not given up, where are they secured? Let the gentlemen show that they are secured in a plain, direct, un-

---

[8] Declaration of Rights, Article IV, 1 Poore 958. Similar provisions were contained in the constitutions of Maryland (1776), Bill of Rights, Article II, 1 Poore 817; New Hampshire (1784), Article VII, 2 Poore 1281; North Carolina (1776), Declaration of Rights, Article II, 2 Poore 1409; Vermont (1777), Declaration of Rights, Article IV, 2 Poore 1859.

[9] Commager 111.

[10] Wilson, 2 Elliot 436; Hamilton, Federalist No. 32 at 194, No. 84 at 558–559; Marshall, 3 Elliot 419; Madison, 3 Elliot 620. In a letter to Lafayette, April 28, 1788, Washington wrote, "the people evidently retained everything that they did not in express terms give up." 4 *Documentary History of the Constitution* 601–602 (1905).

[11] Murphy 403.

[12] C. A. Lofgren, "The Origins of the Tenth Amendment: History, Sovereignty, and the Problems of Constitutional Intention," in *Constitutional Government in America* 331, 344 (R. Collins ed. 1981).

[13] See Thomas Burke, supra Chapter 1, note 29; Mason 8; Wood 21.

[14] 3 Elliot 448.

equivocal manner."[15] So spoke Spencer in North Carolina[16] and the "Centinel" in Pennsylvania.[17] The Tenth Amendment was designed to lay such fears to rest, as Justice Stone noted, and that purpose is not to be defeated by labeling the Tenth Amendment as a "truism." A truism is a proposition that "is so obviously true as not to require discussion."[18] The Tenth Amendment was added to put the obvious beyond peradventure; as Charles Jarvis assured the Massachusetts Convention regarding a proposed amendment: "by positively securing what is not expressly delegated, it leaves nothing to the uncertainty of conjecture, or to the refinements of implication, but is an explicit reservation of every right and privilege which is nearest and most agreeable to the people."[19] That reservation, the Court stated in *Kansas v. Colorado*, "was *made absolutely certain* by the Tenth Amendment."[20] It is strange reasoning that would blur this fundamental demarcation of powers because the Founders took the precaution to put into express terms what had rested on assurances and implication. Who would contend that because Madison told the First Congress that the Bill of Rights "may be deemed unnecessary"[21] the rights guaran-

[15] Id. 266.

[16] 4 Elliot 137.

[17] McMaster & Stone 580. See also Madison, infra note 45. The Tenth Amendment, Story stated, "was framed for the purpose of quieting the excessive jealousies which had been excited." 1 Story, §433 at 311–312.

[18] *Oxford Universal Dictionary* (Rev'd 3d ed. 1955).

[19] 2 Elliot 153.

[20] 206 U.S. 46, 89–90 (1907); see also infra text accompanying notes 27–28. At least as respects the Tenth Amendment, the foregoing materials render William Murphy's assertion untenable: "[T]he fact that amendments limiting national power in favor of state power were considered to be necessary or desirable clearly demonstrates the understanding in the conventions that without the amendments, there would be no such limitations." Murphy 405.

[21] 1 *Annals of Congress* 411 (2d ed. 1834, print bearing running head "History of Congress").

teed by the Bill are therefore put in question? Still less does the "truism" dismissal meet the demand of seven Ratification Conventions for the reservation the Tenth Amendment expresses.[22] Nor is the effect of the Amendment diminished because it is "primarily declaratory." A "declaratory" statute, Blackstone explained, declares "what the common law is and ever has been" in order to avoid "all doubts and difficulties," precisely what the Founders had in mind.[23]

To diminish the Tenth Amendment as merely "declaratory" is likewise to vitiate the supremacy clause and the necessary and proper clause, for each, Hamilton wrote in No. 33 of the Federalist, was merely declaratory. Of both he said, "They are only declaratory of a truth which would have resulted by necessary and unavoidable implication from the very act of constituting a federal government, and vesting it with certain powers. . . . The declaration itself, though it may be chargeable with tautology and redundancy, is at least perfectly harmless." "Why then was it introduced," he asked, and answered, "it could only have been done for greater caution, and guard against cavilling refinements."[24] So too he said of the supremacy clause; what would the laws of the Union "amount to, if they were not to be su-

[22] Murphy 404; six employed the words "expressly" delegated.

[23] 1 William Blackstone, *Commentaries on the Laws of England* 86 (1765–1769).

Lofgren is ambivalent: "The Tenth Amendment argument is easily disposed of—at least superficially. By the historical evidence the Court was correct in labelling the Amendment a 'truism.' Declaratory of the overall constitutional scheme, it had no independent force as originally understood. Accordingly, although merely declaratory, the amendment militates at a deeper level against the central government's compromising the states' constitutional roles." Lofgren, supra note 12 at 350. What Lofgren finds at a "deeper level" is to be found on the face of the text: the federal government may not encroach on powers reserved to the States. A statute is not the less effective because it is "declaratory."

[24] Federalist No. 33 at 199, 200.

preme? . . . A LAW, by the very meaning of the term, includes supremacy."[25] Adherents of "declaratory" deflation
run the risk of throwing the baby out with the bath water.

Seizing on a statement by Justice Story, Walter Berns concluded that the Tenth Amendment merely represents a "rule
of interpreting the Constitution."[26] Story wrote: "This
amendment is a mere affirmation of what, upon any reasoning, is a *necessary* rule of interpreting the constitution. Being
an instrument of limited and enumerated powers, it follows,
irresistibly, that what is not conferred is withheld, and be-
longs to the state authorities."[27] Story underscored his "irresistible" rule by declaring that the Tenth Amendment's
"sole design is *to exclude any interpretation* by which other
powers should be assumed beyond those that are granted."[28]

[25] Id. at 201. Murphy 402 regards such expressions as a "departure
from the requirements of the Articles [of Confederation] that only expressly granted powers could be exercised," repudiating "a strict construction in approach to national power." But the fact remains that the
framers did *not* depend on implication but spelled out the "necessary and
proper" and "supremacy" clauses. Nor can those expressions annul the
repeated assurances that the federal powers were limited and defined.

[26] Walter Berns, "The Meaning of the Tenth Amendment," in *A Nation
of States* 126, 131 (R. A. Goldwin ed. 1961).

[27] 2 Story, §1907 at 652 (emphasis added).

[28] Id., §1908 at 653 (emphasis added). That the purpose of the Tenth
Amendment was to nail down the residuary jurisdiction of the States is
made plain by another Story statement. Quoting from his opinion in
Martin v. Hunter's Lessee, he said:

'It is perfectly clear that the sovereign powers vested in the State governments by their respective constitutions remained unaltered and unimpaired, except so far as they were granted to the government of the
United States.' These deductions do not rest upon general reasons,
plain and obvious as they seem to be. They have been positively recognized by one of the articles in amendment of the Constitution, which
declares that 'the powers not delegated to the United States by the
Constitution, nor prohibited by it to the States, are reserved to the
States respectively, or to the people."

1 Story, §417 at 318.

Then too, the Founders, who insisted on an explicit declaration that the "internal" rights of the States would be shielded from federal intrusion, would hardly have been content with a "rule of interpretation" that placed their rights at the mercy of judicial discretion, for they had a "profound fear" of judicial discretion.[29] True, some preliminary interpretation is required to determine whether a given matter is of national sweep or is local and internal. Once that determination is made, however, "interpretation" is at an end and the mandate of the Tenth Amendment takes over: powers "not delegated" to the federal government are reserved to the States.

Berns argues, however, that the Tenth Amendment

> is not a rule of law of the Constitution, which is to say that no court can base its holding in any case on the Amendment because the Amendment does not contain terms that can provide a rule of law. . . . Unlike the Tenth Amendment, which merely declares that what is not granted is reserved, the commerce clause specifies what commercial powers are granted and, implicitly, what commercial powers are reserved, and thereby provides the terms in which the constitutionality of commercial legislation can be determined. . . . The Tenth Amendment, on the other hand, contains no terms that the courts can use to settle any legal case or controversy.[30]

---

[29] Wood 298, 304. In 1767, Chief Justice Hutchinson of Massachusetts stated, "the *Judge* should never be the *Legislator:* because then the will of the judge would be the Law: and this tends to a State of Slavery." Morton Horwitz, "The Emergence of an Instrumental Conception of American Law, 1780–1820," in 5 *Perspectives in American History* 287, 292 (1971). Chancellor Kent wrote that without the common law, i.e., the precedents, "the courts would be left to a dangerous discretion to roam at large in the trackless field of their own imaginations." 1 James Kent, *Commentaries on the American Law* 373 (9th ed. 1858).

[30] Berns, supra note 26 at 131, 132. The Court experienced no difficulty in holding that the Civil Rights Act of 1875 was "repugnant to the Tenth Amendment." Civil Rights Cases, 109 U.S. 3, 15 (1883).

Thus Berns elevates the *implicit* reservation to the States of *intra*-state commerce above the Tenth Amendment's *express* reservation of powers "not delegated" and concludes without more that that implicit reservation affords the "terms" or guidelines to adjudication. Why does not the express reservation of undelegated powers equally furnish the "terms" of constitutional adjudication? Indeed, the enumeration of the delegated powers in Article I supplies specific guides to what was delegated, whereas no such guide is furnished by commerce "among the States," for the Court has had no end of trouble in its construction, meandering in a tortuous course.[31] Berns' reasoning runs counter to Story's own advice:

> Constitutions are not designed for metaphysical or logical subtleties . . . for elaborate shades of meaning, or for the exercise of philosophical acuteness. . . . The people make them . . . [and] must be supposed to read them, with the help of common sense, and cannot be presumed to admit in them any recondite meaning or any extraordinary gloss.[32]

In fact, Story speaks against Berns:

> It is perfectly clear that the sovereign powers vested in the State governments by their respective constitutions remained unaltered and unimpaired, except so far as they were granted to the government of the United States. These deductions do not rest upon general reason, plain and obvious as they seem to be. They have been positively recognized by one of the articles in amendment of the Constitution, which declares that "the powers not delegated to the United States by the Constitution, nor

[31] Cf. supra Chapter 1, text accompanying notes 4−5; and see supra Chapter 3, text accompanying notes 66−68.

[32] 1 Story, §451 at 345. In *Kansas v. Colorado* the Supreme Court declared, "Article X is not to be shorn of its meaning by any narrow or technical construction, but is to be considered fairly and liberally so as to give effect to its scope and meaning." 201 U.S. 46, 90 (1907).

prohibited by it to the States, are reserved to the *States* respectively, or to the *people*."[33]

As late as 1975 the Court affirmed that "The Amendment expressly declares the constitutional policy that Congress may not exercise power in a fashion that impairs the States' integrity or their ability to function effectively in a federal system."[34]

"EXPRESSLY DELEGATED"

The reservation of undelegated powers to the States by Article II of the Articles of Confederation was accompanied by the words "expressly delegated." That wording was submitted by several Ratification conventions to the First Congress,[35] but the qualification of "not delegated" by "expressly" was omitted from the Tenth Amendment. From this and from several references in the Ratification conventions to "expressly delegated," Charles Lofgren deduces a "contemporary understanding that absent 'expressly' . . . a reserved powers clause would have little meaning."[36] This reduces the Amendment to an exercise in futility. Not for this did the Founders insist on making certain that the powers reserved to the States would be protected from federal invasion. To conclude that the Amendment "probably reaffirmed the centralizing tendencies of the new system"[37] is to stand the Amendment on its head. Central to the constitutional scheme was restriction of the federal government to "few" defined and limited powers, and assurances that the States' "residuary" powers would be "inviolable." As Al-

[33] 1 Story, §417 at 318.
[34] Fry v. United States, 421 U.S. 542, 547 note 7 (1975).
[35] Lofgren, supra note 12 at 345.
[36] Id.
[37] Id. 349.

pheus Mason perceived, the problem was that "Insertion of 'expressly' before 'delegated' would eliminate the . . . *choice of means* for carrying the enumerated grants into execution."[38] That is also the burden of Madison's Federalist No. 44: "Had the Convention attempted a positive enumeration of the powers necessary and proper for carrying their other powers into *effect*, the attempt would have involved a complete digest of laws on every subject to which the Constitution relates."[39]

This, in my judgment, is what Madison had in mind when he stated in the First Congress that "it was impossible to confine a government to the exercise of express powers; there must necessarily be admitted powers by implication, unless the constitution descended to recount every minutiae."[40] Madison, in a word, regarded omission of "expressly" as removal of a bar to the use of necessary and proper *means* to carry granted powers into effect.[41] Illustrative of the concerns that triggered the omission is Randolph's remark that the predecessor "expressly" in the Articles of Confederation "was interpreted to prohibit Congress from granting passports, although such a power was necessarily incident to that of making war."[42] Similarly, Hamilton said in the New York Ratification Convention, "they must do a thousand things not expressly given"; and Justice Yates, an opponent of the Constitution, agreed that "in granting gen-

[38] Mason 48.
[39] Federalist No. 44 at 293 (emphasis added).
[40] 1 *Annals of Congress,* supra note 21 at 761.
[41] In this sense I agree with Lofgren, supra note 12 at 348, that the exclusion of "expressly" "meant that the central government's powers needed no detailed base in the Constitution." The enumeration in Article I, §8 afforded a base of *powers;* it was not necessary to detail the *means* of executing the powers.
[42] 3 Elliot 601.

eral powers—the powers to execute are implied."[43] Omission of "expressly" must be viewed in light of a central purpose of the Founders—the object of construction is to effectuate, not to defeat, that purpose[44]—to make certain that the federal regime would not encroach upon powers reserved to the States. In sum, the reservation made explicit by the Tenth Amendment, as Willard Hurst observed, "represented a political bargain, key terms of which assumed the continuing vitality of the states as prime law makers in most affairs."[45]

THE "NECESSARY AND PROPER" CLAUSE

It has been said that the debates over "the general welfare, necessary and proper, and supremacy clauses—surely sensitized Americans to the potential for a central government under the Constitution with an *expansive reach*."[46] Another commentator regards the necessary and proper clause as "a giant step towards conversion of the 'foregoing' enumerated powers into powers of indefinite scope," and considers "it was clear that the *ends* could be *enlarged* by recourse to the necessary and proper clause."[47] Still another asserts that "on

[43] Quoted by Lofgren, supra note 12 at 346.

[44] United States v. Classic, 313 U.S. 299, 316 (1941).

[45] W. Hurst, *The Legitimacy of the Business Corporation in the Law of the United States* 40 (1970). Jefferson wrote in June 1823, "The States supposed that by their tenth amendment, they had secured themselves against constructive powers." *The Jefferson and Hamiltonian Tradition in American Politics* 104 (Albert Fried ed. 1968). Referring to the various "declarations of rights" submitted by the several ratification conventions, Madison wrote in 1830, "all of them indicating a jealousy of the Federal powers and an anxiety to multiply securities against a constructive enlargement of them." 4 *Letters and Writings of James Madison* 129 (1865).

[46] Lofgren, supra note 12 at 348 (emphasis added).

[47] Mason 49, 50 (emphasis added).

its face it *amplifies* . . . the previously listed specific powers."[48] To my mind, they misconceive the Founders' design
in framing and adopting those clauses.

Article I employs seventeen sections to enumerate the various powers granted, and then by section 18 provides power

> To make all laws which shall be necessary and proper *for carry-
> ing into execution* the foregoing powers and all other powers
> vested by this Constitution in the Government of the United
> States.

Hamilton, Madison, and Wilson corroborated the plain
meaning of the text. In Federalist No. 33, Hamilton wrote:
"What is a power but the ability or faculty of doing a thing?
What is the ability to do a thing but the power of employing
the *means* necessary to its execution? . . . What are the
proper means of executing such a power, but *necessary and
proper laws?*[49] Madison stated that the clause "gives no supplementary power. It only enables them to execute the delegated powers. . . . For when any power is given, its delegation necessarily involves authority to make laws to execute
it."[50] And Wilson said that the clause says "no more than
that the powers we have already particularly given, shall be

[48] Murphy 199.

[49] Federalist No. 33 at 199.

[50] 3 Elliot 438. "As James Madison explained, the Necessary and
Proper Clause is but merely a declaration, for the removal of all uncertainty, that the means for carrying into execution those [powers] otherwise granted are included in the grant." Kinsella v. Singleton, 361 U.S.
234, 247 (1960). Madison explained in Federalist No. 44 at 294:

> Had the Constitution been silent on this head, there can be no doubt
> that all the particular powers requisite as means of executing the gen-
> eral powers would have resulted to the government, by unavoidable
> implication. No axiom is more clearly established in law, or in reason,
> than that wherever the end is required, the means are authorized;
> wherever a general power to do a thing is given, every particular power
> necessary for doing it is included.

effectually carried into execution."[51] He also rejected the argument that the clause gives to Congress "a power of legislating generally."[52] That the clause was not designed to enlarge existing grants was made clear in other conventions. In Virginia, Nicholas stressed that "it was no augmentation of power";[53] Madison maintained that the clause "gives no supplementary powers."[54] In North Carolina, Archibald Maclaine said "the clause gives no new power";[55] and Chief Justice McKean said in Pennsylvania that it "gives to Congress no further powers than those enumerated."[56] Speaking to the clause in North Carolina, Iredell declared, "If Congress, under the pretence of exercising one power, should, in fact usurp another, they will violate the Constitution."[57]

Those who, like Corwin, regard *McCulloch v. Maryland* as exhibiting a "latitudinarian construction of the 'necessary and proper' clause"[58] misread Marshall's opinion. The issue

[51] 2 Elliot 468. In Virginia, George Nicholas stated, "the Constitution had enumerated all the powers which the general government should have, but did not say how they were to be exercised. Does this give any new power? I say not. Suppose it had been inserted, at the end of every power, that they should have power to make laws to carry that power into execution; would that have increased their power?" 3 Elliot 245; and see id. 246.

[52] Id. 488.

[53] 3 Elliot 443. Randolph stated in the Virginia Convention that before the federal Convention "The augmentation of congressional power was dreaded." Id. 188. The "sweeping clause," he said, "does not in the least increase the powers of Congress. It is only inserted for greater caution." Id. 106. These last words meet his subsequent remark that the necessary and proper clause is superfluous if it only pertains to incidental powers. Id. 463.

[54] Id. 438.

[55] 4 Elliot 141.

[56] 2 Elliot 537.

[57] 4 Elliot 179.

[58] E. S. Corwin, "The Passing of Dual Federalism," 36 Va. L. Rev. 1, 17 (1950).

was whether Congress was empowered to establish the
Bank of the United States, and that turned on whether a
bank was a proper *means* for execution of other expressly
granted powers. Marshall reasoned that a government "intrusted with such ample powers" as "the great powers, to
lay and collect taxes; to borrow money; to regulate com-
mece. . . . must also be intrusted with *ample means* for their
execution." Were the Constitution "to contain an accurate
detail of all the *subdivisions* of which its great powers will admit, and of all the *means* by which they may be carried into
execution, [it] would partake of the prolixity of a legal
code."[59] When *McCulloch* came under attack he leapt to its
defense under a pseudonym,[60] insisting that "it does not
contain the most distant allusion to *any extension by construction* of the powers of congress. Its sole object is to remind us
that a constitution cannot possibly enumerate the *means* by
which the powers of government are to be carried into execution."[61] Again and again, he repudiated any intention
to lay the predicate for such "extension by construction."
There is "not a syllable uttered by the court," he said, "that
applies to an enlargement of the powers of Congress."[62] He
rejected any imputation that "those powers ought to be en-

[59] 17 U.S. (10 Wheat.) 316, 407, 408 (1819) (emphasis added). Note
Madison's statement that "powers by implication were necessary to avoid
spelling out 'every minutiae'." Supra text accompanying note 40.

[60] "That famous pronouncement evoked a storm of hostile criticism
from the jealous exponents of states rights, one which did not wholly
abate until his death." Corwin, *Twilight* 7.

[61] *John Marshall's Defense of McCulloch v. Maryland* 185 (G. Gunther ed.
1969).

[62] Id. 182. Marshall's own incautious statement probably invited controversy: the necessary and proper clause, he stated, "purports to *enlarge,*
not to diminish the *powers* vested in the government. It purports to be an
additional power, not a restriction on those already granted." Emphasis
added. McCulloch v. Maryland, 17 U.S. (4 Wheat.) 316, 420 (1819).

larged by construction or otherwise,"[63] and branded as a "palpable misrepresentation" attribution to the Court of the view that the necessary and proper clause "as augmenting those powers and as one which is to be construed 'latitudinously' or even 'liberally'."[64]

The Founders' emphasis that the necessary and proper clause does not confer *additional* powers militates against the doctrine of *implied* powers that go beyond "means." What was denied under that express provision cannot be conjured out of the blue by "implication." The Marshallian "powers may not be enlarged by construction" is not to be circumvented by finding "implied" powers. The "notion of 'implied powers' would be inconsistent with the doctrine of enumerated powers."[65] Of what use were the reiterated assurances that the necessary and proper clause neither conferred new powers nor augmented existing powers, that the federal government's powers were "limited" and "enumerated," and therefore, "everything not expressly mentioned will be presumed to be omitted,"[66] if below the horizon

[63] Gunther, supra note 61 at 184. In fact, establishment of a national bank had unequivocally been rejected by the Convention. See infra Chapter 5, text accompanying notes 31–34, 37.

[64] Gunther 97. Gunthers remarkable discovery has been all but ignored by academe.

[65] David Engdahl, *Constitutional Power: Federal and State in a Nutshell* 11 (1974). "Recognizing this fact the Supreme Court early observed that 'the constitution . . . has not left the right of Congress to employ the necessary means, for the execution of the powers conferred on the government, to general reasoning. To its enumeration of powers is added [the necessary and proper clause]." Id. Murphy recounts that in the Virginia Convention "Marshall wanted to know if powers not specifically bestowed were still implied . . ., 'could any man say that this power was not retained by the states, as they had not given it away? For . . . does not a power remain till it is given away?'" Murphy 361.

[66] Wilson in the Pennsylvania Convention, McMaster & Stone 354; see

lurked "implied" powers which had not been disclosed to the Founders?[67] That would be to eject the devil through the door and permit him to reenter through a window. Then too, as Frankfurter pointed out, "implied restrictions upon the states were necessarily the creatures of judicial discretion"[68]—discretion which they profoundly distrusted.

The Framers did not trust implied powers, as is exemplified by Gorham's successful motion to add "and support" to the "to raise armies" phrase,[69] although a power to raise armies reasonably might have been construed to include the power to support them. That is likewise the lesson of their treatment of federal jurisdiction over places purchased for the erection of forts, arsenals, and other needed buildings. Originally Article I, §8(17) did not contain "by the consent of the Legislature of the State in which the same shall be." When Elbridge Gerry objected that this might be a medium of coercing State obedience, Rufus King "thought the [purchase] provision unnecessary, the power being already involved [i.e., implied]," but moved to insert the "consent" proviso, saying, "This would certainly make the power safe"; his motion was unanimously adopted.[70] Here was a palpably "national" measure that might readily have been deemed a "necessary and proper" means for effectuation of the powers to raise and support armies, to establish post offices, and the like, and yet intrusion into the State domain was specifically made dependent on State consent.

It will profit us to expatiate on what Madison described as the Founders' "cautious definition of federal powers."[71]

Marshall, supra note 65. Compare Washington, supra note 10. On augmentation, see supra text accompanying notes 52–57.

[67] See Madison, supra note 45.
[68] Felix Frankfurter, *The Commerce Clause* 49 (1937).
[69] 2 Farrand 329.
[70] Id. 510.
[71] Infra Chapter 5, text accompanying note 15.

Again and again the framers sought by painstaking drafting to guard against ambiguity that would invite "liberal" interpretations. The word "inhabitant" was substituted for "resident" because it was less liable to misconstruction;[72] "make" war was supplanted by "declare" because "'make' war might be understood to 'conduct' [it] which was an Executive function."[73] The draft of the Supreme Court's jurisdiction reading that "it shall be appellate" was changed "to 'the supreme Court shall have appellate jurisdiction,' in order to prevent uncertainty whether 'it' referred to the *supreme Court,* or to the *Judicial power.*"[74] Mason's suggestion that "maladministration" be made cause for impeachment was changed to "high crimes and misdemeanors" because Madison urged that "maladministration" was a "vague" term.[75] In the Pennsylvania Convention, Wilson emphasized "the care that the convention took in selecting their language. The words are 'the *migration* or IMPORTATION' of such persons [slaves] shall not be prohibited by Congress prior to the year 1808, but a tax or duty may be imposed on such IMPORTATION," migration being dropped for purposes of taxation.[76] And although Madison argued that the power "to regulate commerce" restrained States from "laying tonnage duties," the Convention adopted an express provision: "no State shall lay any duties on tonnage without the consent of Congress."[77] This provision at the tail end of the Convention strikingly exhibits its unwillingness to permit encroachment on States' Rights under cover of the commerce clause without explicit sanction. In short, the care of the Framers precisely to delineate the bounds of delegated

[72] 2 Farrand 217–218.
[73] Id. 319.
[74] Id. 437.
[75] Id. 550.
[76] 3 Farrand 161.
[77] 2 Farrand 625.

power[78] militate against the presupposition that those powers were to be "liberally" construed and thus set their fastidious labors at naught. And the explicit reservation to the States by the Tenth Amendment of rights not delegated further argues against a liberal interpretation of the delegated powers. These facts go far to rebut an inference that the door was left wide open for resort to "implied" powers.

The records further indicate that the Ratifiers associated implied powers with the *means* essential to execute granted powers. That association emerges in discussion of the omission of the word "expressly." Commenting on Randolph's reference to passport denials, though passports were essential to war making, Patrick Henry said, "Passports would not be given by Congress—Why? Because there was a clause in the Constitution which denied them *implied* powers."[79] In New York, Justice Robert Yates agreed that "in granting genl. powers—the powers to execute are *implied*."[80] Such views had been anticipated by Madison in Federalist No. 44. Addressing the necessary and proper clause, he wrote, "[W]herever the end is required, the means are authorized; wherever a general power to do a thing is given, every particular power necessary for doing it is included."[81] It is in this sense that Marshall's statement in *McCulloch v. Maryland*—"there is no phrase in the instrument which, like the articles of confederation, [by "expressly" delegated] excludes incidental or implied powers"[82]—is to be read. For

[78] In Federalist No. 33 at 202, Hamilton emphasizes that the supremacy clause "*expressly* confines this supremacy to laws made *pursuant to the Constitution*" and is "merely an instance of the caution in the Convention; since that limitation would have been . . . understood, though it had not been expressed."
[79] 3 Elliot 623.
[80] Lofgren, supra note 12 at 346.
[81] Federalist No. 44 at 294.
[82] 17 U.S. at 406; see also supra note 65.

McCulloch, as Marshall himself explained, was concerned with the *means* of executing (allegedly) "ample powers."

In his index to the records of the Convention, Max Farrand, who was steeped in the history of the Constitution, lists twelve instances under "Implied Powers,"[83] all but two of which refer to powers necessary and proper to effectuate those granted. Of the two, the Sherman reference breathes of a granted power that would embrace a proposed project: "It was mentioned in the general convention—but it was not thought necessary or proper to insert it in the Constitution, for Congress would have sufficient power to adopt it."[84] The other reference is to Mason's insistence that the objects of federal government "be expressly defined instead of indefinite powers under arbitrary construction of general clauses."[85] He objected that *granted* powers could be arbitrarily construed, not dreaming that additional "implied" powers would be claimed. If there are any references in the sources to implied powers other than those constituting means for effectuating granted powers, they have escaped my attention. My own reading confirms Farrand's identification of implied powers with "means," not additional powers.[86]

In sum, the records make plain that the necessary and proper clause was merely designed to specifically authorize

[83] 4 Farrand 162.

[84] 3 Farrand 362.

[85] 4 Farrand 56–57. So too, Gerry complained that "some powers of the legislature are ambiguous, and others are indefinite and dangerous." 3 Farrand 128.

[86] This was likewise Hamilton's opinion in his 1791 opinion on the constitutionality of the Bank:

a power of erecting a corporation may as well be *implied* as any other thing; it may as well be employed as an instrument or *means* of carrying into execution any of the specified powers.

Respecting the "necessary and proper" clause, he said,

the employment of *means* to effectuate, to carry into execution, granted powers, not to augment them; and they
strongly read against the doctrine of implied *powers*. Such
was the view expressed by the Supreme Court in the *Curtiss-
Wright* case: the test of an implied power is whether it
is "necessary and proper to carry into effect" an express
grant.[87] To go beyond this is to collide with Justice Story's
statement in *Gelston v. Hoyt* that "it is certainly against the
general theory of our institutions to create great discretion-
ary powers by implication."[88]

THE SUPREMACY CLAUSE

By way of background, it will be recalled that the Constitution set up a federal government that was to be supreme in
its sphere, leaving the States supreme with respect to undelegated powers.[89] Delegation of a power deprived the
States of supremacy in that sphere, and there federal would
override State laws. Madison put the matter succinctly: "If
the power was not given, Congress could not exercise it; if
given, they might exercise it, although it should interfere
with the laws or even the Constitution of the States."[90] But
each government, Hamilton assured the New York Ratification Convention, was supreme in its sphere, stressing
that "this balance between the National and State govern-

---

it will not be contended . . . that the clause in question gives any *new*
or *independent* power. But it gives an explicit sanction to the doctrine
of *implied* powers.

8 *The Papers of Alexander Hamilton* 100, 106 (H. C. Syrett & J. E. Cooke
eds. 1965).
   [87] United States v. Curtiss-Wright Export Corp. 299 U.S. 304, 316
(1936).
   [88] 16 U.S. (3 Wheat.) 246, 332–333 (1818).
   [89] Supra Chapter 3, text accompanying notes 52–63.
   [90] 2 *Annals of Congress* 1897 (1791).

ments . . . is of the utmost importance. . . . It forms a double security to the people."[91] The Tenth Amendment and the supremacy clause are nicely geared to reflect this equilibrium—the former to preserve to the States powers *not delegated* to the United States, the latter to make *delegated* powers supreme. Corwin states, however, that the "theory of two mutually exclusive, reciprocally limiting fields of power" was twice rejected by Chief Justice Marshall in *McCulloch v. Maryland* and *Gibbons v. Ogden*.[92] In *McCulloch* Marshall observed that "the government of the Union, though limited in its powers, is *supreme within its sphere of action*."[93] The corollary is that it is not supreme beyond that sphere. It is true that in *Gibbons* counsel "contended that if a law, passed by a State in the exercise of its acknowledged sovereignty comes into conflict with a law passed by Congress in pursuance of the Constitution," they stand "like equal opposing powers." But as Marshall pointed out, laws passed "in pursuance of the Constitution" are declared "supreme law" by the supremacy clause.[94] Only *delegated* powers, however, were made "supreme"; the Founders meant to protect the States' *undelegated* powers from federal intrusion, as Article VI makes quite clear.[95]

[91] 2 Elliot 257.

[92] Corwin, *Commerce* 135. Yet he wrote, "*The most persistent problem of American constitutional law arises from the fact that to a multiplicity of state legislatures has been assigned the most important powers over private rights.*" (emphasis in orginal). Corwin, *Twilight* 90.

[93] 17 U.S. (4 Wheat.) 315, 405 (1819) (emphasis added). See also Marshall, supra Chapter 3, note 52.

[94] 22 U.S. (9 Wheat.) 1, 210 (1824).

[95] Corwin's statement that "Dual federalism cannot be squared logically with the 'supremacy clause,'" overlooks State supremacy in its undelegated sphere. Corwin, *Twilight* 182–183. His misconception is underscored by his argument that "subordinating ['national legislative power'] to the reserved powers of the States . . . revers[es] the supremacy clause." Corwin, *Commerce* 215.

Article VI, §2 provides: "This Constitution and the laws of the United States . . . *in pursuance* thereof . . . shall be the supreme law of the land." The key words are "in pursuance thereof." Elsewhere I have documented the Founders' understanding that "in pursuance" meant consistent with the Constitution; if a law was inconsistent therewith, it was not "in pursuance of the Constitution," and therefore not "supreme."[96] To that proof may be added several confirmatory statements.

In Federalist No. 33, Hamilton wrote that laws "which are not *pursuant* to its constitutional powers, but which are *invasions* of the residuary authorities" of the States "will be merely acts of usurpation," not "the supreme law of the land."[97] In Virginia, Marshall assured the Ratifiers that the supremacy clause did not extend to all cases, that a federal "law not warranted by any of the enumerated powers" would constitute "an infringement of the Constitution."[98] Davie, discussing the supremacy clause in North Carolina, said a federal law "can be supreme only in cases consistent with

---

Justice McLean better understood that "the federal government is supreme within the scope of its *delegated* powers, and the State governments are equally supreme in the exercise of those powers *not delegated* by them." The License Case, 46 U.S. (5 How.) 504, 588–589 (1847). This reiterates the earlier holding in New York v. Miln, 36 U.S. (11 Pet.) 102, 139 (1837): "[A] State has the same undeniable and unlimited jurisdiction over all persons and things, within its territorial limits, as any foreign nation; where that jurisdiction is *not surrendered* or restrained by the Constitution." See supra Chapter 3, text accompanying notes 52–63. Madison justly considered that "the residuary and inviolable sovereignty" of the State results in a "limitation" on the powers of the federal government. Corwin, *Twilight* 3. For if the State retained exclusive jurisdiction in a given sphere, that jurisdiction was not "surrendered" to the federal government. See also Madison infra Chapter 8, text accompanying note 67.

[96] Raoul Berger, *Congress v. The Supreme Court* 228–234 (1969).

[97] Federalist No. 33 at 201–202. In No. 27 at 169, Hamilton emphasized that the federal government's laws "as to the *enumerated* and *legitimate* objects of its jurisdiction, will become the SUPREME LAW of the land."

[98] 3 Elliot 553.

the powers specially granted, and not in usurpations."[99] Iredell explained that the supremacy clause meant only that "when Congress passes a law consistent with the Constitution, it is to be binding on the people."[100] And he emphasized that "the question, then, under this clause, will always be whether Congress has exceeded its authority."[101] Charles Pinckney referred to the regulations of Congress "in pursuance of *their powers*."[102] And Chief Justice McKean told the Pennsylvania Ratification Convention that the meaning of the supremacy clause "is simply this, that the Congress have the power of making laws upon any subject over which the proposed plan gives them a jurisdiction, and that those laws thus made in pursuance of the Constitution, shall be binding upon the States."[103] Twice Chief Justice Marshall so construed "in pursuance." In *Marbury v. Madison* he concluded that "laws . . . made in pursuance of the Constitution" strengthen the principle that "a law *repugnant* to the Constitution is void."[104] And in *Gibbons v. Ogden* he said, "The nullity of any act *inconsistent* with the Constitution, is produced by the declaration that the Constitution is the supreme law."[105] In short, as Alpheus Mason stated, "Even the supremacy clause could not extend the operation of supreme national law beyond the confines of national power, constitutionally granted."[106]

[99] 4 Elliot 182.
[100] Id. 179.
[101] Id.
[102] 3 Farrand 117.
[103] McMaster & Stone 277.
[104] 5 U.S. (1 Cranch) 137, 180 (1803) (emphasis added).
[105] 22 U.S. (9 Wheat.) 1, 210 (1824) (emphasis added).
[106] Mason 49.

CHAPTER FIVE

The "General Welfare" Clause

ARTICLE I, §8(1) of the Constitution provides that

> The Congress shall have power:
> To lay and collect taxes, duties, imposts and excises, to pay the debts and provide for the common defence and general welfare of the United States; . . . .

It is followed by the enumeration of seventeen specific powers, and the issue is whether the enumeration restricts the generality of the preceding clause.

Corwin, after vigorously defending a broad construction of the "general welfare" clause, laments that "the success of the spending power in eluding all constitutional snares, goes far to envelop the entire institution of judicial review, as well as its product, constitutional law, in an atmosphere of unreality, even of futility."[1] Thereby he vindicates Madison's prophetic vision: were the clause construed to give Congress "a general power of legislation," "no adequate landmarks would be left by the constructive extension of the power of Congress."[2] Madison echoed the deep-seated aversion of the Founders to the delegation of unlimited power;

[1] Corwin, *Twilight* 153–154, 178–179.
[2] Elliot 469–470.

this was probably their deepest fear, and it should constitute the starting point of analysis.

Instead, the long-accepted approach has been to weigh the opposing arguments of Madison and Hamilton and to award the palm to Hamilton,[3] as if the issue were merely one of forensics. But more than balancing arguments is involved. What Madison wrote in Federalist No. 41 represented the opinion of the Framers,[4] whereas Hamilton's 1791 argument departed from their opinion and merely represented his own. Moreover, No. 41 constituted a *representation* to the Ratifiers, designed to capture votes for adoption of the Constitution. Corwin correctly observed that

> While adoption of the Constitution was pending some of the opponents made the charge that the phrase "to provide for the general welfare" was a sort of legislative joker which was designed, in conjunction with the "necessary and proper" clause, to vest Congress with the power to provide for whatever it might choose to regard as the "general welfare" by any means deemed by it to be "necessary and proper." The suggestion was promply repudiated by advocates of the Constitution.[5]

[3] Corwin, *Twilight* 154–156.

[4] Jefferson regarded the Federalist as "evidence of the general opinion of those who framed" the Constitution. Clinton Rossiter, *Alexander Hamilton and the Constitution* 52, 227 (1964). Commenting on the Federalist and the views Hamilton repeated in the New York Convention, Chancellor Kent stated, "These opinions may be regarded as the best evidence of the sense of the authors of that instrument [the Constitution] . . . and the most accurate contemporary exposition to which we can recur." Livingston v. van Ingen, 9 Johns 507, 516, 517 (1812). Corwin wrote, "It cannot reasonably be doubted that Hamilton was . . . endeavoring to represent the matured conclusions of the Convention itself." E. S. Corwin, *The Doctrine of Judicial Review* 44 (1914).

Given that the Federalist represents the views of the framers and is frequently cited, on what theory can access to the framers' own recorded intentions be barred, particularly when confirmed by the Federalist?

[5] E. S. Corwin, "The Passing of Dual Federalism," 36 Va. L. Rev. 1, 5 (1950).

Contemporaries understood that such representations were designed to garner votes, as may be gathered from Rutledge's remarks in the Senate on January 13, 1802. He said that the three authors of the Federalist "who had the most agency in framing this Constitution, finding that objections had been raised against its adoption, and that much of the hostility produced against it had resulted from a misunderstanding of its provisions, united in the patriotic work of explaining the true meaning of its framers."[6] As Justice Story—whose espousal of the Hamilton view is often cited—wrote in another context, "If the Constitution was ratified under the belief, sedulously propagated on all sides, that such protection was afforded, would it not now be a fraud upon the whole people to give a different construction to its powers?"[7]

A contemporary assurance as to the limited scope of the general welfare clause is that of Madison in Federalist No. 41:

> It has been urged and echoed, that the power "to lay and collect taxes . . . to pay the debts, and provide for the common defence and the general welfare of the United States amounts to an unlimited commission to exercise every power which may be alleged to be necessary for the common defence or general welfare. No stronger proof could be given of the distress under which these writers labor for objections, than their stooping to such a misconstruction. . . . But what color can this objection have, when a specification of the objects alluded to by these general terms immediately follows, and is not even separated by a longer pause than a semicolon? . . . For what purpose could the enumeration of particular powers be inserted, if these and all others were meant to be included in the preceding general power. . . . But the idea of an enumeration of particulars which neither explain nor qualify the general meaning . . . is an absurdity.[8]

[6] 4 Elliot 446.
[7] 2 Story, §1084 at 33.
[8] Id. 268–269 (emphasis added). In the Virginia Convention, Madison reiterated that "the powers of the federal government are enumerated;

Madison also stressed that the "language used by the Convention is a copy from the Articles of Confederation," and asked, "what would have been thought" of the Continental Congress if, in disregard of the "specifications which ascertain and limit" the import of "those general expressions," they "had exercised an unlimited power of providing for the common defence and general welfare?"[9] This was not a fleeting representation for the purpose of garnering votes for ratification of the Constitution, but an enduring article of Madison's faith.[10] In his veto message of March 3, 1817,

---

it can only operate in certain cases; it has legislative powers on defined and limited objects, beyond which it cannot extend its jurisdiction." 3 Elliot 95. For a similar expression by Edmund Randolph in the Virginia Convention, see infra text accompanying notes 25–26. See also Wilson in the Pennsylvania Convention, 2 Elliot 454. This seems the soundest common sense. What need was there expressly to provide power to "raise and support armies," to "provide and maintain a navy," and so on, if they were comprehended in to "provide for the common defense"? Again, why express provisions for coining money, fixing weights and measures, establishing post offices, if these were embraced by the provision of the "general welfare"? Such specificity, to my mind, reveals anxiety to circumscribe the generality of the "general welfare" clause in order to assure the Ratifiers that only what was thus specified was to be surrendered.

[9] Federalist No. 41 at 269.

[10] In the First Congress, Madison, discussing the proposal to incorporate a Bank of the United States in light of the general welfare clause, stated:

The powers as to these general purposes was limited to laying taxes for them; and the general purposes themselves were limited and explained by the particular enumeration subjoined. To understand these terms in any sense that would justify the power in question, would give to Congress an unlimited power; that would render nugatory the enumeration of particular powers; would supersede all the powers reserved to the State Governments. These terms are copied from the articles of Confederation; had it ever been pretended that they were to be understood otherwise than as here explained?

2 *Annals of Congress* 1896 (1791). In his 1791 Philadelphia Lectures, Justice James Wilson, who was second only to Madison as an architect of the

President Madison said that he could not locate provision for internal improvements either in the commerce or the general welfare clauses. To rely on the latter, he wrote, would render

> the special and careful enumeration of powers which follow the clause nugatory and improper. Such a view of the Constitution would have the effect of giving to Congress a general power of legislation instead of the defined and limited one hitherto understood to belong to them, the terms "common defense and general welfare" embracing every object and act within the purview of a legislative trust.

The path to change, he pointed out, was by amendment.[11] Identification of the general welfare clause with that of the Articles of Confederation was likewise made by Roger Sherman and Oliver Ellsworth in a letter transmitting the proposed Constitution to the Governor of Connecticut,[12] and by George Nicholas in the Virginia Ratification Convention.[13] The common complaint against the Articles of Confederation was the impotence of Congress. That impotence was not merely due to the absence of taxing power. War making could be fettered by the States; Congress was unable to curb internecine exactions by the States; there was no national judiciary, no coinage, no postal system, and so

---

Constitution, stated, "The national government was intended 'to promote the general welfare.' For this reason Congress have power to regulate commerce. . . ." 1 J. Wilson, *Works of James Wilson* 434 (R. McCloskey ed. 1967).

[11] 1 James Richardson, *Messages and Papers of the Presidents* 584–585 (1896). In his Second Inaugural Address, March 4, 1805, Jefferson asked for an amendment to apply revenues to "rivers, canals, roads, arts, manufactures, education, and other great objects within each state." *The Jeffersonian and Hamiltonian Tradition in American Politics* 79–80 (A. Fried ed. 1968).

[12] 3 Farrand 99.

[13] 3 Elliot 245.

on. If Congress had at hand an unlimited power to provide for the "common defence and general welfare," all the to-do about adopting a new Constitution was superfluous. Adoption of that phraseology in the Constitution carried with it the construction put upon it by the Continental Congress.[14] Where is the evidence that the Framers meant to give it a broader meaning?

It is most significant that in its progress through the Convention the clause excited no comment. The explanation was furnished by Madison; writing in 1830 he said,

> these terms copied from the Articles of Confederation, were regarded in the new as in the old Instrument, merely as general terms, explained & limited by the subjoined specifications; and therefore requiring no critical attention or studied precaution. . . . [I]t exceeds the possibility of belief, that the known advocates, in the Convention, for a jealous grant & cautious definition of federal powers, should have silently permitted the introduction of words or phrases in a sense rendering fruitless the restrictions & definitions elaborated by them.[15]

Story rejects reference to the Articles of Confederation because "the clause has no reference whatsoever to the con-

[14] Chief Justice White said of the Article IV provisions of the Articles of Confederation and of the Constitution, "There can be but little question that the purpose of both of these provisions is the same, and that the privileges and immunities intended are the same in each." United States v. Wheeler, 254 U.S. 281, 296 (1920).

[15] 3 Farrand 483, 487, 488. In a similar situation Martin van Buren observed in 1827:

> We know with what jealousy, with what watchfulness, with what scrupulous care, its minutest provisions were examined, discussed. . . . But of this highly consequential provision . . . no complaints were heard, no explanation asked, no remonstrance made. . . . It is most mysterious, if the Constitution was then understood as it now is, that this was so.

4 Elliot 486. For the Founders' minute scrutiny, see supra Chapter 4, text accompanying notes 68–77.

federation."[16] By this test a court may not look to Blackstone to find the meaning of a common law term employed in the Constitution, e.g., ex post facto, although the Framers themselves did so.[17] So did the Court, as when Chief Justice White assimilated the "privileges and immunities" of Article IV to those of the Articles of Confederation.[18] Moreover, No. 41 of the Federalist advised the Ratifiers that the clause "is a copy of the Articles of Confederation," as did Ellsworth, Sherman, and Nicholas.[19] Story also differs with Madison's construction of the Articles. Assume that Madison may have been mistaken; nevertheless, as Charles Evans Hughes said in addressing the colonists' reliance on Magna Charta: "It matters not whether they were accurate in their understanding, for the point is . . . what the colonists thought it meant."[20] More importantly, Story does not meet Madison's argument that "it exceeds the possibility of belief, that the known advocates, in the Convention, for a jealous grant & cautious definition of federal powers, should have silently permitted the introduction of words or phrases in a sense rendering fruitless the restrictions and definitions elaborated by them."[21] Men do not use words to defeat their purposes; and courts seek rather to effectuate, not to defeat, the legislative purpose.[22]

Madison tellingly emphasized that among the many amendments submitted by the several States, "intended to circumscribe the powers granted" by them, not one touched the "general welfare" clause though it was "evidently more alarming in its range, than all the powers objected to put

[16] 1 Story, §917 at 669.
[17] See 2 Farrand 448.
[18] See supra note 14.
[19] Supra, text accompanying notes 9, 12, 13.
[20] C. E. Hughes, *The Supreme Court of the United States* 186 (1928).
[21] Supra, text accompanying note 15.
[22] United States v. Classic, 313 U.S. 299, 316 (1941).

together." This demonstrated that "it was taken for granted that the terms were harmless; because explained & limited, as in the 'Articles of Confederation,' by the enumerated powers which followed them."[23] Story does not comment on the extraordinary absence from the many amendments proffered by the Ratifiers of one circumscribing the "general welfare" clause. At no stage did any advocate of adoption intimate that the clause enlarged the granted powers. On the contrary, Nicholas, speaking in the Virginia Convention, rejected the argument of the clause's opponents that "its dangers . . . resulted from its . . . extension, of the powers granted in the other clauses," maintaining that it was not united "to the general power of legislation."[24] There too Randolph dismissed "the dangers of giving the general government an indefinite power of providing for the general welfare. I contend that no such power was given." After reading the clause he asked, "Is this an independent, separate power, to provide for the general welfare of the United States? No sir."[25] As he said in rejecting a reading of the related "necessary and proper" clause as vesting "complete and unlimited" legislative power in Congress, "its powers are enumerated. Is it not, then, fairly deducible, that it has no power but what is expressly given it? For if its powers were to be general, an enumeration would be needless."[26]

Turning his back on the representations made to the Ratifiers, Hamilton (as co-author of the Federalist he was at least aware of Madison's representation in No. 41) argued in 1791 that the "phrase is as comprehensive as any that could have been used, because it was not fit that the constitutional authority of the Union to appropriate its revenues should

[23] 3 Farrand 489–490.
[24] 3 Elliot 443.
[25] Id. 466.
[26] Id. 464.

have been restricted within narrower limits than the general welfare."[27] In the Convention, however, he had proposed that he would give Congress "the unlimited power of passing *all* laws without exception," but confessed that he "was aware that [his plan] went beyond the ideas of most members."[28] His 1791 construction was therefore at war with his admission that such "unlimited power" was unacceptable to the Convention. Henry St. George Tucker bitingly commented that "Mr. Hamilton having failed to secure to Congress the power to legislate in all matters which Congress might deem of benefit or interest to the United States, has sought to attain the same end by giving the words 'common defence and general welfare' that broad significance which would embrace the power denied by the Convention in its rejection of his plan."[29] Tucker is confirmed by Hamilton himself. Urging his fellow delegates to sign the Constitution, he said, "No man's ideas were more remote from the plan than his own were known to be."[30]

   Hamilton's attempt to secure by "interpretation" what the Convention had rejected is illustrated by his argument that Congress was empowered to establish a national bank. Let the record speak. On August 18, Madison proposed that among other powers Congress be authorized "to grant char-

[27] Corwin, *Twilight* 156.

[28] 1 Farrand 300, 291.

[29] H. Tucker, "The General Welfare," 8 Va. L. Rev. 167, 168 (1922). Corwin tells us that in Federalist Nos. 30 and 34 Hamilton assigned the words of the "general welfare" clause "their most liberal meaning." Corwin, *Twilight* 154. Both deal with taxation; neither mentions the clause. No. 34 treats the concurrent State and federal power to tax, and stressed the need to provide for payment of debts incurred by wars (page 206). No. 30 refers to provision for the expense of raising troops, building fleets, "all matters which call for disbursements out of the national treasury" (page 182).

[30] 2 Farrand 645–646.

ters of incorporation in cases where the public good may require them, and the authority of a single State may be incompetent." This, and Pinckney's proposal "to grant charters of incorporation,"[31] were referred to the Committee of Detail. The resultant report on August 27 omitted any such provision.[32] Three days before the Constitution was signed, on September 14, Madison suggested that Dr. Franklin's motion to add "a power to provide canals where deemed necessary" be enlarged into a

"power to grant charters of incorporation where the interests of the U.S. might require & the legislative provisions of individual States may be incompetent." His primary object was however to secure an easy communication between the States which the free intercourse now to be opened, seemed to call for—The political obstacles being removed, a removal of the natural ones as far as possible ought to follow. Mr Randolph 2ded the proposition.

Mr. King thought the power unnecessary.

Mr. Wilson. It is necessary to prevent a *State* from obstructing the *general* welfare.

Mr. King—The States will be prejudiced and divided into parties by it—in Phila. & New York, it will be referred to the establishment of a Bank, which has been the subject of contention in those Cities. In other places it will be referred to mercantile monopolies.

Mr. Wilson mentioned the importance of facilitating by canals, the communication with the Western settlements—As to Banks he did not think with Mr. King that the power in that point of view would excite the prejudices & parties apprehended. As to mercantile monopolies they are already included in the power to regulate trade.

Col. Mason was for limiting the power to the single case of Canals. He was afraid of monopolies of every sort, which he

[31] Id. 325.
[32] Id. 366.

did not think were by any means already implied by the Constitution as supposed by Mr. Wilson.

The motion being so modified as to admit a distinct question specifying & limited to the case of canals.

The vote was 3 for and 8 against.[33] In sum, even when "limited to the case of Canals," excluding the controversial Bank, the motion failed. Presumably Hamilton was present on the 14th for he signed the Constitution on the 17th.[34]

In his 1791 Opinion on the constitutionality of the Bank, Hamilton pretended to find the facts confused, saying that some consider that the Convention's action "was confined to the opening of canals . . . others that it embraced banks; and others that it extended to the power of incorporation generally"; still others "thought it improper to vest in Congress a power of erecting corporations." He ended by saying, "whatever may have been the intention of the framers of a constitution, or of a law . . . that intention is to be sought in the instrument itself,"[35] ignoring that the common law had long been to the contrary.[36] Subsequently Framers Abraham Baldwin and Wilson, now a Justice, recapitulating these facts, agreed that "a *bank* had been the great bone of contention between the two parties of [Pennsylvania] . . . that therefore, to insert this power, would instantly enlist against the whole instrument, the whole of the anti-bank party in Pennsylvania. Whereupon it was rejected."[37]

By far the most extended discussion of the clause is that of Justice Story, focused almost entirely on the text and constituting a formidable exercise in exegesis if only because it

[33] Id. 615–616, 620.
[34] Id. 641, 664.
[35] 8 *Papers of Alexander Hamilton* III (H. Syrett & J. Cooke eds. 1965).
[36] See Appendix.
[37] 3 Farrand 373, 376.

runs to some thirty pages in his *Commentaries on the Constitution of the United States.*[38] Although he cites Madison's Federalist No. 41, he treats it as an *argument,* ignoring its weight as a *representation* meant to garner the Ratifiers' votes, to repudiate which, by his own testimony, would be a fraud upon the people. And though he also cites Elliot's *Debates,* he likewise takes no account of similar representations by Randolph and Nicholas in the Virginia Ratification Convention.[39] Intent on rebutting the argument that the clause conferred a "substantive power," he declared that

> The Constitution was, from its very origin, contemplated to be a frame of a national government, of special and enumerated powers, and *not general or unlimited powers. . . .* If the clause "to pay the debts and provide for the common defence and general welfare of the United States," is construed to be an independent and substantive grant of power, it not only renders wholly unimportant and unnecessary the subsequent enumeration of specific powers; but it plainly extends far beyond them, and creates a general authority in congress to pass all laws, which they may deem for the common defence or general welfare. Under such circumstances, the constitution would practically create an unlimited national government.[40]

And he picked up Madison's "For what purpose could the enumeration of particular powers be inserted, if these and all others were meant to be included in the preceding general power? Nothing is more natural or common than first to use a general phrase and then to qualify it by a recital of particulars."[41]

Thus Story maintains that the general welfare phrase is

[38] 1 Story, §905 at 661 et seq.

[39] Story traces the progress of the clause through the several drafting stages, in which he is "substantially" in agreement with Madison. Id., §930 at 682 note 1.

[40] Id., §909 at 663.

[41] Id., §911 at 664.

limited by the subjoined enumeration for purposes of re-
futing the "substantive power" argument. But he shifts
ground when he examines the phrase in relation to the
taxing power, rejecting the argument that "the clause is connected with any subsequent specifications," and insisting
that "it stands entirely disconnected from every subsequent
clause, both in sense and punctuation."[42] This, he explains,
is because the enumeration is not preceded by the words
"In the manner following, viz."[43] But that lack equally undermines his "substantive power" argument that the "general
welfare" phrase is limited by the subjoined enumeration. In
truth he has employed a double standard. The words "general welfare" in one and the same clause cannot have two opposite meanings in the absence of compelling evidence that
such was the intention. Nor may a rule of construction
be manipulated as a desired course may dictate. Story has
opened the door to the very unlimited power he decried. To
urge that the "general welfare" phrase is a qualification that
"limits the taxing power to objects for the common defence
or general welfare"[44] is to indulge in delusory rhetoric. For
he himself urged that if "general welfare" is not qualified by
the subsequent enumeration, Congress is left with boundless discretion to decide what is for the general welfare and
common defense.[45]

[42] Id., §913 at 665. It is worth noting that in the penultimate version of
Article I, §8, every clause was puncutated by a period, 2 Farrand 594–596,
whereas the final version substituted semicolons for periods, suggesting
that the general welfare clause was not meant to be disconnected from the
subjoined enumeration. Id. 655–656.

[43] 1 Story, §913 at 665.

[44] Id., §911 at 664.

[45] Supra, text accompanying note 40. The provision in the New Jersey
Plan that the revenues shall "be applied to such federal purposes as [Con-
gress] shall deem proper & expedient," 1 Farrand 243, fell by the wayside,
as did Hamilton's wish to give Congress "the unlimited power of passing
all laws without exception." Id. 300.

Still other difficulties are posed by Story's arguments. Repeatedly he emphasizes that the "general welfare" phrase does not constitute an "independent and substantive grant of power," but is merely a "qualification or limitation of the power to lay taxes."[46] He rejects a construction of the phrase as "an independent and substantive grant of power,"[47] saying it "contains no grant of any power whatsoever."[48] In short, the phrase does not give Congress general welfare *power;* it serves only to limit the power to tax. But if there is no general welfare power then unless resort be had to the enumerated powers there is no subject of taxation. Taxation does not exist in a vacuum; it serves only to pay for carrying out granted powers. Without substantive powers taxation has no purpose.[49] Conversely, to argue that Congress can tax

[46] 1 Story, §909 at 663 (emphasis added). Replying to Timothy Pickering, who had consulted the first edition of the Journals of the Convention, as printed in 1787, and found that "to pay the debts," etc., was preceded by a comma, not a semicolon, Chief Justice Marshall wrote, "I have always supposed that there ought to be a comma instead of a semi-colon after the word excises. I have never believed that the words 'to pay the debts . . .' were to be considered as a substantive grant of power, but as a declaration of objects for which taxes &c. might be levied." James McClellan, *Joseph Story and the American Constitution* 303–304 (1971).

[47] 1 Story, §909 at 663.

[48] Id. §911 at 664.

[49] Thomas Cooley considered that the federal government is empowered to tax for "all national purposes," the "general outline of these is to be found in the federal constitution," e.g., "it may raise and support armies, create and maintain a navy." T. Cooley, *A Treatise on the Law of Taxation* 110 (2d ed. 1886). To argue that the authorization "to provide money for the common defense and general welfare," 1 Story, §925 at 676, "is a mere expression of the ends and purposes to be effected by the preceding power of taxation," id., is empty rhetoric. The purpose to "provide for the common defence" is clothed in substantive power to do so, e.g., "to raise and support armies." A "purpose" unaccompanied by a power is unimplemented. If, as Story maintains, "to provide for the common defence" does not constitute a "substantive grant" of power, how can taxes be levied for that "purpose"? Nor may we overlook that "Con-

and spend for the general welfare is to endow Congress with a welfare *power*. Story himself denied that "a mere power to lay taxes . . . for the common defence and general welfare, does include all the other powers of government; or even does include the other enumerated powers (limited as they are)."[50] Since he maintains that the general welfare clause "stands *entirely disconnected* from every subsequent clause,"[51] it follows that the power to tax is divorced from *all* subsequent powers. That, if I do not misunderstand Story, is a startling result: where can the federal government look to pay, for example, the costs of the army? That the power of taxation, however, was not "entirely disconnected," for example, from the provision to "raise and support armies" is evidenced by the Article I, §8(12) provision that no appropriation of money "shall be for a longer term than two years." And Federalist No. 30 explains that taxation is essential to cover the expenses of raising troops, building fleets, and the like.[52]

Then too, the last clause of §8 empowers Congress "To make all laws which shall be necessary and proper to carry

---

gress is not empowered to tax for those purposes which are within the exclusive province of the States." Gibbons v. Ogden, 22 U.S. (9 Wheat.) 1, 199 (1824).

Tested by Story's own illustration, the general welfare clause has become virtually illimitable. As an object "wholly extraneous" to the "general welfare," he instanced "propagating Mahometanism among the Turks [today paying for birth control in undeveloped countries], or giving aids and subsidies to foreign nations to build palaces for its kings." 1 Story, §922 at 673. Is aid to African nations employed to erect stadia also "wholly indefensible upon Constitutional principles"?

[50] Id., §923 at 674.

[51] Id., §913 at 665.

[52] After enumerating certain powers vested in the federal government, James Wilson said, "for the accomplishment of the foregoing purposes, a revenue is unquestionably indispensable." Quoted in H. Tucker, "Judge Story's position on the So-Called General Welfare Clause," 13 A.B.A.J.465, 466 (1927).

into execution the foregoing Powers." Given that law making is explicitly limited to effectuation of the granted powers, is it conceivable that taxation, the subject of bitter dispute, was meant to range beyond the law-making power? It is also difficult to conceive that those who were at pains to authorize Congress to "make rules for the government and regulation of the land and naval forces," Article I, §8(14), meant to confer unlimited power by the general welfare clause.

Jefferson was closer to the Founders' thinking than Story. Story cites him for interpretation of the clause "as a qualification of the power to lay taxes," but does not appreciate his anticipation of Story's view that the clause does not confer unlimited power. Jefferson rejected the view that the general welfare clause conferred a

> distinct and independent power to do any act they might please for the good of the Union, [it] would render all the preceding and subsequent enumerations of power completely useless. It would reduce the whole instrument to a single phrase, that of instituting a Congress with power to do whatever would be for the good of the United States. . . . Certainly no such universal power was intended to be given them. It was intended to lace them up strictly within the enumerated powers, and those without which, as *means,* those powers could not be carried into effect.[53]

[53] 1 Story, §926 at 677 (emphasis added). Story stated,

There can be no doubt that an affirmative grant of powers in many cases will imply an exclusion of all others. As, for instance, the Constitution declares that the powers of Congress shall extend to certain enumerated cases. This specification of particulars evidently excludes all pretensions to a general legislative authority. Why? Because an affirmative grant of special powers would be absurd, as well as useless, if a general authority was granted.

Citing Federalist No. 83 at 541; 1 Story, §448 at 343.

Others have also rejected constructions that "would practically create an unlimited government." 1 Story, §909 at 663; which result that there is "no part of the conduct of life with which on similar principles Congress

In light of the records of the several Conventions, that seems to me all but incontestable. Born of distrust of "indefinite" grants, the drive for enumeration was meant to circumscribe the delegated powers, and that purpose is not to be frustrated by a paper restriction—that the power to tax is "limited" to the "general welfare"—itself as illimitable as the wide blue sky. The grant of power to tax was bitterly contested, and as Story mildly puts it, there was a "desire . . . to introduce some restriction upon the power to lay taxes in order to allay jealousies and suppress alarms."[54] His interpretation sets that "desire" at naught.

Madison's summation in 1792 in the House seems just: the clause is "a sort of caption, or general description of the specified powers . . . having no further meaning, and giving no further powers, than what is found in that specification."[55] This reflected his Federalist No. 41; and it can hardly be denied that Madison was better situated to appreciate the thinking of the Founders than Story, who wrote at a remove of 40 years, seeking to deduce their intention from the text

---

might not interfere." Justice Holmes dissenting in Northern Securities Co. v. United States, 193 U.S. 197, 403 (1903); or "to find immediacy or directness here is to find it almost everywhere." Justice Cardozo, joined by Justice Stone, concurring in Schecter Poultry Corp. v. United States, 295 U.S. 495, 554 (1935). See also Chief Justice Hughes, *Schecter*, id. at 550; Kidd v. Pearson, 128 U.S. 1, 21 (1888).

[54] 1 Story, §930 at 681.

[55] Id., §919 at 671 note 2. Madison forcefully argued, "Money cannot be applied to the general welfare, otherwise than by application of it to some particular measure, conducive to the general welfare. Whenever, therefore, money has been raised by the general authority, and is to be applied to a particular measure, a question arises, whether the particular measure be within the enumerated authorities vested in the Congress. . . . An appropriation of money to the general welfare would be deemed rather a mockery than an observation of this constitutional injunction" that "no money shall be drawn from the treasury but in consequence of appropriations by law." Id., §918 at 670.

by rules of grammar, punctuation, and rules of construction without heeding the record they left of their intentions. Story's arguments run counter to the Founder's rejection of unlimited power, to the representations to the Ratifiers that the clause conferred no such power, and to the absence of objections in the Ratifying Conventions to so wide-ranging a power in the midst of objections to far less formidable powers.

When the Court "at last came to grips with the constitutional issue" in 1936,[56] it adopted Hamilton's view, noting that it was espoused by Story.[57] Instead of seeking to find the intention of the draftsmen as was long its practice,[58] particularly when a "literal" construction would conduce to unlimited power, the Court weighed the opposing Madison-Hamilton arguments, and without a glance at the representations made to the Ratifiers, concluded that Story's reading was "the correct one" never mind that Story himself branded repudiation of representations made to the Founders as a fraud upon the people. The Court dismissed Madison's statement in Federalist No. 41 (without mention of its source),

[56] Corwin, "The Passing of Dual Federalism," supra note 5 at 1, 11.

[57] United States v. Butler, 297 U.S. 1, 65 (1936). This is a strange case on which to erect a far-reaching doctrine, for those remarks were sheerest dictum: "We are not now required to ascertain the scope of the phrase 'general welfare of the United States' to determine whether an appropriation in aid of agriculture falls within it. Wholly apart from that question, another principle embedded in the Constitution prohibits enforcement of the Agricultural Adjustment Act. The Act invades the reserved rights of the States. It is a statutory plan to regulate and control agricultural production, a matter beyond the powers delegated to the federal government." Id. at 68. It follows, although Justice Roberts did not perceive the logical consequence of his reasoning, that if a power was reserved to the States, it lies outside the scope of the general welfare clause.

[58] Hawaii v. Mankichi, 190 U.S. 197, 212 (1903); Rhode Island v. Massachusetts, 37 U.S. (12 Pet.) 657, 721 (1838). And see Appendix, text accompanying notes 34–40.

that the "power to tax and spend must be confined to the enumerated" powers, saying, "In this view the phrase is a mere tautology, for taxation and appropriation are or may be necessary incidents of the exercise of the enumerated legislative powers."[59] If it be tautologous in relation to the enumerated powers, it is equally tautologous as to the "general welfare" clause. In truth, however, the power to tax, among the most hotly debated issues in the several conventions, was deemed too crucial to be left to inference. It was "one of the most important," Madison told the Virginia Ratification Convention, "that can possibly engage our attention," "essential to salvation of the Union," "indispensable . . . to the existence of any efficient or well-organized system of government."[60] It speaks volumes for the improvisatory nature of constitutional law making that the Court should reduce so vital a power to a mere "incident" of the "enumerated legislative powers."

It bears repetition that Story himself rejected a construction that converted the general welfare clause into a grant of unlimited power, stating that if the clause is

> construed to be an independent and substantive grant of power [rather than a mere qualification of the power to tax], it not only renders unimportant and unnecessary the subsequent enumeration of specific powers, but it plainly extends far beyond them and creates a general authority in Congress to pass all laws which they may deem for the common defence or general welfare.[61]

[59] 297 U.S. at 65.

[60] 3 Elliot 248. In Federalist No. 30 at 182, Hamilton wrote, "Money is . . . the vital principle of the body politic. . . . A complete power, therefor, to procure a regular and adequate supply of it . . . may be regarded as an indispensable ingredient in every constitution."

[61] 1 Story, §909 at 663.

Finally, the Tenth Amendment, the Supreme Court declared, "disclosed the widespread fear that the National Government might, under the pressure of the supposed general welfare, attempt to exercise powers which had not been granted."[62]

[52] Kansas v. Colorado, 266 U.S. 46, 90 (1907).

CHAPTER SIX

The "Commerce" Clause

*The meaning of the power to regulate commerce is to be
sought . . . in the objects generally to be embraced when
it was inserted in the Constitution.*

—JAMES MADISON *

THE commerce clause, Felix Frankfurter wrote,
"has throughout the Court's history been the chief source of
its adjudications regarding federalism."[1] The story "is one of
aggrandizement,"[2] resulting in "the gargantuan power of
Congress to regulate people and business *within* the States."[3]
Imagine the bemusement of a Founder upon learning of the
several ways the federal government can now regulate the
functioning of a janitor of a State building,[4] an activity far

---

* 3 *Letters and Other Writings of James Madison* 521 (1865).

[1] Felix Frankfurter, *The Commerce Clause* 66–67 (1937). Yet, "the commerce clause rarely receives much attention from constitutional theorists." F. Schauer, "Easy Cases," 58 S. Cal. L. Rev. 399, 400 note 2 (1985).

[2] Corwin, *Commerce* xi.

[3] J. H. Choper, "Federalism," in *Constitutional Government in America* 373, 374 (R. Collins ed. 1981) (emphasis added).

[4] Dissenting in National League of Cities v. Usery, 426 U.S. 833 (1976), Justice Stevens declared, "The Federal Government may . . . require the State to act impartially when it hires or fires the janitor"; it may have him "observe safety regulations when he is performing his job"; it

removed from the contemplation of the Founders, who jealously clung to sovereignty over all matters of local, internal police. The path to the janitor was carved out by a process satirically portrayed by Jefferson in a comment on an 1800 proposal to incorporate a copper mining company:

> Congress are authorized to defend the nation. Ships are necessary for defence; copper is necessary for ships; mines are necessary for copper; a company necessary to work the mines; and who can doubt the reasoning who has ever played at— "This is the House that Jack Built." [5]

More soberly, Madison wrote that the "inevitable tendency . . . must be to convert a limited into an unlimited government." For, "in the great system of political economy, having for its general objects the national welfare, everything is related immediately or remotely to every other thing; and consequently, a power over any one thing, if not limited by some obvious and precise affinity, may amount to a power over every other." [6] Pressed to its logical conclusion, such reasoning collides with the Founders' categorical rejection of unlimited federal power and their unyielding resolve to retain State control over internal matters.

Not unreasonably, therefore, did Justice Lamar conclude that if "commerce" be held to include

---

can forbid him "from burning too much soft coal in the capitol furnace." Id. at 880. These are worthy objectives, but is the federal government authorized to govern such internal matters? Justice Cardozo answered, concurring in Schecter Poultry Co. v. United States, 295 U.S. 495, 554 (1935): "I find no authority in the commerce clause for the regulation of wages and hours of labor in the intrastate transactions that make up the defendant's business."

[5] 1 Charles Warren, *The Supreme Court in United States History* 501 (1922). See Justice Cardozo, infra text accompanying note 156. The Convention rejected a proposal to authorize the congressional charter of corporations. Supra Chapter 5, text accompanying notes 31–34, 37.

[6] Corwin, *Twilight* 10.

the regulation of all such manufactures as are intended to be subject of commercial transactions in the future, it is impossible to deny that it would also include all productive industries that contemplate the same thing. The result would be that Congress would be invested, to the exclusion of the States, with the power to regulate, not only manufactures, but also agriculture, horticulture, stock raising, domestic fisheries, mining—in short, every branch of human industry.[7]

When a row of such declarations was given fresh currency in *Carter v. Carter Coal Co.,*[8] the New Dealers—of whom I was one—greeted them with imprecations, rejoicing when the Court reversed its course and breathed life into Lamar's prophetic vision. Herbert Wechsler, one of the most careful scholars in the field, was led to refer in 1959 to "the virtual abandonment of limits to the federal commerce clause."[9] In the result, a proponent of current over-generous construction wrote, "the interstate commerce clause is deleted from the Constitution."[10] With Charles Lofgren, I consider that "the constitutional meaning" of "commerce" calls for "rethinking."[11]

[7] Kidd v. Pearson, 128 U.S. 1, 20–21 (1888). Lamar might have cited Chief Justice Marshall in *Gibbons v. Ogden*. Referring to State inspection laws, part of the "immense mass of legislation" which was "not surrendered to the general government," Marshall amplified, "their purpose is "to fit [articles] for exportation. . . . They act upon the subject, before it becomes an article of foreign commerce . . . and prepare it for that purpose." 22 U.S. at 203.

[8] 298 U.S. 238 (1936).

[9] Herbert Wechsler, "Toward Neutral Principles of Constitutional Law," 71 Harv. L. Rev. 1, 23–24 (1959).

[10] Martin Shapiro, "American Federalism," in *Constitutional Government in America* 359, 361 (R. Collins ed. 1981). Shapiro adds that judicial construction "for the most part has lead only to the abolition of the constitutional provisions guaranteeing federalism." Id.

[11] Charles A. Lofgren, "The Origin of the Tenth Amendment: History, Sovereignty and the Problem of Constitutional Intention," in *Con-*

Article I, §8(3) of the Constitution gives Congress power "to regulate commerce with foreign nations, and among the several States, and with the Indian tribes." In seeking the meaning of these terms, we should not impose "upon the past a creature of our own imagining,"[12] but rather ask what did the words mean to those who employed them?[13] To begin with "commerce," Samuel Johnson's famous 1755 Dictionary defines it as "Intercourse, exchange of one thing for another, interchange of anything; trade; traffick."[14] The several examples he cites, for example, Locke, refer to "commerce with the rest of the world," that is, foreign commerce. Given the independence of the colonies and nascent States from each other, this concept extended to commerce of one State *with* another, and early proposals, as will appear, reflect this understanding, that is, interstate commerce.

---

stitutional Government in America 331, 350 (R. Collins ed 1981). "Reexamination of first principles is always hard, and often unpleasant, especially if it entails a change in orientation or commitment." R. A. Epstein, "Common Law, Labor Law and Reality," 92 Yale L.J. 1435 (1983).

[12] H. G. Richardson and G. O. Sayles, "Parliament and Grand Councils in Medieval History," 77 L.Q. Rev. 213, 224 (1961). That is historical fallacy.

[13] See supra Chapter 1, text accompanying note 55. Thomas Rutherford, whose writings were known to the colonists, said, "The end, which interpretation aims at, is to find out what was the intention of the writer, to clear up the meaning of his words." 2 Thomas Rutherford, *Institutes of Natural Law* 309 (1754–1756). On the heels of the Convention, Justice James Wilson, who had been a leading Framer and Ratifier, wrote, "The first and governing maxim of interpretation of a statute is to discover the meaning of those, who made it." 1 *The Works of James Wilson* 75 (R. McCloskey ed. 1967). Story likewise wrote that "The first and fundamental rule in the interpretation of all instruments is, to construe them according to . . . the intention of the parties." 1 Story, §400 at 305. Hawke v. Smith, 253 U.S. 221, 227 (1920): "What it meant when adopted, it still means for the purpose of interpretation."

[14] Samuel Johnson, *Dictionary of the English Language* (3d ed. 1765).

"Commerce *among* the States," Chief Justice Marshall observed, "must, of necessity, be commerce *with* the states."[15] When Marshall, in *Gibbons v. Ogden,* brushed aside the argument that the word "commerce" signified traffic in goods, saying "it is something more; it is intercourse," comprehending "every species of commercial intercourse,"[16] he overlooked that Dr. Johnson wedded "intercourse" to "traffick," "the interchange of *anything,*" that is, of merchandise. And he ignored as well Hamilton's explanation in Federalist No. 11 that "An unrestrained intercourse between the States themselves will advance the trade of each by an interchange of their respective productions."[17] Marshall's version of commerce was an importation; it did not correspond to the accepted usage at the time the Constitution was adopted.[18] Economic expansion cannot alter the meaning the constitutional terms had for the Founders, particularly

[15] Gibbons v. Ogden, 22 U.S. (9 Wheat.) 1, 196 (1824) (emphasis added).

[16] Id. at 189, 193. The latter was uttered in the context of foreign commerce.

[17] Federalist No. 11 at 68. Writing in No. 22 at 132, of the "commerce of the German empire" between the several principalities, Hamilton again referred to "the merchandise passing through their territories."

[18] Ernest Brown called attention to the Oxford Dictionary definition of "commerce" "based on usages through several centuries, gives as a leading definition 'exchange of merchandise, esp. as conducted on a large scale between different countries or districts." Ernest Brown, "Book Review," 67 Harv. L. Rev. 1439, 1448 (1954).

In the Massachusetts Convention, Caleb Strong stated, "Gentlemen have said, the proposed Constitution was in some places ambiguous. . . . I think the whole of it is expressed in the plain, common language of mankind," 3 Farrand 248. There too, Rufus King said, "it was the intention and honest desire of the Convention to use those expressions that were most easy to be understood and least equivocal in their meaning." Id. 268. In North Carolina, William Lenoir remarked that "A Constitution ought to be understood by every one." 4 Elliot 201. And Iredell emphasized that it was to be read by "any person." Id. 172.

when alteration results in a takeover of internal functions which the States did not dream of surrendering. Courts may not expand constitutional terms by "interpretation,"[19] as Chief Justice Marshall acknowledged in his defense of *McCulloch v. Maryland:* the judicial power "cannot be the assertion of a right to change that instrument."[20]

It is not easy to maintain that the interchange of goods—traffic in things—comprehends the movement of people. The great domestic evil which, with foreign commerce, was the source of the clause, was the States' erection of obstacles against the passage of goods from one State to another. Madison wrote in Federalist No. 42, "A very material object of this [commerce] power was the relief of the States which import and export through other States, from the improper contributions levied on them by the latter."[21] Personal freedom to go from one State to another had been guaranteed by Article IV of the Articles of Confederation: "the people of each State shall have free ingress and egress to and from any other State."[22] That was picked up by the privileges and immunities of Article IV of the Constitution,[23] so that inclusion of such freedom in the commerce clause would have been supererogatory. Justice Robert H. Jackson observed that "the migrations of a human being . . . do not fit easily into my notions of what is commerce."[24] Nor did it comport with Dr. Johnson's definition which was before the Framers. As Zechariah Chafee noted, "Though much was said about barriers at State lines against goods, nobody spoke

[19] S. Johnson's *Dictionary,* supra note 14, defines "To interpret: To explain, to translate, to decipher . . . to expound," not to alter or expand.

[20] *John Marshall's Defense of McCulloch v. Maryland* 209 (Gerald Gunther ed 1969).

[21] Federalist No. 42 at 274.

[22] Commager III.

[23] See supra Chapter 5, text accompanying note 18.

[24] Edwards v. California, 314 U.S. 160, 182 (1941), concurring opinion.

about barriers against persons,"[25] presumably because the Framers assumed such barriers had been razed by Article IV.

Consider next the words "among the several States." In 1785 it was proposed in the Continental Congress to regulate "the trade of the States, as well with foreign nations as *with each other*," and a similar recommendation was made in 1786.[26] The New Jersey Plan likewise proposed "the regulation of trade & commerce as well with foreign nations as with each other,"[27] and such language appeared in a draft of the Committee on Detail.[28] A subsequent draft employed the language "with foreign nations & amongst the several States."[29] Inferably the change was merely stylistic in order to employ the same structure throughout. "With the several States" might have raised the question of who is to trade with them, an ambiguity that the earlier "trade of the States . . . with each other" had avoided. At any rate, the shift to "amongst" met with no objection, suggesting it was not considered a substantive change from regulating the trade of the States "with each other" to commerce *within* a State.

The latter possibility was first intimated by Marshall's 1824 statement that "The word 'among' means intermingled with. A thing which is among others is intermingled with them. . . . Commerce among the States cannot stop at the external boundary lines of each State, but may be introduced into the interior."[30] Now to "intermingle" is "to mingle together," and to "mingle" is "to unite together . . .

[25] Zecheriah Chaffee, *Three Human Rights in the Constitution of 1787*, at 186 (1956).
[26] Corwin, *Commerce* 55, 56 (emphasis added).
[27] 1 Farrand 243.
[28] 2 Farrand 157; see also Chief Justice Marshall, supra text accompanying note 15.
[29] 2 Farrand 167.
[30] Gibbons v. Ogden, 22 U.S. (9 Wheat.) 1, 194 (1824).

become mixed . . . to blend."[31] That suggests an erasure of
State lines. Commerce, however, Marshall continued, is "restricted to that commerce which concerns more States than
one," not "the exclusively internal commerce of a State."[32]
For the moment let me defer closer examination of Marshall's
dicta in *Gibbons v. Ogden* and return to the Founders.

Roger Sherman made the first relevant comment on the
clause, referring to "the power to regulate trade *between* the
States";[33] most of the references thereafter likewise employed "between," indicating that the Founders assimilated
"among" to "between," echoing trade of the States "with
each other." Thus, Madison referred to the "regulation of
trade between State and State," and pointed up the Founders' identification of "between" and "among" by speaking of
the "injurious retaliation *among* the States on each other."[34]
One of Dr. Johnson's definitions of "between" is "from
one to another," whereas he defined "among" as "mingled
with . . . conjoined with others," which presumably gave
rise to Marshall's "intermingled." But under "Between"
Johnson explained that it "is properly used of two," and
"*among* of more, but perhaps this accuracy is not always observed."[35] The Committee's resort to "among" may therefore be explicable as embracing thirteen rather than two
States. To my mind, the Founders' frequent use of "between" rather than "among" indicates that their conception

[31] Funk & Wagnalls, *Desk Standard Dictionary* (1946).
[32] Gibbons v. Ogden, 22 U.S. at 194–195.
[33] 2 Farrand 308 (emphasis added).
[34] Id. 361, 451 (emphasis added). For similar use of "between," see
Ellsworth, 2 Farrand 359–360; James McHenry, id. 504; Madison, id. 589;
Hamilton, Federalist No. 11 at 68; Madison, Federalist No. 42 at 274;
Charles Pinckney, 4 Elliot 335; John Jay, 2 Elliot 283.
[35] Emphasis added. Ernest Brown noted that "among" had long been
regarded as a synonym for "between." Supra note 18 at 1450–1451.

of commerce was "from one to another," not federal governance of internal commerce, still less as "mingled with each
other."

According to a centuries-old rule of interpretation, an en-
actment is to be construed in light of the evil it was designed
to remedy, and the rule h'as often been applied by the federal
courts.[36] At times that objective has been met under a different rubric, as in *Church of the Holy Trinity v. United States*.
There the church had hired an English clergyman to serve as
rector; the statute made it unlawful to assist the migration
of an alien to "perform labor or service of any kind." Although the case was "within the letter of this section," the
Court held that it was not within "the intention of the law"
because Congress sought "to stay the influx of this cheap
unskilled labor, not ministers."[37] Similarly, the all but exclusive domestic concern of the Founders was exactions by
States from their neighbors. Madison said, "it would be unjust to the States whose produce was exported by their

[36] Matthew Bacon, *A New Abridgment of the Laws of England,* "Statutes" (4) (3d ed. 1768). Madison wrote, "In expounding the Constitution
and deducing the intention of its framers, it should never be forgotten,
that the great object of the Convention was to provide, by a new Constitution, a remedy for the defects of the existing one." 3 Farrand 520. In the
Slaughter-House Cases, 83 U.S. (16 Wall.) 36, 72 (1873), the Court stated
that in construing the Reconstruction amendments, "it is necessary to
look to . . . the evil which they were designed to remedy." United States
v. Champlin Refg. Co., 341 U.S. 290, 297 (1951): "The statute cannot be
divorced from the circumstances existing at the time it was passed, and
from the evils which Congress sought to correct and prevent." See also
Knowlton v. Moore, 178 U.S. 41, 95 (1900). The "purpose of a statutory
provision is the best test of the meaning of the words chosen." Cawley v.
United States, 272 F.2d 443, 445 (2d Cir. 1959), per Learned Hand, J.

[37] 143 U.S. 457, 464, 472 (1892). The Court also stated that "another
guide to the meaning of the statute is found in the evil it was designed to
remedy; and for this the court properly looks at contemporaneous events,
the situation as it existed, and as it was pressed upon the attention of the
legislative body." Id. at 463.

neighbors, to leave it subject to be taxed by the latter."[38] Wilson "dwelt on the injustice and impolicy of leaving N. Jersey, Connecticut &c any longer subject to the exactions of their commercial neighbors."[39] John Mercer and McHenry in the Convention,[40] Dawes in Massachusetts, Ellsworth in Connecticut, Patrick Henry in Virginia, and Davie in North Carolina spoke to the same effect.[41] That the commerce clause was meant to remedy this evil was made unmistakably clear: Madison stated it was necessary to remove "existing & injurious retaliations *among* the States";[42] McHenry said, "Perhaps a power to restrain any State from demanding tribute from citizens of another State . . . is comprehended in the power to regulate trade *between* State and State."[43] Madison amplified: "[P]erhaps the best guard against an abuse of power of the States on this subject, was the right in the Genl. Government to regulate trade *between* State and State."[44] So too, Sherman stated that "The oppression of the uncommercial States was guarded agst. by the power to regulate *trade between* the States."[45] And Ellsworth said that "The power of regulating *trade between* the States will protect them agst. each other."[46] It is food for

[38] 2 Farrand 306.

[39] Id. 307.

[40] Id. 307, 504.

[41] Thomas Dawes, 2 Elliot 57−58; Ellsworth, id. 189, 192; Patrick Henry, 3 Elliot 158.

[42] 2 Farrand 451 (emphasis added).

[43] Id. 504 (emphasis added).

[44] Id. 588−589 (emphasis added).

[45] Id. 308 (emphasis added).

[46] Id. 359−360 (emphasis added). In his influential "Letters of a Federal Farmer," Richard Henry Lee acknowledged that among the clearly internal objects that should be lodged in the federal government was power "to regulate trade between the States," which "may be exercised without essentially affecting the internal police of the respective states." Murphy 272. This history was epitomized in Justice William Johnson's

thought that Story, writing in 1833, 44 years after the Constitution was adopted, should say that "A very material object of this [interstate] power is the relief of the States which import and export through other States, from the levy of improper contributions by the latter,"[47] without mention of any other objective. It is reasonable to infer that for 44 years no other purpose had been thought of.[48]

Marshall enunciated a broader rule in the *Dartmouth* case (1819):

> It is not enough to say, that this particular case was not in the mind of the Convention, when the article was framed. . . . It is necessary to go farther, and to say that, had this particular case been suggested the language would have been varied so as to exclude it.[49]

Is it conceivable, for example, that the Founders would have accepted federal regulation of the janitor of a State building,

---

concurring opinion in *Gibbons:* the State conflicts led to calling the Convention; they were "the evils existing," and the commerce clause had the "purpose of remedying those evils." 22 U.S. at 225–226. Corwin acknowledges that "The restraints imposed by the States upon one another's commerce were one of the immediate causes of the Convention of 1787." Corwin, *Commerce* 56. Frankfurter summed up: the commerce power "was an authorization to remove those commercial obstructions and harassments to which the militant new free states subjected one another, and to enable the community of the states to present a united commercial front to the world." Frankfurter, supra note 1, at 13.

[47] 2 Story, §1066 at 10.

[48] Such of the amendments proposed by the State Ratification Conventions as mentioned commerce, were concerned with avoiding monopolistic grants. Massachusetts, 2 Elliot 177; New York, id. 407. Frankfurter observed, "The records disclose no constructive criticisms by the states of the commerce clause as proposed to them. Their only recommendations were amendments requiring a two-thirds vote to pass 'navigation laws, or laws regulating commerce,' and forbidding Congressional grants of monopolies." Frankfurter, supra note 1, at 12.

[49] Trustees of Dartmouth College v. Woodward, 17 U.S. (4 Wheat.) 517, 644 (1819).

or of a farmer's produce for his own use? The answer is in part supplied by another remarkable fact: among the multitudinous objections to this or the other provision—McKean ticked off 19 in Pennsylvania [50]—not one protest was voiced that the commerce clause invaded State control over internal affairs. The reason, to borrow from Madison in Federalist No. 45, was that "no apprehensions are entertained" with respect to the "regulation of commerce." [51] Neither Hamilton nor Madison dreamed "that a central authority could or would descend to enforcement of local laws." [52] So too, Davie stated in the North Carolina Ratification Convention: "There is not one instance of a power given to the United States, whereby the internal policy or administration of the states is affected." [53] The Founders' repeated assurances that internal functions were reserved to the States, their categorical rejection of unlimited federal power, their emphasis that the delegated powers were specifically enumerated, indicate that had such federal intrusion been proposed it would have been roundly condemned. Marshall himself recurred to the "remedy the evil" rule in the very context of the commerce clause: if

> there should be serious doubts respecting the extent of any given power, it is a well settled rule, that the *objects* for which it was given . . . should have great influence in the construction. . . . We know of no rule for construing the extent of such powers, other than is given by the language which confers them, taken in connection with the *purposes* for which they were conferred. [54]

[50] McMaster & Stone 366–368.
[51] Federalist No. 45 at 303; see also Pinckney, 3 Farrand 116.
[52] Supra Chapter 2, text accompanying note 116; and see id., text accompanying notes 117–121.
[53] 4 Elliot 110.
[54] Gibbons v. Ogden, 22 U.S. at 188–189 (emphasis added).

We are therefore justified in confining interstate commerce to the mischief it was meant to remedy—internecine exactions.

Another fact needs to be noticed—many, indeed most, of the references to a commerce clause were in terms of foreign commerce, responding to English usage. In presenting the Virginia Plan, Randolph spoke of the need for "counteraction of the commercial regulations of other nations";[55] among "the objects of the Union," Sherman listed "regulating foreign commerce."[56] George Clymer of Pennsylvania stressed the need of the States "to defend themselves against foreign regulation."[57] In Federalist No. 11, Hamilton dwelt on "commerce in our own bottoms," that is, foreign trade, on our trade with the West Indies, but also referred to an "*unrestrained* intercourse between the States themselves [which] will advance the trade of each by an interchange of their respective productions."[58] In the New York Ratification Convention, however, he adverted to the "regulation of commerce—that is, the whole system of foreign intercourse."[59] And in North Carolina, Davie, addressing "the regulation of commerce," said, "The United States should be empowered to compel foreign nations into commercial regulations. . . . Is not our commerce abroad equally un-

[55] 1 Farrand 19.

[56] Id. 133. In Connecticut, Sherman repeated that "The great end of the federal government is to protect the several states . . . against foreign invasion . . . and to regulate and protect our foreign commerce with foreign nations." Herbert Storing, "The 'Other' Federalist Papers: A Preliminary Sketch," 6 Pol. Sci. Reviewer 215, 224 (1976). Mason stated in the Virginia Convention that Congress is "to get [power] of regulating commerce with foreign nations." 3 Elliot 523. Storing considers that "in the main . . . the objects of the Union are described [by the Federalists] in terms like those of Roger Sherman." Storing, id.

[57] 2 Farrand 450.

[58] Federalist No. 11 at 63, 64, 68 (emphasis added).

[59] 2 Elliot 350.

protected?"[60] Such utterances gave no inkling that the power to "regulate commerce with foreign nations," or to curb exactions by sister States, could be turned against the internal affairs of the States themselves.[61] They could only lull the delegates into a belief that State control of internal affairs was left untouched.

GIBBONS V. OGDEN

Gibbons v. Ogden[62] long has cast a shadow over exposition of the commerce clause. New York had granted an exclusive right to navigate in its waters, and the holder thereof sought to enjoin Gibbons from operating his ferryboats between Elizabethtown, New Jersey, and New York City. Gibbons defended under a federal license for carrying on coastwise trade. Consequently the case could have turned on whether this was *inter*-state commerce[63] and, if so, whether a State was empowered to grant a monopoly therein. On this, as well as other grounds, much of Marshall's discussion went "beyond the necessities of the case."[64] Marshall himself had

[60] 4 Elliot 18.

[61] In his 1791 Opinion on the Constitutionality of the Bank, Jefferson stated, "[T]he power given to Congress by the Constitution does not extend to the internal regulation of commerce of a state . . . which remains exclusively with its own legislature; but to its external commerce only, that is to say, its commerce with another state or with a foreign nation." Commager 159.

[62] 22 U.S. (9 Wheat.) 1 (1824).

[63] In a concurring opinion, Justice Johnson "rested the invalidity of the New York statute on its invasion of a field exclusively committed to Congress." Frankfurter, supra note 1 at 17.

[64] Id. 44. There is no need to follow the convolutions of Marshall's opinion, which Frankfurter considers "was either unconsciously or calculatedly confused." Id. 17. Marshall's "discussion of the relation of the commerce clause to the reserved powers of the states," Frankfurter wrote, "was logically irrelevant to Marshall's holding." Id. 17–18.

brushed aside his own dicta in *Marbury v. Madison* on the sound ground that general expressions "which go beyond the case" are "seldom completely investigated."[65] Decided in 1824, *Gibbons* was 36 years removed from adoption of the Constitution. Felix Frankfurter, an ardent Marshall devotee, wrote that the momentum he gave "to the doctrine that state authority must be subject to such limitations as the Court finds it necessary to apply for the protection of the national community . . . was an audacious doctrine, which, one may be sure, could hardly have been publicly avowed in support of the adoption of the Constitution."[66] In fact, it ran counter to assurances made by proponents of adoption that the States' control of internal affairs was amply guarded.[67] But, as Frankfurter points out, "Local government was associated in his mind with the party bickerings of narrow ambition and a dangerous indifference to the rights of property. The need of a strong central government, as the indispensable bulwark of the solid elements of the nation, was for him the deepest article of his political faith."[68]

Consider his construction of the federal Coasting Act as a grant of free passage over the navigable waters of the United States, which supplants conflicting state legislation. He himself had emphasized that commerce "which is carried on between different parts of the same State" is not comprehended by the commerce clause.[69] Yet he declared that "If Congress licenses vessels to sail from one port to another *in the same State,* the act is supposed to be, necessarily, inciden-

[65] Cohens v. Virginia, 19 U.S. (6 Wheat.) 264, 399–400 (1821).

[66] Frankfurter, supra note 1 at 19.

[67] Corwin holds that "It may justly be said that Marshall's greatest service consisted precisely in the uphill fight with he maintained for years against the trend of his times." Corwin, *Twilight* 6.

[68] Frankfurter, supra note 1, at 14.

[69] 22 U.S. at 194; see infra text accompanying note 72.

tal to the power expressly granted to Congress."[70] What Founder conceived that transportation from Boston to Plymouth, Massachusetts by wagon train was *intra*-state commerce, whereas it became *inter*-state commerce if transportation was by coastwise vessel?[71] Whatever the scope of federal jurisdiction of navigable waters, it needs to be asked whether it overrides the reserved *intra*-state commerce.

For all his "audacious" departure from the Founders' design, Marshall cautiously paid tribute to the State's internal powers. The commerce clause does not "comprehend that commerce which is completely internal, which is carried on . . . between different parts of the same State, and which *does not* extend to or *affect* other States." It does not embrace "the completely interior traffic of a State"; the "enumeration presupposes something not enumerated; and that something . . . must be the exclusively internal commerce of a State. . . . The completely internal commerce of a State, then, may be considered as reserved for the State itself." But he threw in a foggy caveat: protected internal concerns were such as "do not *affect* other States, and with which it is not necessary to interfere for the purpose of executing some of the general powers of the government."[72] "Commerce among the States," he said, "cannot stop at the external boundary line of each State, but may be introduced into the interior."[73] "Can a trading expedition between two adjoining States," he asked, "commence and terminate outside of

[70] 22 U.S. at 204 (emphasis added).

[71] Earlier, Chancellor James Kent had pointed out that the statute disentitled an unlicensed ship "from the privileges of *American* vessels, but [it] must pay the same fees and tonnages as foreign vessels." Ogden v. Gibbons, 4 Johns. Chancery 150, 156 (New York 1819). See Frankfurter, supra note 1, at 15.

[72] 22 U.S. at 194−195 (emphasis added).

[73] Id. at 194.

each? And if the trading intercourse be between two states remote from each other, must it not commence in one, terminate in the other, and probably pass through a third?"[74] Undeniably, interstate commerce presupposes uninhibited passage through the third State, and entry into the second. But how far does "introduc[tion] into the interior" reach? Marshall's extrapolation that Congress' power must be exercised "*within* the territorial jurisdiction of the several states" is too sweeping by far.[75]

To begin with, Marshall's context was "trading," a limited concept which the modern cases have left far behind. Then, too, the penetration was limited under the "original package" doctrine—*Brown v. Maryland,* based on both the prohibition of State "duties on imports and exports" and on the commerce clause.[76] Maryland had required a license for all importers of certain goods; Marshall, reasoning from *Gibbons* that the commerce clause "reaches the interior of a State and may there be exercised," concluded that the power "must be capable of authorizing the sale of those articles which it introduces." He held the goods were nontaxable so long as they were "in the original form or package in which it was imported." At the same time, however, he distinguished imports which had been "mixed up with the mass of property" and "lost its distinctive character as an import."[77] Such goods were taxable. Patently "introduction into the interior" did not extend very far. Application of this doctrine to *interstate* commerce was overruled in *Woodruff v. Parham,* which held that the commerce clause did not forbid imposition of a sales tax on the sale of goods in their

[74] Id. at 196.
[75] Id. (emphasis added).
[76] 25 U.S. (12 Wheat.) 419, 437, 445 (1827).
[77] Id. at 446, 441–442.

original package.[78] It may be thought that *Woodruff* was limited to State freedom to tax, not to regulate, because *Leisy v. Hardin* applied the "original package" doctrine to a shipment of a barrel of beer from Illinois to Iowa, where its sale was prohibited.[79] But Chief Justice Fuller "did not explain why the original package doctrine should have vitality in cases of state regulation, but not in cases of state taxation of interstate commerce."[80] There is no need to follow the vagaries of subsequent adjudications,[81] for few who have studied the historical records would conclude that the States would have surrendered the right to prohibit the sale of liquor or drugs within a State's boundaries if such prohibition did not discriminate against shipments from sister States,[82] for that would constitute the very exaction that the commerce clause was intended to strike down. These facts illustrate the danger of uncritical reliance on Marshall's dictum—Congress' power "must be exercised *within* the territorial jurisdiction of the several states."

Consider another oft-quoted *Gibbons* dictum: if commerce comprehends "every species of commercial intercourse" as applied "to foreign nations, it must carry the same meaning throughout the sentence, and remain a unit, *unless* there be some plain intelligible cause which alters

[78] 75 U.S. (8 Wall.) 123 (1868).
[79] 135 U.S. 100 (1890).
[80] E. Barrett, P. Bruton, and J. Honnold, *Constitutional Law: Cases and Materials* 359 note 1 (2d ed. 1963).
[81] Id. 359 note 3.
[82] In 1784 Madison advanced in the Virginia House of Delegates an instruction to propose in Congress "That no State be at liberty to impose duties on any goods" imported "from any other state, but may altogether prohibit the importation from any State" of any goods "of which the importation is at the same time prohibited from all other places whatsoever." Quoted in Knowlton v. Moore, 178 U.S. 41, 100 (1900).

it."[83] Corwin concludes that "*it is one and the same power,* and that the power to regulate commerce among the States is of equal scope with the power to regulate foreign commerce."[84] But the foreign commerce power was explained in broadest terms—to enable the federal government to meet regulation by other nations on equal terms,[85] whereas the explanation of the inter-state power was restrictive—to bar impositions by one State on another. A distinction was drawn by Madison in the Virginia Ratification Convention: "Would it not be considered as a dangerous principle in the British Government were the king to have the same power in internal regulation as he has in the external business of treaties?"[86] He was not therefore launching a new interpretation when he wrote in 1829 that

---

[83] 22 U.S. at 193–194 (emphasis added). Chief Justice Taney spoke to the same effect: "The power to regulate commerce among the several States is granted to Congress in the same clause, and by the same words, as the power to regulate commerce with foreign nations, and is coextensive with it." The License Cases, 46 U.S. (5 How.) 504, 578 (1847).

[84] Corwin, *Commerce* 254.

[85] Supra text accompanying notes 55–60.

[86] 3 Elliot 515. Madison had distinguished the federal jurisdiction of "external objects" such as "foreign commerce" from the States' "internal order." Supra Chapter 3, text accompanying note 114.

He also stated, however, that a protective tariff could affect the internal economy of the States, arguing that the power to regulate *foreign* commerce included the "encouragement of domestic manufactures," and that "few regulations of foreign commerce . . . do not operate on internal pursuits." Corwin, *Commerce* 184, 185. Traditionally commerce revenue measures had been employed to encourage manufactures, so that the foreign commerce power may be taken to extend thereto. 2 Story, §1082 at 30–31. The States, he argued, could not act in the premises because of the limitations placed on State levies of duties on imports or exports by Article I, § 10(2), and because as a practical matter they could not effectively deal with the situation. Corwin, *Commerce* 185.

Whether Madison would have extrapolated this reasoning to action under the interstate power is debatable. He considered the power over

> Being in the same terms with the power over foreign commerce
> the same extent, if taken literally, would belong to [inter-state
> commerce]. Yet it is very certain that it grew out of the abuse of
> the power by the importing States in taxing the non-importing,
> and was intended as a negative and preventive provision against
> injustice among the States themselves, rather than as a power to
> be used for the positive purposes of the General Government.[87]

Madison is richly confirmed by the records of the several
conventions. And as architect of the Constitution he is entitled to more credit on this issue than Marshall, who spoke
long after the event, let alone that in espousing the cause of
increased centralization for protection of "the solid elements
of the country" Marshall was departing from the Founders'
assurances that the "internal" powers of the States were
amply shielded against federal invasion, a departure that was
even out of tune with his own times.[88]

To Corwin,

> the paradoxical nature of this [Madison] theory is evident on a
> moment's reflection. It is contended, in effect, that the grant of
> a power to regulate commerce among the States merely took
> this power from the States without vesting the equivalent
> power in Congress. The net result of the transfer is therefore
> that both the States from which the power was taken and Con-
> gress to which it was in explicit terms given, have equal power

---

external affairs greater than over internal, and he explained that the interstate power was designed to prevent exactions by one State from another.
This does not extend to federal imposition of its economic policies on the
States. I put to one side out-of-state shipments of articles which place sister States at a competitive disadvantage and concern myself with federal
regulation which prevents a State from regulating matters within its own
borders.

[87] 3 Farrand 478.

[88] "'States rights' had become, to a greater or lesser degree, the constitutional creed of the entire country even before Marshall's death, a fact
which he recognized and deplored." Corwin, *Commerce* 132.

to regulate commerce among the States "for positive purposes"—which is to say no power.[89]

This misconceives the issue. Undoubtedly Congress has
power to govern commerce *between* the States and the States
have not. So Corwin's charge of "no power" in the premises
goes too far. Nor was the inter-state grant all-embracing.
The "police" power, for example, was not conferred upon
the federal government but was retained by the States. Regulation of interchange of products did not extend to moral
conduct. Story, a vigorous proponent of centralized national government, wrote that among the powers that

> are entirely distinct in their nature from that to regulate com-
> merce . . . [are] inspection laws, health laws, . . . all of which
> . . . are not so much regulation of commerce as of police, and
> may truly be said to belong, if at all to commerce, to that which
> is purely internal.[90]

Were such a federal power desirable, that would not make
out a grant.[91] Corwin's paradox assumes the very point at
issue: that the commerce clause embraced "positive purposes," whereas the Founders were solely concerned with
preventing exactions by one State from another.

The Founders' anxiety to safeguard the States' police
powers—protection of the health, safety, and morals of
their citizens—from federal "intermeddling" is well documented.[92] It should require more than the colorless "commerce among the several States" to demonstrate their intention sub silentio to act in derogation of assurances to allay
such fears. Yet the Court, without reference to the historical

[89] Id. 25.
[90] 2 Story, §1070 at 14. See also supra Chapter 3, text accompanying
notes 89–105.
[91] See infra note 132.
[92] Supra Chapter 3, text accompanying notes 89–105.

sources, has laid claim to a federal police power. In *Brooks v. United States,* Chief Justice Taft declared that the commerce clause can be employed to prevent "immorality, dishonesty, or the spread of any evil or harm to the people of other States" in "exercising the police power . . . within the field of interstate commerce," citing derivatively only to Cooley's *Constitutional Limitations,* which asserts the proposition without discussion or citation of authorities.[93]

Earlier, in *New York v. Miln* (1839), the Court sustained the right of New York to exclude immigrant paupers as an appropriate exercise of the "power to regulate their own internal police," saying that since the power "undeniably existed at the formation of the Constitution" it was not "taken from the States" by the commerce power.[94] These views were reiterated in seriatim opinions in the 1849 *Passenger Case.*[95] In

[93] 267 U.S. 432, 436, 437 (1925). Gloucester Ferry Co. v. Pennsylvania, 114 U.S. 196, 215 (1885): "Congress may establish police regulations as well as the States." On the other hand, Patterson v. Kentucky, 97 U.S. 501, 503 (1878), quoted Cooley: "the power to establish the ordinary regulations of police has been left with the individual States, and cannot be assumed by the national government. Cooley, Const. Lim. 574."

[94] 36 U.S. (11 Pet.) 102, 141, 132 (1837). Corwin opines that "the Miln decision was practically overturned" in Henderson v. New York [92 U.S. 259 (1875)]." Corwin, *Commerce* 146. But in New Orleans Gas Co. v. Louisiana Light Co., 115 U.S. 650, 661 (1885), the Court said Henderson "declin[ed] to decide whether in the absence of action by Congress, the States can . . . protect themselves against actual paupers." See also Railroad Co. v. Husen, 95 U.S. 465, 471 (1877).

[95] 48 U.S. (7 How.) 283 (1849). In the Slaughter-House Cases, 83 U.S. (16 Wall.) 36, 63 (1873), the Court cited *New York v. Miln* for the propostion that the exercise of State police power was unaffected by the commerce clause. See also id. 62.

The impact of the commerce clause on the police power should be measured in terms of Pierson v. Ray, 386 U.S. 547, 554–555 (1967). After adverting to the common law immunity of judges from suits for acts performed in their official capacity, the court stated, "We do not believe that this settled principle was abolished by sec. 1983, which makes liable 'every

1887 the Court quoted Justice McLean in the *License Cases* (1847): "A State regulates . . . all internal matters which relate to its moral and political welfare. Over these subjects the Federal government has no power."[96] From the same case the Court quoted Justice Grier: "The police power, which is exclusively in the States, is alone competent to correction of these great evils."[97] And in *Keller v. United States* (1909), the Court stated, "there is in the Constitution no grant to Congress of the police power,"[98] reaffirming what Justice Story had said on behalf of the Court in *Prigg v. Pennsylvania* (1842)[99]: "The police power extends over all subjects within the territorial limits of the States and has never been con-

---

person' who under color of law deprives another person of his civil rights. . . . The immunity of judges . . . [is] well established and we presume that Congress would have specifically so provided had it wished to abolish the doctrine." Curtailment of the all-inclusive "every person" in the interest of a common law immunity counsels an even more exacting standard for preservation of the Founders' jealous solicitude to safeguard "internal," "local" State sovereignty.

[96] Mugler v. Kansas, 123 U.S. 623, 658 (1887). Chief Justice Fuller said as much for the Court in United States v. E. C. Knight Co., 156 U.S. 1,11 (1895): "It cannot be denied that the power of a State to protect the lives, health . . . and the public morals . . . is a power originally and always belonging to the States, nor surrendered by them to the general government, nor directly restrained by the Constitution of the United States, and essentially exclusive." Among the "immense mass of legislation . . . not surrendered to the general government," said Chief Justice Marshall, were "health laws of every description." Gibbons v. Ogden, 22 U.S. (9 Wheat.) 1, 203 (1819).

[97] Mugler v. Kansas, 123 U.S. 623, 658–659 (1887).

[98] 213 U.S. 138, 148 (1909).

[99] 41 U.S. (16 Pet.) 539, 625 (1842). I am therefore at a loss to account for Corwin's reference to a "*new* doctrine that there is a field of jurisdiction which is exclusively reserved to the States and to which for that reason, Congress' power over *interstate* commerce cannot constitutionally extend." Corwin, *Commerce* 126–127 (emphasis added). For if an area "is exclusively reserved to the States," it lies outside the interstate power. Certainly Corwin's "new" doctrine cannot be laid at the door of his cited

ceded to the United States." Such statements more accurately reflect the Founders' design than does the Court's off-the-cuff utterance in *Brooks*.[100]

The untenable lengths to which the Court has pushed the alleged federal "police" power is illustrated by *McDermott v. Wisconsin*.[101] Defendant, a retail grocer in Wisconsin, received cans of "Karo corn syrup" from a Chicago wholesaler properly labeled under federal law but mislabeled under the Wisconsin statute. He was convicted in a State court for violation of State law. The Supreme Court reversed, saying the federally required label "must be upon the packages intended to reach the purchaser" for his protection.[102] The retail sales, however, were purely *intra*-state, and protection of the safety of its citizens was left entirely with the State. That, the evidence shows, was the intention of the Founders. Judge Pendleton, it will be recalled, assured the Virginia Ratification Convention that the Constitution "does not intermeddle with the local, particular affairs of the State."[103] And Framer William Davie stated in the North Carolina Convention, "There is not one instance of a power given to the United States whereby the internal

---

License cases. Id. 126. See supra Chapter 3, text accompanying notes 89–105.

[100] In a letter to Joseph E. Cabell, September 18, 1824, Madison said of a construction by the First Congress confirmed by an unbroken practice of forty years, "No novel construction, however ingeniously devised . . . can withstand the weight of such authorities, or the unbroken current of so prolonged and universal a practice." 4 Elliot 602. See also infra Chapter 9, note 24.

[101] 228 U.S. 115 (1913).

[102] Id. at 131. Commenting on some Marshall opinions, Frankfurter wrote, "Except in the limited field of the tariff and hotly contested proposals for internal improvements, government was not yet thought of as directing agent of social and economic policies." Frankfurter, supra note 1, at 39.

[103] See supra Chapter 3, text accompanying note 104.

policy . . . of the State is affected."[104] Consequently, any exercise of the commerce power which invades the State's reserved police power goes beyond the powers delegated.[105]

To plod through the multitude of interstate commerce

[104] Id note 106. Iredell also assured the North Carolina Convention that "With the mere local concern of a State, Congress are to have nothing to do." Id. note 105. See also infra text accompanying note 122.

[105] See Lee, supra note 46. United States v. Dewitt, 76 U.S. (9 Wall.) 41 (1869) so held. A federal safety measure governed sales of certain petroleum oils for illuminating purposes. The act was held unconstitutional: "power to regulate commerce among the States has always been understood as limited by its terms; and as a virtual denial of any power to interfere with the internal trade and business of the separate States: except, indeed, as necessary and proper measure for carrying into execution some other power expressly granted or vested. . . . [I]t is plainly a regulation of police. . . . As a police regulation, relating exclusively to the internal affairs of the States . . . it can have no constitutional operation." Id. at 44, 45. See supra note 96; and see Justice Cardozo in Schecter, infra, text accompanying note 156. McDermott, in my judgment, ran counter to the counsel of Justice Story, himself a dyed-in-the-wool nationalist: "The sovereignty of a State, in the exercise of legislation, is not to be impaired, unless it be clear, that it has transcended its legitimate authority; nor ought any power to be sought . . . in favor of the United States, unless it be clearly within the reach of its constitutional charter." Houston v. Moore 18 U.S. (5 Wheat.) 1, 48 (1820), dissenting opinion. "The most persistent problem of American constitutional law arises from the fact that to multiplicity of state legislatures has been assigned the most important powers of government over private rights." Corwin, *Twilight* 90. It was not given to the Court to solve that problem by judicial amendment of this constitutional distribution.

Misuse of the commerce power is likewise exemplified by Leisy v. Hardin, 135 U.S. 100 (1890), which held that the Iowa prohibition law could not bar importation of beer from Illinois because it was an article of commerce which could freely enter from another State. Federal intrusion is not always on the side of the angels, as is illustrated by Hall v. De Cuir, 95 U.S. 485 (1878). A Louisiana statute forbade segregation on public conveyances; Mrs. De Cuir, a colored passenger, complained that the owner of a vessel plying the Mississippi between Louisiana and Mississippi had denied her access to a cabin reserved for white passengers. The Court held that the statute constituted a burden on interstate commerce.

cases, testing them by the yardsticks herein suggested, would be an herculean undertaking. From such a daunting task an octagenarian may be excused, the more because the Court's meandering course generally responded to changing of the guard and shifting political currents.[106] Professors Edward Barrett, Paul Bruton and John Honhold remarked with respect to the conflict between "the established net-work of local controls" and "hostile state regulation" which burdened interstate commerce, that "the intellectual resources of most members of the Court" were "hardly adequate to deal with this problem."[107] Such stuff does not lend itself to distillation of perdurable principles. Instead, I shall examine a few cases in which the Court has intruded into the realm of morals in order to illustrate how fleeting are the morals the Court sought to bolster.

Under the White Slave Traffic Act, *Hoke v. United States* sustained the conviction of a person who induced a woman to go from Louisiana to Texas for purposes of prostitution. The Court said that "there is no word of limitation" in the commerce grant, that it includes transportation "of persons and property," and that the exercise of the commerce power "may have the quality of police regulation."[108] Commerce, it will be recalled, connoted the exchange of goods, not the movement of persons.[109] Another intrusion on moral grounds is exemplified by the *Lottery Case (Champion v. Ames)*, which held that the carriage of lottery tickets by

[106] Cf. supra Chapter 1, text accompanying notes 4–5. "The precedents available to the Court as it faced the New Deal in the 1930s were rather varied, and not very consistent with each other." Christopher Wolfe, *The Rise of Modern Judicial Review* 170 (1986).

[107] Supra note 80 at 165.

[108] 227 U.S. 308, 320, 323 (1913).

[109] Supra text accompanying notes 21–25. Gooch v. United States, 297 U.S. 124 (1936), sustained a death penalty for transportation of a kidnapped person held for ransom in interstate commerce.

an express company from one state to another may be barred by Congress under the commerce clause.[110] If, the Court asked, a State may suppress "lotteries within its own limits . . . why may not Congress, invested with the power to regulate commerce along the several States, provide that such commerce shall not be polluted by the carrying of lottery tickets from one State to another?"[111] The well-documented answer is that the police power remained the exclusive province of the States.[112] The lottery, prostitution, and contraception[113] cases illustrate the questionable wisdom of bending equivocal constitutional language to govern morals. Given the looser sexual mores of today, would the transportation of a woman by her lover from Connecticut to Long Island for sexual "debauchery" be viewed as a criminal offense? Today many States resort to large-scale lotteries to help cover rising expenses—would interstate shipment of lottery tickets may be viewed as "polluting" the stream of commerce? Moral issues, I suggest, are best left to the States, precisely as the Founders intended.

A word as to the related resort to the tax power for analogous purposes. In *McCray v. United States*[114] the federal government placed a tax of 10 cents per pound on yellow margarine, a substitute for butter, responding, one may

[110] 188 U.S. 321 (1903). This was a 5-to-4 decision.

[111] Id. at 356.

[112] See Story, supra text accompanying note 90, and Chapter 3, text accompanying notes 93–110.

[113] Rebuffing a claimed conflict with the State police power, United States v. Popper, 98 Fed. 423 (D.N.D. Cal. 1899), sustained an indictment under a federal prohibition of transportation in interstate commerce of anything "intended for the prevention of conception." James Wilson, speaking of "the great objects of the Genl. Government," assured the Pennsylvania Ratifiers that "All of them are connected with money." Supra Chapter 3, note 112.

[114] 195 U.S. 27 (1904).

conjecture, to pressure from the powerful dairy lobby. To-day margarine is a familiar staple. The Court declared that the power to tax is given with "only one exception and only two qualifications. Congress cannot tax exports, and it must impose direct taxes by the rule of apportionment, and indirect taxes by the rule of uniformity. Thus limited, and thus only, it reaches every subject, and may be exercised at discretion."[115] Even Story maintained that the tax power was limited to "the common defence and general welfare," while Madison more properly held that it was limited by the subsequent enumeration of powers.[116] Chief Justice Marshall declared in *Gibbons v. Ogden* that "Congress is not empowered to tax for those *purposes* which are within the exclusive province of the States."[117] What was not delegated by enumeration was retained by the States. The manufacture and sale of margarine *within* a State assuredly is "within [its] exclusive province." So too, Marshall stated in *McCulloch v. Maryland*, "should Congress, under the pretext of executing its powers, pass laws for the accomplishment of objects not entrusted to the government," the act would be held invalid.[118] How is one to decide whether the tax is a "pretext" without looking to the motive behind the tax? Yet it has become judicial habit to disclaim the right to look for the motive of Congress.[119] Harking back to the Marshall view, Justice Frankfurter, in dissent, stated that "what was formally a means of raising revenue for the Federal Government was es-

[115] Id. at 56.

[116] Supra Chapter 5, text accompanying notes 7, 28, 32, 47.

[117] 22 U.S. at 199 (emphasis added). McCray was not "within an acknowledged field of national jurisdiction." Corwin, *Commerce* 229.

[118] 17 U.S. (4 Wheat.) 316, 423 (1819) (emphasis added). For a similar statement by Iredell in the North Carolina Ratification Convention, see supra Chapter 4, text accompanying note 54.

[119] United States v. Darby, 312 U.S. 100, 115 (1941).

sentially an effort to check if not to stamp out professional gambling."[120] "When oblique use," he stated, is "made of the taxing power as to matters which substantively are not within the powers delegated to Congress, the Court cannot shut its eyes to what is obviously, because designedly, an attempt to control conduct which the Constitution left to the responsibility of the States, merely because Congress wrapped the legislation in the verbal cellophane of a revenue measure."[121] No one who has studied the historical records can ingenuously conclude that the federal government was given control over gambling by means of the tax power. Wagering was intrinsically a local problem, left to the States.

One of the soundest generalizations in the field is that of Justice Jackson in *H. P. Hood & Sons v. DuMond*:

> The distinction between the power of the States to shelter its people from menaces to their health or safety and from fraud, even when those dangers emanate from interstate commerce, and its lack of power to retard, burden or constrict the flow of such commerce for their economic advantage, is one deeply rooted in both our history and our law. . . . There was no desire to authorize federal interference with social conditions or legal institutions of the states.[122]

It is true that economic discrimination or reprisals were the mischief the Founders meant to remedy; how then can one account for Jackson's subsequent opinion in *Wickard v. Filburn?*[123] That case arose under the Agricultural Adjustment Act of 1938, designed in part "to avoid surpluses and shortages and the consequent abnormally low or high wheat prices and obstructions to commerce." The Act extended "federal regulation to production not intended in any part

[120] Dissenting in United States v. Kahriger, 345 U.S. 22 (1953).
[121] Id. at 38.
[122] 336 U.S. 525, 533, 534 (1949).
[123] 317 U.S. III (1942).

for commerce but *wholly for consumption on the farm*," apparently because nation-wide such consumption constituted about 20% of production.[124] Bearing in mind that the Founders were assured that the delegated powers would not extend to agriculture,[125] it is in the highest degree unlikely that they meant to grant power to regulate a farmer's production for his own consumption, even though that wheat, in conjunction with that of farmers in others States, might "overhang the market." As late as 1904, the Court, per Justice, later Chief Justice, White, cited as a horrible example a congressional regulation that "the farmer in sowing his crops should be limited to a certain production because overproduction would give power to affect commerce."[126] *Wickard* acknowledged that

> Certain activities such as "production," "manufacturing," and "mining" were occasionally said to be within the province of state governments and beyond the power of Congress under the Commerce Clause. . . . These earlier pronouncements also played an important part in several of the five cases in which this Court later held that Acts of Congress under the Commerce Clause were in excess of its power.[127]

But, as Justice Frankfurter earlier stated, "A reversal of a long current of decisions can be justified only if rooted in the Constitution itself."[128] Instead *Wickard* proceeded from

[124] Id. at 115, 118, 127 (emphasis added).
[125] Supra Chapter 3, text accompanying notes 122–123."[I]n the late eighteenth century, the food produced by farmers could often be shipped to other states without it occurring to anyone . . . that the farming itself became subject to federal regulation." Wolfe, *Modern Judicial Review* 175–176 (1986).
[126] Dissenting in Northern Securities Co. v. United States, 193 U.S. 197, 364, 397 (1904).
[127] 317 U.S. at 121, 122.
[128] Graves v. New York *ex rel*. O'Keefe, 306 U.S. 466, 488 (1939), concurring opinion.

the "Court's [quite recent] recognition of the relevance of the economic effects in the application of the Commerce Clause."[129] Economic developments do not confer power that was withheld.[130]

For its "broader interpretation," *Wickard* cited Holmes' "commerce among the States is not a technical legal conception, but a practical one drawn from the course of business."[131] That was extracted from *Swift & Co. v. United States*,[132] where, as Holmes made plain, cattle undeniably were in the stream of commerce:

> When cattle are sent for sale from a place in one State, with the expectation that they will end their transit, after purchase, in another, and when in effect they do so, with only the interruption necessary to find a purchaser at the stockyards, and when this is a typical, constantly recurring course, the current thus existing is a current of commerce among the States, and the purchase of the cattle is a part and incident of such commerce.[133]

Sending cattle to another State is poles removed from a farmer's production for his own use within the State. The Court would have been better advised to be guided by its later utterance, speaking by Justice Frankfurter: "It is not for us to make inroads upon our federal system either by indifference to its maintenance or excessive regard for

[129] 317 U.S. at 123.

[130] See Madison, infra text accompanying note 168. The courts have held that "judges cannot remedy political imperfections, nor supply legislative omissions." United States v. Worral, 2 U.S. (2 Dall.) 384, 395 (C.C.D. Pa. 1798), per Justice Chase. See also supra Chapter 1, note 32; and Justice Iredell, infra, note 168; infra Chapter 9, note 41.

The Court itself has stated that "if in the future further powers seemed necessary they should be granted by the people in the manner they had provided for amending" the Constitution. Kansas v. Colorado, 206 U.S. 46, 90 (1907).

[131] 317 U.S. at 122.

[132] 196 U.S. 375 (1905).

[133] Id. at 398.

the underlying forces of modern technology." The "inter-penetrations of modern society have not wiped out state lines."[134] In its exuberant overturn of its laissez faire dogmas, the "reconstructed" Court[135] went too far.

GUIDING PRINCIPLES OF CONSTRUCTION

The "Marshall system of constitutional interpretation," Corwin tells us, was *National power was to be liberally construed and effectively implemented, regardless of the coexistence of State powers.*"[136] He also cites Hamilton's 1791 opinion as to the constitutionality of the Bank of the United States, wherein, speaking of the word "necessary," he wrote, "the powers contained in a constitution of government ought to be construed liberally in advancement of the public good."[137] But Marshall, in defending *McCulloch v. Maryland,* branded as a "palpable misrepresentation" attribution to the Court of the view that the "necessary and proper clause" "is to be construed 'latitudinously' or even 'liberally'."[138] Hamilton was addressing *means* rather than powers, for he said in the same document, "If the *end* be clearly comprehended within any of the specified powers, and if the measure have an obvious relation to that end"—in other words, if the means obviously effectuate the power—then it "may safely be deemed to come within the compass of the national authority."[139] Moreover, Hamilton was an extreme nationalist

[134] Polish National Alliance v. N.L.R.B., 322 U.S. 643, 650 (1944).

[135] Graves v. New York *ex rel.* O'Keefe, 306 U.S. 466, 487 (1939).

[136] Corwin, *Commerce* 124; Mason 187: "Marshall established the proposition that national power must be liberally construed."

[137] Corwin, *Commerce* 217.

[138] *John Marshall's Defense of McCulloch v. Maryland* 97. Marshall likewise recognized the sovereignty of a State in its own sphere; supra Chapter 3, note 52.

[139] Corwin, *Commerce* 219.

whose own views fell on deaf ears in the Convention,[140] and whose advocacy of the Bank flew in the face of its unmistakable rejection of a national bank,[141] as he well knew, presumably being present at the time.[142] The Founders' profound distrust of judicial discretion,[143] their substitution of a detailed enumeration of powers for a loose federal authority "in all cases to which the separate States are incompetent,"[144] indicates that they had no stomach for a "liberal" interpretation, an approach that ill-accorded with their jealousy of federal encroachment on States' rights. Federal powers were "defined and limited" precisely to forestall such intrusion.

Construction of both the commerce and general welfare clauses should proceed from Madison's assurances in the Federalist. The federal jurisdiction, he stated in No. 39, "extends to certain enumerated objects only, and leaves to the States a residuary and *inviolable* sovereignty over all other objects."[145] Particularizing in No. 45, he said federal power "will be exercised principally on *external* objects as war, peace, negotiations and foreign commerce. . . . The powers reserved to the several States will extend to all objects which . . . concern . . . the *internal* order . . . of the State."[146] To repudiate such representations to the Ratifiers is, as Story wrote, to commit a fraud upon the American people.[147]

[140] In the Convention, Dr. William Johnson said, "The Gentlemen from NYk is praised by every gentleman, but supported by no gentleman." 1 Farrand 366. Hamilton himself "confess[ed]" that his own plan was "very remote from the idea of the people." Id. 301.

[141] Supra Chapter 5, notes 31–34, 37.

[142] Madison's proposal of national incorporation and its rejection took place on September 14, 1787. 1 Farrand 615–616. Hamilton signed the Constitution on September 17, id. 664–665.

[143] Supra Chapter 1, text accompanying notes 42–43.

[144] 2 Farrand 17.

[145] Federalist No. 39 at 349.

Earlier, two guides to construction were suggested: the Founders' emphases upon the *limited* nature of federal delegations and upon the *inviolable* State control of its internal affairs.[148] Any construction which conduces to unlimited federal power, to invasion of that inviolable domain, therefore violates the original design. A row of early cases rejected interpretations which would have swallowed the States' residuary powers.[149] In its recoil from the "no-man's land" excesses of its laissez faire predecessors,[150] the Court went too far, as the "janitor" cases exemplify. Apprehension of that danger was shared by some highly regarded "liberal" Justices. Dissenting in *Maryland v. Wirtz,* wherein the Court held that the Fair Labor Standards Act minimum wages applied to employees of State hospitals and schools,[151] Justice Douglas declared, "the national Government could devour the essentials of State sovereignty, though that sovereignty is attested by the Tenth Amendment."[152] In *Oregon v. Mitchell,* Justice Black cautioned against pushing the logic of the analogous equal protection provision too far lest the federalism envisioned by the Constitution be destroyed and the States reduced to "impotent figureheads."[153] And Justice Harlan rejected recent opinions in favor of federalism re-

[146] Id. No. 45 at 303.

[147] Supra Chapter 5, text accompanying note 7.

[148] Supra Chapter 3, text accompanying notes 74–76. See also Story, supra Chapter 5, text accompanying notes 28, 55.

[149] New York v. Miln, 36 U.S. (11 Pet.) 102, 141, 132 (1837); supra text accompanying note 94; Veazie v. Moore, 55 U.S. (14 How.) 568, 573–574 (1852); Kidd v. Pearson, 128 U.S. 1, 20–21 (1888); United States v. E. C. Knight Co., 156 U.S. 1, 11–15 (1895); supra note 96.

[150] Supra Chapter 1, text accompanying note 5.

[151] 392 U.S. 183 (1968); but see Justice Cardozo, infra, text accompanying note 156.

[152] 392 U.S. at 205.

[153] 400 U.S. 112, 126 (1970).

quirements.[154] At the turn of the century Justice Holmes, in
a dissent joined by Chief Justice Fuller and Justices White
and Peckham, rejected "an indirect effect upon commerce
not shown to be certain," saying, "I can see no part of the
conduct of life with which on similar principle Congress
might not interfere."[155] In the midst of the New Deal's fever-
ish efforts to stem the ravages of the Depression, Justice
Cardozo joined in invalidating application of the National
Industrial Recovery Act to poultry bought by the Schecters
from local commission men who had brought it into New
York, saying, "There is a view of causation that would obliterate the distinction between what is national and what is
local in the activities of commerce."[156] Justice Frankfurter
declared on behalf of the Court that "Scholastic reasoning
may prove that no activity is isolated within the boundaries
of a single State, but that cannot justify absorption of legislative power by the United States over every activity."[157]
Such an array of respectable opinion may not be dismissed
as divorced from present-day realities, particularly since it
responds to the clearly articulated aims of the Founders. In
sum, an interpretation which tends to unlimited federal
power and correspondingly invades the "inviolable" domain
of the States must be avoided.[158]

It is not too much to insist that those who would curtail
the State's "reserved" powers under cover of amorphous
terms such as "commerce" have the burden of proof that
such was the Founders' design. Writing in 1954, Herbert

[154] Id. at 217, 218.
[155] Northern Securities Co. v. United States, 193 U.S. 197, 402–403
(1904).
[156] Schecter Poultry Co. v. United States, 295 U.S. 495, 554 (1935).
[157] Polish National Alliance v. N.L.R.B., 322 U.S. 643, 650 (1944).
[158] Compare the express provision for tonnage duties despite the plea
that it was comprehended in the power to regulate commerce. Supra
Chapter 4, text accompanying note 76.

Wechsler stated that there is "a burden of persuasion on those favoring national intervention"[159]; he observed that "national action has always been regarded as exceptional in our polity, an intrusion to be justified by some necessity, the special rather than the ordinary case."[160] The exceptional nature of federal intervention was underlined by Justice Brandeis: the Constitution "preserves the autonomy and independence of the States"; federal supervision of their actions "is in no case permissible *except* as to matters specifically . . . delegated to the United States. Any interference . . . *except* as thus permitted, is an invasion of the authority of the State."[161] In other words, the federal powers are an exception from those retained by the States. Again and again the Founders stressed that the States were to *retain* powers not delegated, that each State would be "*giving up* a portion of its sovereignty," "retaining all the rights of supreme sovereignty *except* such as ought to be contributed to the union."[162] In the Virginia Ratification Convention,

[159] Herbert Wechsler, "The Political Safeguards of Federalism: The Role of the States in the Composition and Selection of the National Government," 54 Colum. L. Rev. 543, 545 (1954).

[160] Id. 544. I would emphasize proof of surrender of State powers rather than practical necessity. See also R. Nagel, "Federalism as a Fundamental Value: National League of Cities in Perspective," Supreme Court Rev. (1981) 81, 104.

[161] Erie Railway Co. v. Tompkins, 304 U.S. 64, 78–79 (1938) (emphasis added). See also Story, supra chapter 3, text accompanying note 64.

[162] Supra Chapter 3, text accompanying notes 26–31, 36. John Marshall said in the Virginia Convention, "Could any man say that this power was not retained by the states, as they had not given it away? For, says he, does not a power remain till it is given away?" 3 Elliot 419. There too, Henry Lee stated, "the limited powers were only an exception to those which rested in the people," that is, were "retained by the people." Id. 186. Those, said Justice Story, who "set up any such exception, must establish it as being within the words as well as within the reason thereof." United States v. Dickson, 40 U.S. (15 Pet.) 141, 165 (1841). See also United States v. First City National Bank, 386 U.S. 361, 366 (1967); Rheem Manufacturing

Marshall asked, "Could any man say that this power was not retained by the states, as they had not given it away? For . . . does not a power remain till it is given away?"[163] Chief Justice Stone regarded it as "a truism that all is retained *which has not been surrendered*."[164] The threshold question must always be, therefore, did the States surrender a power claimed by the federal government,[165] and it is incumbent on the claimant to prove the surrender—a "burden of persuasion" implicitly imposed by the Founders.

Such reasoning undermines the federal exclusion, for example, of deleterious foods, drugs, and the like from interstate commerce, and is therefore likely to raise the hackles of

---

Co. v. Rheem, 295 F.2d 473,477 (9th Cir. 1961). See also Pierson v. Ray, supra note 95.

Jefferson, in reply to a request from Justice William Johnson "to examine the question whether the Supreme Court has advanced beyond its constitutional limits, and trespassed on those of the State authorities," stated on June 12, 1823, "there are two canons which will guide us safely, 1st, The capital and leading object of the constitution was to leave with the States all authorities which respected their own citizens only, and to transfer to the United States those which respected citizens of foreign or other States: to make us several as to ourselves, but one as to all others." *The Jeffersonian and Hamiltonian Tradition in American Politics* 18 (Albert Fried ed. 1968).

[163] Murphy 361.

[164] Supra Chapter 4, text accompanying note 2.

[165] Speaking to the supremacy clause, James Iredell said, "the question . . . will always be, whether *Congress* has exceeded its authority." 4 Elliot 178 (emphasis added).

Justice Miller refused to embrace a construction of the Fourteenth Amendment that would subject the State's local concerns to "the control of Congress . . . in the absence of language which expressed such a purpose too clearly to admit of doubt." Slaughter-House Cases, 83 U.S. (16 Wall.) 36, 78 (1872). See Pierson v. Ray, supra note 95.

Edward Corwin adjured the Court to abandon its attempt "to supervise national legislative policies on the basis of a superconstitution which in the name of the Constitution, repeals and destroys the historical document." Corwin, *Twilight* 182.

those who equate what is desirable with what is constitutional. But as James Wilson stated in the Federal Convention, "Laws may be unjust, may be unwise, may be dangerous, may be destructive, and yet not so unconstitutional as to justify the Judges in refusing to give them effect."[166] And Chief Justice Marshall stated, "The peculiar circumstances of the moment may render a measure more or less wise, but cannot render it more or less constitutional."[167] Because a vital power may be lacking, it does not follow that the Court is authorized to supply it. Madison said, "Had the power of making treaties . . . been omitted, however necessary it might have been, the defect could only have been lamented, or supplied by amendment of the Constitution."[168] To confuse what *is* with what *ought to be* is to engage in wishful thinking.

[166] 2 Farrand 73.

[167] Gunther, supra note 138 at 190–191. Professor Frankfurter observed that "wisdom and justice are not the test of constitutionality." Felix Frankfurter, "Can the Supreme Court Guarantee Toleration?" 43 New Republic 85, 86 (1925). In Missouri Pacific Ry. Co. v. Humes, 115 U.S. 512, 520–521 (1885), the Court, per Justice Field, stated that "the hardship, impolicy or injustice of State laws is not necessarily an objection to their constitutional validity," and that "This Court is not a harbor where refuge can be found from every act of ill-advised and oppressive State legislation."

[168] 2 *Annals of Congress* 1900–1901 (February 2, 1791). Justice Iredell, who led the fight for adoption of the Constitution in the North Carolina Convention, stated that the argument "that because it [a power] was proper to be given, therefore, it was actually given, [is] a position which, as it would lead to dangerous and inadmissible consequences, cannot be the ground of a legitimate argument." Penhallow v. Doane, 3 U.S. (3 Dall.) 54, 92 (1795). See infra Chapter 9, note 41.

CHAPTER SEVEN

The Impact of the Fourteenth Amendment

AN indissoluble Union was forged in the fires of the Civil War. But that, the Court declared in *Texas v. White* (1868), "by no means implies the loss of distinct and individual existence or of the right of self-government by the States."[1] For notwithstanding that the States' Rights doctrine had been badly tarnished by its association with secession, there remained a deep-seated attachment to State sovereignty. On the eve of the Civil War Lincoln stated in his First Inaugural Address, "The right of each State to order and control its own domestic institutions according to its own judgment exclusively is essential to the balance of powers on which the perfection and endurance of our political fabric depends."[2] That view survived the Civil War. Roscoe

[1] 74 U.S. (7 Wall.) 700, 725 (1868). The Republican Party Platform of May 16, 1860, provided "That the maintenance inviolate of the rights of the States, and especially the right of each State to order and control its own domestic institutions according to its own judgment exclusively, is essential to the balance of power." *The Jeffersonian and Hamiltonian Tradition in American Politics* 232 (Albert Fried ed. 1968).

[2] Quoted in *Cong. Globe* 2096 (39th Cong. 1st Sess. 1866). In 1865 Governor Yates of Illinois, soon to be Senator, said, "I am for unlimited state sovereignty in the true sense, in the sense that the State is to control all its municipal and local legislation, and I would be the first to resist all attempts on the part of the Federal Government to interpose tyrannical

Conkling, a member of the Joint Committee on Reconstruction, stated in the 39th Congress which drafted the
Fourteenth Amendment, "The proposition to prohibit
States from denying civil or political rights to any class of
persons encounters a great objection on the threshold. It
trenches upon the principle of existing local sovereignty."[3]
Samuel Marshall of Illinois stated, "It is a fundamental principle of American law that the regulation of the local police
of all the domestic affairs of a State belong to the State itself,
and not to the Federal Government."[4] The draftsman of the
Fourteenth Amendment, John Bingham, said, "the care of
the property, the liberty, and the life of the citizen . . . is in
the States and not in the federal government. I have sought
to effect no change in that respect."[5] "The radical leaders,"
Harry Flack observed, "were aware as anyone of the attachment of a great majority of the people to the doctrine of
States rights . . . the right of the States to regulate their own
internal affairs."[6] These sentiments were accurately summarized by Justice Miller in 1872, shortly after adoption of the
Fourteenth and Fifteenth Amendments: "Under the pres-

usurpations of power in controlling the legislation of States." P. Paludan,
A Covenant With Death 34 (1975).
    [3] *Cong. Globe* 358 (39th Cong. 1st Sess. 1866); see also Columbus
Delano, id. *Globe* App. 158.
    [4] Id. 627.
    [5] Id. 1292. Bingham repeated, "I have always believed that the protec-
tion in times of peace within the State of all the rights of persons and
citizens was of the powers reserved to the States." Id. 1293.
    [6] H. Flack, *The Adoption of the Fourteenth Amendment* 81 (1908).
Harold Hyman concluded, "One reason the Reconstruction of the South
loomed so high to northerners was less that blacks were involved than
that everyone understood the pre-eminence of states . . . in affecting all
their citizens lives." H. Hyman, *A More Perfect Union* 246 (1973). "A heavy
phalanx of Republican politicos, including Sherman and Trumbull [chair-
man of the Senate Judiciary Committee] were states rights nationalists,
suspicious of any new functional path the nation travelled." Id. 304.

sure of all the excited feeling growing out of the war, our
statesmen have still believed that the existence of the states
with power for domestic and local government . . . was
essential to the perfect working of our complex form of
government."[7]

What then did the Fourteenth Amendment accomplish?
The answer is to be sought in the association of the Civil
Rights Act of 1866 with the Amendment; they proceeded on
parallel tracks in the 39th Congress. "Over and over in this
debate" on the amendment, said Charles Fairman, "the correspondence between Section One of the Amendment and
the Civil Rights Act is noted. The provisions of the one are
treated as though they were essentially identical with those
of the other."[8] Flack, a devotee of a broad construction of
the Amendment, wrote, "nearly all said that it was but an
incorporation of the Civil Rights Bill . . . there was no controversy as to its purpose and meaning."[9] Justice Bradley
summed up in the *Civil Rights Cases* what is plain from the
face of the Act,[10] that the 1866 Act sought to secure "those

---

A broad constructionist of the Fourteenth Amendment, Howard Jay
Graham, said, "No one reading the debates carefully will question the
framer's devotion to federalism, even the extreme radicals." H. J. Graham,
Everyman's Constitution 312 (1968).

[7] The Slaughter-House Cases, 83 U.S. (16 Wall.) 36, 82 (1872).

[8] C. Fairman, "Does the Fourteenth Amendment Incorporate the Bill
of Rights," 2 Stan. L. Rev. 5, 44 (1949).

[9] Flack, supra note 6, at 81; see also id. at 54, 79. Henry Raymond of
New York stated in the 39th Congress that by the Civil Rights Bill Congress "proposed to exercise precisely the powers which that amendment
was intended to confer." Cong. Globe, supra note 3, at 2502. An ardent
advocate of an abolitionist reading of the Amendment, Howard Jay
Graham, said, "virtually every speaker in the debates . . . said or agreed
that the Amendment was designed to embody or incorporate the Civil
Rights Act." Graham, *Everyman's Constitution* 291, note 73. Motives were
mixed; some wanted to assure a sound constitutional basis for the Act;
others to prevent its repeal. Berger 23, note 12.

[10] Berger, supra note 9 at 24.

fundamental rights which are the essence of civil freedom, namely, the same right to make and enforce contracts, to sue . . . to inherit, purchase . . . property as is enjoyed by white citizens. . . . Congress did not assume . . . to adjust what may be called the social rights of men . . . but only to declare and vindicate these fundamental rights."[11] Without them the emancipated blacks could not exist or would be returned to serfdom. That the "legislative history of the 1866 Act clearly indicates that Congress intended to protect a limited category of rights" was repeated 100 years later by the Court in *Georgia v. Rachel.*[12] In 1870 Justice Bradley stated that "the civil rights bill was enacted at the same session, and but shortly before the presentation of the fourteenth amendment . . . was in para materia . . . the first section of the bill covers the same ground as the fourteenth amendment."[13] Although the four dissenters in the *Slaughter House Cases,* speaking by Justice Field, read the Amendment more broadly than the majority, they too indicated that the Civil Rights Act of 1866 covered the same ground as the Amendment.[14]

The framers underscored their narrow goals by the exclusion of suffrage and segregation from the scope of the amendment. There is no need here to recapitulate the his-

[11] Civil Rights Cases, 109 U.S. 3, 22 (1883).

[12] 384 U.S. 780, 791 (1966).

[13] Live Stock Dealers' & Butchers' Ass'n v. Crescent City Live-Stock Landing and Slaughter-House Co., 15 F. Cas. 649, 655. (C.C.D. La. 1870) (No. 8,408). Michael Perry agrees that by the Fourteenth Amendment the framers "meant only to protect against state action discriminating on the basis of race, a narrow category of 'fundamental' rights: those pertaining to the physical security of one's person, freedom of movement, and capacity to make contracts . . . and to acquire, hold or transfer chattels and land—'life, liberty, and property' in the original sense." Perry, "Interpretivism, Freedom of Expression and Equal Protection," 43 Ohio St. L. Rev. 261, 273 (1981).

[14] 83 U.S. (16 Wall.) 36, 96 (1872).

tory that richly documents the exclusion of suffrage, which the one man-one vote decisions flagrantly reversed. Justice Harlan justly affirmed that those decisions flew "in the face of irrefutable and still unanswered history to the contrary."[15] Activist Louis Lusky considers that Harlan's demonstration is "irrefutable and unrefuted."[16] Another activist, Nathaniel Nathanson, noted the "general understanding" of the framers "and probably most of the ratifying legislatures . . . that it would not require school desegregation or negro suffrage."[17] The framers of the Fifteenth Amendment, which outlawed discrimination with respect to suffrage, made plain that it was required to fill a gap in the Fourteenth.[18] Next to no reference to this history will be found in the Court's majority opinions because it stands

[15] Griswold v. Connecticut, 381 U.S. 479, 501 (1965), concurring.

[16] Lusky, "Book Review," 6 Hastings Const. L.Q. 403, 406 (1979). Even that superheated activist, Paul Brest, grudgingly concedes that "the adopters of the equal protection clause probably intended it not to encompass voting discrimination at all." P. Brest, "The Misconceived Quest for the Original Intention," 60 B.U. L. Rev. 204, 234 note 115 (1980). Summing up, Robert Bork stated, "The principle of one man, one vote . . . runs counter to the text of the fourteenth amendment, the history surrounding its adoption and ratification and the political practice of Americans from Colonial times up to the day the Court invented the new formula." Bork, "Neutral Principles and Some First Amendment Problems," 47 Ind. L.J. 1, 18 (1971).

[17] Nathanson, "Book Review," 56 Tex. L. Rev. 579, 580–581 (1978). See also Abraham, "Book Review," 6 Hastings Const. L.Q. 467–468 (1978); Mendelson, "Book Review, id. 437, 453. Activist Michael Perry concluded that "the framers specifically intended that the fourteenth amendment would not diminish any state's plenary control over suffrage," and that "they did not intend that the amendment would diminish any state's plenary control over education . . . or judicial proceedings." Perry, "Book Review," 78 Colum. L. Rev. 685, 687 (1978).

[18] Raoul Berger, "The Fourteenth Amendment: Light From the Fifteenth," 74 Nw. U. L. Rev. 311, 321–323 (1979).

athwart its busy creation of rights that cannot be found in the Constitution.[19]

In short, the reader will vainly search in the legislative history of the Amendment for evidence that surrender of the State's police power over internal affairs under the rubric of "commerce" or any other rubric—putting contracts, ownership of property, and access to the courts to one side—was contemplated by the framers. To the contrary, as Justice Field declared on behalf of the Court in 1885, "Neither the [Fourteenth] amendment . . . nor any other amendment, was designed to interfere with the power of the State, sometimes termed its police power, to prescribe regulations, to promote health, . . . education . . . good order of the people."[20]

---

[19] For citations see Raoul Berger, "Michael Perry's Functional Justification for Judicial Activism," 8 U. Dayton L. Rev. 465, 466 note 12 (1983). Arthur R. Miller of Harvard Law School observed, "we have engaged in twenty years of 'right creation frenzy'." 77 Harv. L. Record 2 (December 9, 1983). "We are not at liberty," Justice Story declared, "to add one jot of power to the national government beyond what the people have granted in the Constitution." Houston v. Moore, 18 U.S. (5 Wheat.) 1, 48 (1820). See also Raoul Berger, "Insulation of Judicial Usurpation: A Comment on Lawrence Sager's Court-Stripping Polemic," 44 Ohio St. L.J. 611, 615 note 44 (1983). See also infra, Chapter 9 note 36.

[20] Barbier v. Connolly, 113 U.S. 27, 31 (1885).

CHAPTER EIGHT

Is Municipal Mass Transit "Interstate Commerce"?

Garcia v. San Antonio Metropolitan Transit Authority (1985) decided by 5-to-4 that municipal mass transit is governed by federal minimum wages and hours standards.[1] Hailed by the *New York Times* as a "welcome return to sensible federalism," *Garcia*, Dean John C. Pittenger remarked, marks "the end of federalism as a notion with any support in the Constitution," and he chided the *Times* for not flatly stating that "federalism is obsolete."[2] But federalism is embedded in the Constitution and is beyond the Court's power to discard. Justice Powell, dissenting, justly stated that *Garcia* rejected "the history of our country and the intention of the Framers of our Constitution."[3] And it did so on grounds that cannot withstand scrutiny, once more evidencing that the Constitution is merely what any given set of Justices say it is.

In 1976 *National League of Cities v. Usery*[4] held that application of the Fair Labor Standards Act to the "traditional governmental functions" of State and local governments was unconstitutional. That "traditional functions" test plunged

[1] 105 S. Ct. 1005, hereinafter cited as *Garcia*.
[2] New York Times, March 25, 1985, A–18.
[3] *Garcia* 1032.
[4] 426 U.S. 833 (1976).

164

the courts into an interpretive quagmire, proving itself, said Justice Blackmun, "both impracticable and doctrinally barren."[5] He had joined in the *Usery* decision, but now threw up his hands and concluded that the task had better be left to Congress, saying that any such rule of state immunity "inevitably invites an unelected judiciary to make decisions about which state policies it favors and which ones it dislikes."[6] Dissenting, Justice Powell justifiably observes that the "extent to which the States may exercise their authority, when Congress purports to act under the Commerce Clause, henceforth is to be determined from time to time by political decisions made by members of the federal government, decisions the Court says will not be subject to judicial review,"[7] thus leaving federal officials "the sole judges of the limits of their own power."[8] This is a glaring departure from the established course, and it places the States at the mercy of Congress, precisely what the Founders meant to avoid.[9]

Not that judicial review has served to impede the expansion of the commerce clause; on the contrary, the Court made that expansion possible. Justice O'Connor adverts to the Court's "increasingly generous . . . interpretation of the commerce power" whereby "Congress has been given an ability lacking prior to the emergence of an integrated national economy," justly labeling it a "breathtaking expan-

[5] *Garcia* 1011–1016, 1021.

[6] Id. 1015.

[7] Id. 1023. Van Alstyne observes that "Stripped of its elegance, *Garcia* proposes the piecemeal repeal of judicial review." Van Alstyne, "The Second Death of Federalism," 89 Mich. L. Rev. 1709, 1724 (1985).

[8] *Garcia* 1026. Justice Powell correctly comments that "the Court's view of federalism appears to relegate the States to precisely the trivial role that opponents of the Constitution feared that they would occupy," id. 1020, and that proponents of the Constitution assured them was contrary to the fact.

[9] Supra Chapter 6.

sion."[10] Economic integration does not confer constitutional power. Nevertheless, abuse of the judicial power cannot deny its place in the constitutional structure. Since Justice Blackmun pins his case to the curbs he derives from that structure, it will not be amiss to rehearse the place of judicial review therein.

Hamilton rejected the argument that "the legislative body are themselves the constitutional judges of their own powers";[11] and he assured the Ratifiers that the courts were to keep Congress "within the limits assigned to their authority" and to be the "bulwarks of a limited Constitution against legislative encroachments."[12] In "controversies relating to the boundaries between the two jurisdictions"—State and federal—he said, "[T]he tribunal which ultimately is to decide, is to be established under the general government,"[13] that is, the Supreme Court. In Federalist No. 33, he said that "invasion of the residuary authorities of the smaller societies . . . will be merely acts of usurpation";[14] and such usurpations, he stated in No. 16, were to be pronounced "unconstitutional and void" by the courts.[15] Similar statements were made in State Ratification Conventions by Samuel Adams, Oliver Ellsworth, and George Nicholas.[16] Let Wil-

[10] *Garcia* 1034, 1035.
[11] Federalist No. 78 at 506.
[12] Id. 506, 508.
[13] Id., No. 39 at 249.
[14] Id., No. 33 at 202.
[15] Id., No. 16 at 100. Madison also stated in Federalist No. 39 (page 249) that there must be a tribunal empowered to decide "controversies relating to the boundaries between the two jurisdictions."
[16] Raoul Berger, *Congress v. The Supreme Court* 8–16 (1969). The popular mood is reflected in Hamilton's remarks in the New York Assembly just before the Convention: "Upon every occasion . . . we hear a loud cry about the dangers of intrusting powers to the Congress." Clinton Rossiter, *Alexander Hamilton and the Constitution* 168 (1964).

son sum up. In his 1791 Lectures—he was then a Justice of the Supreme Court—Wilson stated that the legislative power is subject to "control by the judiciary department, whenever the laws . . . are found to be contradictory of the Constitution." The "bounds of the legislative power" are "distinctly marked," and provision is made that "every transgression of those bounds shall be adjudged vain and fruitless. What a noble guard against legislative despotism."[17] The stubborn State insistence that initial arbitrament of federal-State conflicts be lodged in the State courts sprang from the fervent belief, voiced by William Grayson in the Virginia Convention, that "State courts were the principal defence of the states," their "only defensive armor."[18] Justice Powell therefore spoke truly in stating that the majority "ignores the role of judicial review in our system of government."[19] Worse, it abdicated a duty the Constitution imposes.[20]

The "traditional governmental functions" test was *Usery*'s timorous response to the compulsions of the Tenth Amendment. Of course, mass transit was not a "traditional governmental function"; there was no need for it in the eighteenth-century towns and villages. Justice Powell rightly dismissed the Court's emphasis that

> municipal operation of an intracity mass transit system is relatively new in the life of our country. It nevertheless is a classic example of the type of service traditionally provided by local government. It is *local* by definition. It is indistinguishable

[17] Berger, supra note 16 at 151. If Congress "steps outside of its constitutional limitations . . . the courts are authorized to . . . annul its enroachments upon the reserved power of the States and the people." United States v. Reese, 92 U.S. 214, 221 (1875).

[18] Berger, supra note 16 at 263.

[19] *Garcia* 1023.

[20] Panama Refining Co. v. Ryan, 293 U.S. 388, 421 (1935).

in principle from the traditional services of providing and maintaining streets, public lighting, traffic control, water and sewerage services. Services of this kind are precisely those "with which citizens are more 'familiarly minutely conversant'. The Federalist No. 46."[21]

In light of the Founders' jealous solicitude for local control over internal matters, it is simply inconceivable that they would have ceded to the remote federal government control over transportation of persons within town boundaries, whether by privately owned coaches or by those the town might choose to furnish. It needs no "*a priori* definitions of state sovereignty"[22] to reject federal intrusion into the "local" domain, for the Founders little heeded abstract definitions of "sovereignty,"[23] but fixed their attention on safeguarding the States' "local" functions. Whatever the broader dimensions of "sovereignty," minimally it meant governance of "internal," "local" affairs.

There is no need to re-traverse the evidence of the Founders' deep attachment to their local institutions, their "deeply rooted distrust of central power,"[24] their anxiety to "limit" federal power. We have seen their unmistakable intention to retain "internal police" power, power in "cases purely local,

---

[21] *Garcia* 1032. Powell reminded the Court that *Usery* "spoke of fire prevention, police protection, sanitation, and public health as 'typical of [the services] performed by state and local governments in discharging their dual functions of administering the public law and furnishing public services. . . . Not only are those activities remote from any normal concept of interstate commerce, they are also activities that epitomize the concerns of local, democratic self-government." *Garcia* 1031. This, we have seen, was the long-held view of the Court. And as the Court itself has said, "the State's regulation of its relationship with its employees is an 'undoubted attribute of state sovereignty'." FERC v. Mississippi, 456 U.S. 742, 764 note 28 (1982).

[22] *Garcia* 1016.

[23] Supra Chapter 3, text accompanying notes 12–16.

[24] Id., text accompanying notes 42–49.

applying to their internal policy,"[25] and have noted assurances on all sides that they would do so. To recall only a few citations: in Federalist No. 17 Hamilton dismissed federal intrusion into "the mere domestic police of a State."[26] In the North Carolina Ratification Convention, William Davie, who had been a delegate to the Federal Convention, declared, "There is not one instance of power given to the United States, whereby the internal policy of administration of the State is affected."[27] Herbert Storing's recent comprehensive survey of the Federalist-antifederalist debate concluded that the *proponents* of the Constitution considered that "each State will retain sovereignty in what concerns its own internal sovereignty."[28] Nor was the meaning of "internal" wrapped in mystery. James Wilson stated in the Pennsylvania Ratification Convention that "Whatever object of government is confined in its operation and effect, *within the bounds* of a particular State, should be considered as belonging to the government of that State; whatever the object of government extends, in its operation, *beyond the bounds* of a

[25] Id., text accompanying notes 101–110. "It is simply the tradition of state and (more typically) of local governments to supply public services that they find consistent with the public welfare and unsuitable to leave to other providers. . . . If (but only if) their operations can fairly be described as somehow interfering with commerce (whether interstate or foreign) within Congress' power to control, may they properly be restricted, albeit, of course, only to the extent of their interference with that commerce." Van Alstyne, supra note 7 at 1719–1720. See also Howard, "*Garcia* and the Values of Federalism: On the Need for a Recurrence to Fundamental Principles," 19 Ga. L. Rev. 789 (1985).

[26] Federalist No. 17 at 101.

[27] Supra Chapter 3, text accompanying note 106. So too, Judge Pendleton assured the Virginia Ratification Convention that the Constitution "does not interfere with the local particular affairs of the State." Id., text accompanying note 104.

[28] Id., text accompanying note 109. Throughout the nineteenth century the Court recognized that the States had exclusive power in this domain.

particular state, should be considered as belonging to the government of the United States."[29]

To do Blackmun justice, San Antonio had not claimed immunity from federal regulation "on the ground that it is a local transit system engaged in intrastate commercial activity."[30] But the jurisdictional boundary issue stared the Court in the face and could not, in good conscience, be ducked. Justice Blackmun acknowledged that the transit "operations might well be characterized as 'local.' Nonetheless, it long has been settled that Congress' authority under the Commerce Clause extends to intrastate economic activities that *affect* interstate commerce."[31] Manifestly, mass transportation from 42d Street to 72d Street has no effect "beyond the bounds" of New York City, and therefore it does not "affect" interstate commerce. Like Jefferson's and Madison's analogous remarks,[32] O'Connor observed that "virtually every State activity . . . arguably 'affects' interstate commerce,"[33] so that "affects" cannot be given unlimited scope without violating the Founders' determination to withhold illimitable power. Instead of explaining how purely local transit "affects" interstate commerce, Blackmun argues that a similar operation by a private company undeniably would be governed by the commerce clause, so that San Antonio's claim must rest on its "status as a governmental entity rather than on the 'local' nature of its operation."[34] But federal control of private, purely local transportation itself would invade State control of local matters, so that Blackmun would rest a fresh usurpation on a prior arrogation.

[29] Id., text accompanying note III (emphasis added); see also id. at notes 112–126.

[30] *Garcia* 1010.

[31] Id.

[32] Supra Chapter 6, text accompanying notes 5–6.

[33] *Garcia* 1035.

[34] Id. 1010.

Justice Blackmun agrees that "The essence of our federal system is that within the realm of authority left open under the Constitution, the States must be equally free to engage in any activity that their citizens choose for the common weal." And he adds, "The States unquestionably do 'retain a significant measure' of sovereign authority. . . . They do so, however, only to the extent that the Constitution has not divested them of their original powers and transferred those powers to the federal Government."[35] Thus we are brought to the core issue: how far does "commerce among the several States" divest the States of jurisdiction of local transit?

True it is that "the Commerce Clause by its specific language does not provide any special limitation on Congress' actions with respect to the States."[36] "Commerce," however, is not self-defining, and we must therefore look to the constitutional history which, as has been noted, discloses that "commerce among the States" was not meant to comprehend purely local matters.[37] Blackmun himself acknowledges that "the text of the Constitution provides the beginning rather than the final answer to every inquiry into questions of federalism," for "[b]ehind the words of the constitutional provisions are *postulates which limit* and control."[38] Among those postulates is "inviolable" State control of internal police,[39] as Chief Justice Marshall recognized in the *Dartmouth College* case: "That the framers of the Constitution did not intend

[35] Id. 1015, 1017.
[36] Id. 1016.
[37] Supra Chapter 6.
[38] *Garcia* 1016.
[39] The Court's slighting reference to preservation of "a sacred province of state autonomy," *Garcia* 1017, is at war with its citation to the Federalist's assurance that the States were left with "a residuary and inviolable sovereignty" over all unenumerated objects. Id., Federalist No. 39 at 249. "Inviolable" is defined by the *Oxford Universal Dictionary* as "to be kept sacredly free from profanation, infraction or assault."

to restrain the States in the regulation of their civil institutions, adopted for internal government, and that the instrument they have given us, is not to be so construed, may be
admitted."[40] Blackmun agrees that "the composition of the
Federal Government was designed in large part *to protect the
States from overreaching by Congress*"[41]: he recognizes that
"the States occupy a special and specific position in our
Constitutional system and that *the scope of Congress' authority*
under the Commerce Clause *must reflect that position.*"[42] In
other words, interpretation of the clause must respect the
States' inviolable residuary authority over internal affairs.

But he looks through the wrong end of the telescope in
assuming that State exemption from federal statute must be
justified, and in singling out "certain underlying elements
that are deemed essential to the States' 'separate and independent existence'."[43] He forgets that the States grudgingly
delegated to the suspect federal newcomer only so much as
was necessary to carry out national purposes such as war
and the like, leaving other State powers "unimpaired,"[44] and
implicitly imposing a "burden of persuasion" on one who

[40] Dartmouth College v. Woodward, 17 U.S. (4 Wheat.) 518, 629 (1819).
[41] *Garcia* 1018 (emphasis added). Powell finds that "federal overreaching under the Commerce Clause undermines the constitutionally man-
dated balance of power between the States and the federal government, a
balance designed to protect our fundamental liberties." Id. 1029.
[42] Id. 1020 (emphasis added).
[43] Id. 1018. He also states, "The point of the injury, however, has remained to single out particular features of a State's internal governance
that are deemed to be intrinsic parts of state sovereignty." Id. 1016. So too,
he considers that "any constitutional exemption from the requirements of
the FLSA therefore must rest on SAMTA's status as a governmental entity
rather than on the 'local' nature of its operations." Id. 1010.
[44] James Wilson assured the Pennsylvania Ratification Convention that
the Framers were anxious to "preserve the State governments unimpaired." McMaster & Stone 265.

would curtail a given State power.[45] Justice O'Connor commented that "In 1954, one could still speak of a 'burden of persuasion' on those favoring federal intervention," but "the burden of persuasion has surely shifted."[46] It was shifted, however, by the Court, in disregard of the historical evidence that federal intrusion was to be the exception rather than the rule, leaving to the States, as Marshall noted, the "immense mass of legislation, which embraces everything within the territory of a State, *not surrendered* to the general government."[47]

But Justice Blackmun maintains that "the principal and basic limit on the federal commerce power is that inherent in all congressional action—the built-in restraints that our system provides through *state participation* in federal government."[48] The "breathtaking expansion" of congressional intrusion into the State domain[49] shows that those "built-in restraints" have been ineffectual. On Blackmun's reasoning, moreover, provision of judicial review to police congressional boundaries was superfluous. Yet the records disclose that the Founders relied on the courts to curb congressional excesses.[50] For his argument that the Framers relied on the

[45] Supra Chapter 6, text accompanying notes 159–165.

[46] *Garcia* 1037.

[47] Gibbons v. Ogden, 22 U.S. (9 Wheat.) 1, 203 (1824) (emphasis added).

[48] *Garcia* 1020: "[T]he principal means chosen by the Framers to ensure the role of the States in the federal system lies in the structure of the Federal government itself." Id. 1018. For a vigorous criticism of Blackmun's "erroneous suppositions about the way in which nation's political process actually works," see Howard, supra note 25 at 792–793.

[49] Blackmun notes that the expansion is of "recent vintage": "Most of the Federal Government's current regulatory activity orginated less than 50 years ago with the New Deal, and a good portion of it has developed within the past two decades." Id. 1014. Thus the Court belatedly discovered in the Constitution what had gone unnoticed for 150 years.

[50] Supra text accompanying notes 11–17.

structure of the federal government "to insulate the interests of the States," Blackmun cites some general remarks, such as that of Madison in Federalist No. 46: "the Federal Government will partake sufficiently of the spirit [of the States] to be *disinclined* to invade the rights of the individual States."[51] This sounds in federal self-restraint rather than State "participation." That Madison did not rely on State "participation" to limit Congress is demonstrated by his statement in the same No. 46 that "ambitious encroachment of the federal government, on the authority of the State governments . . . would be the signal of general alarm. . . . Plans of resistance would be concerted."[52] Another Blackmun citation is to Federalist No. 62 wherein Madison spoke of "equal representation of the States in the Senate, which he saw as 'at once a constitutional recognition of the portion of sovereignty remaining in the individual States and *an* instrument for preserving that residuary sovereignty'."[53] "Equal representation," Madison observed, was a "compromise between the opposite pretensions of the large and small States."[54] This was the "great compromise" which was designed to protect the small States from the large,[55] *not* from Congress. Blackmun overlooked Madison's statement in Federalist No. 44 that "In the first instance, the success of the [congressional] usurpation will depend on the executive and the judiciary departments . . . in the last resort a remedy must be obtained from the people."[56] Thus, judicial review had the primary role. In the Virginia Ratification Convention, Madison stated that "explication" of the fed-

[51] *Garcia* 1018 (emphasis added).
[52] Federalist No. 46 at 309.
[53] *Garcia* 1018.
[54] Federalist No. 62 at 401.
[55] S. E. Morison, *The Oxford History of the American People* 308 (1965).
[56] Federalist No. 44 at 395.

eral authority was to be submitted "to the judiciary of the United States."[57] Patently Madison is poor authority for Blackmun's argument that State participation in Congress provided "the principal and basic limit" on congressional invasion of States' Rights.

Blackmun's reliance on a paraphrase of James Wilson in the Pennsylvania Convention is no more reliable: "'it was a favorite object in the Convention' to provide for the security of the States against federal encroachment and that the structure of the Federal Government itself served that end."[58] Wilson was rebutting the argument that the very existence of the States was threatened, pointing out that the qualifications of the electors of the House of Representatives were tied to those of the State legislatures, that electors of the President were to be chosen as those legislatures shall direct. Consequently, he concluded the idea "of the *existing* government of the States, is presupposed in the very mode of constituting the legislative and executive departments of the general government." The "*continuance* of the State governments," he stated, was "a favorite object in the Convention."[59] Wilson did not refer to federal "encroachments" on the States' internal functions, nor to State participation in Congress as a bar to such encroachments. For, like other Founders, he considered that if the legislature "transgress the bounds assigned to it," it is the judges' "duty to pronounce it void," a "noble guard against legislative despotism."[60] Blackmun's reliance on "structure" would rest more solidly on the structural provision for judicial review.

[57] 3 Elliot 352. He had stated in Federalist No. 39 that the federal courts were to be the arbiters in conflicts between the federal and State governments." See supra note 15.

[58] *Garcia* 1018.

[59] 2 Elliot 438–439.

[60] Id. 446; see supra text accompanying note 17. Van Alstyne observes

Justice Powell truly states that the majority "rejects almost 200 years of the understanding of the constitutional status of federalism."[61] But Justice Blackmun revealingly asserts that the "most obvious defect of a historical approach to state immunity is that it prevents a court from accommodating changes in the historical function of the States."[62] This claims for the Court the right to go contrary to the Founders' intention, to revise the Constitution. He maintains that a "reasonably objective measure for State immunity, is illusory."[63] Not so. State control over janitors of its schools or hospitals is incontrovertibly "local," as is transportation of people solely within town confines, having no effect on "interstate" transportation. The "local" test is that of the Founders, and it is far more tangible and soundly based than Blackmun's cobwebby inferences from dicta about "structure." It is illustrative of judicial myopia that Blackmun should note "the general conviction that the Constitution precludes 'the National Government [from] devour[ing] the essentials of state sovereignty,"[64] while in fact fulfilling Justice Douglas' prophecy that the Court had embarked on a course that enabled "the National Government [to] devour the essentials of State sovereignty, though that sovereignty is attested by the Tenth Amendment."[65]

The generality of "commerce" must be read against Madison's assurances in Federalist No. 39 that the federal "jurisdiction extends to certain enumerated objects only, and leaves to the several States a residuary and inviolable sover-

---

that the other "safeguards" of the constitutional plan are "merely additional to, and not in substitution of, substantive judicial review." Van Alstyne, supra note 7 at 1724.

[61] *Garcia* 1023.
[62] Id. 1014.
[63] *Garcia* 1014.
[64] Id. 1016.
[65] Maryland v. Wirtz, 392 U.S. 183, 205 (1968), dissenting opinion.

eignty over all other objects."[66] There too, as Justice Powell notes, Madison stated that "local or municipal authorities . . . [are] no more subject within their respective spheres to the general authority than the general authority is subject to them, within its own sphere."[67] Not content with assurances that the federal government was not authorized to invade such "residuary" powers, the States insisted on a written guarantee, the Tenth Amendment, which was added to make that protection "absolutely certain."[68] History richly confirms Powell's statement that "the Tenth Amendment was adopted specifically to ensure that the important role promised [in fact 'reserved' to] the States by proponents of the Constitution was realized."[69] Nevertheless, as he notes, "there is only a single passing reference to the Tenth Amendment" in the majority opinion; it "barely acknowledges that the Tenth Amendment exists," and ignores "its integral role."[70] In the teeth of history, Blackmun "effectively reduces the Tenth Amendment to meaningless rhetoric when Congress acts pursuant to the Commerce Clause,"[71] lending fresh credibility to the argument that the Amendment is "but an empty caboose."[72] The *Garcia* majority needs to take to heart Justice Harlan's stern reproof: "When the Court disregards the express intent and understanding of the Framers, it has invaded the realm of the political process to which the amending procedure was committed, and it has violated the constitutional structure which is its highest duty to protect."[73]

[66] Id. at 249.
[67] *Garcia* 1028.
[68] Supra chapter 4, text accompanying note 20.
[69] *Garcia* 1027; supra Chapter 4, text accompanying notes 1–44.
[70] *Garcia* 1023, 1030, 1028.
[71] Id. 1022.
[72] *Newsweek,* March 4, 1985, at 20.
[73] Oregon v. Mitchell, 400 U.S. 112, 203 (1970), dissenting in part.

CHAPTER NINE

Conclusion

WHAT is to be done? Judged by the historical facts, many of the Supreme Court's recent "interpretations" of the constitutional terms exemplify its ongoing revision of the Constitution, representing yet another usurpation of a function the people reserved to themselves by Article V—the amendment process. Apologists for the Court's revisionist decisions parade the horrors of insisting "that the 'original understanding' be honored across the board."[1] They reproach me for not disclosing how much standing "law" I

---

[1] Gerald Lynch, "Book Review," 63 Cornell L. Rev. 1091, 1094 (1978). The "consequences . . . would be that the States need not enforce the Bill of Rights, protect first amendment freedoms or abandon 'de jure schools segregation'." Lynch is horrified that "Berger's constitutional theory would deny us *Brown*," the "touchstone of constitutional theory," by which he would have it that if a result is benign, ergo, it is constitutional. Among activist scholars who recognize that the Fourteenth Amendment left segregation untouched is Michael Perry: "Berger makes it painfully clear that the Framers of the fourteenth amendment did not mean to prohibit segregated public schooling, or segregation generally . . . [a] tragic morally indefensible consensus," but a consensus nonetheless. M. Perry, "Interpretivism, Freedom of Expression and Equal Protection," 42 Ohio St. L.J. 361,295 (1981). For citations to similar recognition, see R. Berger, "The Activist Legacy of the New Deal Court," 59 Wash. L. Rev. 751, 759–760 (1984).

would repudiate.[2] Insofar as a legal scholar would adhere to the scholarly standards that scientists so brilliantly exemplify, he must hew to the facts, lead where they may. He may not let his reasoning be swayed by the prospect of an unpalatable result.[3] Intellectual honesty therefore constrains me to be prepared to overrule all decisions that departed from the original design, just as *Erie Railway Co. v. Tompkins*[4] unsparingly overruled the century-old doctrine of *Swift v. Tyson*,[5] so deeply embedded in past judicial practice. The modern commerce cases are not as firmly anchored in the Court's precedents, for from Chief Justice Taney onward the Court paid homage to the reserved rights of the States.[6]

But while decisions can be overruled, past events are not

[2] E.g., Sanford Levinson, "Book Review," *The Nation* 248, 250 (February 26, 1983).

[3] See Sullivan, supra Chapter 1, text accompanying note 11. At the height of the Darwinian controversy Thomas Huxley said, "my colleagues have learned to respect nothing but evidence, and to believe that their highest duty lies in submitting to it, however it may jar against their inclinations." Quoted in Homer W. Smith, *Man and His Gods* 372 (1953).

Long since Cervantes wrote that the historian's duty is to relate matters "as they were really transacted without adding or omitting anything, upon any pretence whatever," 3 Miguel de Cervantes, *The History of the Ingenious Gentleman, Don Quixote of La Mancha* 46 (P.A. Motteux trans. 1924), anticipating Ranke's dictum: the duty of an historian is to tell it as it actually was. "It is the importation of meaning, opinion, and the intellectual world of here and now which makes evidence inconclusive, muddies understanding, and shunts inquiry to false leads." Walton Hamilton and Douglas Adair, *The Power to Govern* 104 (1937).

[4] 304 U.S. 64, 79 (1938). Justice Brandeis adopted Justice Holmes' earlier statement that *Swift v. Tyson* was "an unconstitutional assumption of power by the courts of the United States which no lapse of time or respectable array of opinion should make us hesitate to correct."

[5] 41 U.S. (16 Pet.) 1 (1842).

[6] Charles Lofgren, "The Origin of the Tenth Amendment: History, Sovereignty and the Problem of Constitutional Intention," in *Constitutional Government in America* 331 (R. Collins ed. 1981).

so easily undone. Like poured concrete, they have hardened, so that overruling decisions cannot restore the status quo ante. "The past," the Court observed, "cannot always be erased by a new judicial declaration,"[7] though it would not rock American society to overrule such departures as the janitor, the farmer's production for use, and like cases. But to accept unerasable ends on practical grounds is *not to condone continued employment of unlawful means.* The practical difficulty of a rollback cannot excuse the *continuation,* the ever-expanding resort to such unconstitutional practices. "Go and sin no more" does not signify acceptance of illegitimate acts, but counsels, rather, do not continue to apply unconstitutional doctrine in ever-expanding fashion.[8] From the beginning, fidelity to the Constitution, not to what the judges say it is, has been my fundamental concern, overriding my personal predilections.[9]

Does long-standing adherence of the Court to an unconstitutional course, allegedly "acquiesced" in by Congress

[7] Chicot County Drainage District v. Baxter State Bank, 308 U.S. 371, 374 (1940).

[8] In the Convention, Franklin and Sherman among others held that "the past omission of a duty could not justify a further omission." 1 Farrand 452.

The above amplification of my views was published in Raoul Berger, "The Fourteenth Amendment: Light From the Fifteenth," 74 Nw. L. Rev. 311, 364 (1979), and Raoul Berger, "Michael Perry's Functional Justification for Judicial Activism," 8 U. Dayton L. Rev. 465, 486 (1983). Notwithstanding, Dallin Oaks, then a Justice of the Utah Supreme Court, reechoed the charge that I back "away from the [practical] implications" of my "theory." D. Oaks, "Judicial Activism," 7 Harv. J. Law & Pub. Policy 1, 2–3 (1984). A Canadian scholar, H. Scott Fairlie, states, however, that "To his credit. Berger is willing to accept these implications without flinching, no matter how unpalatable they may seem." H. Fairlie, "Constitutionally Legitimate Judicial Review and Death Penalties: Some Lessons From Abroad," 6 S. Ct. Rev. 467, 479 (1984).

[9] Cf. R. Berger, "Constructive Contempts: A Post-Mortem," 9 U. Chi. L. Rev. 601 (1942). Still less would I shrink from overriding departures

and the people, sanction it? Gerald Lynch would extenuate
departures "from the text as well as from the original understanding" on the ground of "adherence to long-standing
constitutional doctrines,"[10] and he asserts that "the people
have implicitly ratified the role the Court has assumed over
the last century."[11] In an analogous case Charles Black argued that judicial review of Congress had been legitimized
by popular acquiescence, that "the people have precisely
through the political process, given the stamp of approval in
the only way they could give approval to an institution in
being—by leaving it alone."[12] To this Leonard Levy replied,
"The simple fact is that at no time in our history have the
American people passed judgment, pro or con, on the mer-
its of judicial review over Congress. Consent freely given, by
referendum, by legislation, or amendment, is simply not the
same as failure to abolish or impair."[13] Lynch would substitute tacit acquiescence in judicial revision for the constitutional Article V change by amendment. Neglect or inac-
tion would excuse noncompliance with the Constitution;

---

from the Constitution because of the predilections of others, even though
it entailed "the wholesale overruling of precedents." Oaks, supra note 8 at
5. Although activists shrink from such overruling, they complacently accept the wholesale reversal of precedents by the Warren court. "The list of
opinions destroyed by the Warren Court," Philip Kurland observed,
"reads like a table of contents from an old constitutional law casebook."
Philip Kurland, *Politics, the Constitution and the Warren Court* 90 (1970).
   [10] Lynch, supra note 1 at 225.
   [11] Id. 218. To begin with, many of the post–New Deal commerce cases
overturned long-standing precedents. The "separate but equal" cases
reach back before the Civil War. R. Berger, "The Activist Legacy of the
New Deal," 59 Wash. L. Rev. 751, 792–793 (1985). Plessy v. Ferguson, 163
U.S. 537 (1896), was almost 60 years old when it was overturned by Brown
v. Board of Education, 317 U.S. 483 (1954). Which is the more weighty
"practice"?
   [12] Leonard Levy, *Judicial Review and the Supreme Court* 30–31 (1967).
   [13] Id. There is "an essential difference," Justice Story stated, "between
silence and abolition." 1 Story, §448 at 343.

usurpation would be legitimized by inertia.[14] But, as Hamilton stated in Federalist No. 78, the Constitution is binding "until the people have, by some solemn and authoritative act, annulled or changed the established form."[15]

To read popular "acquiescence" in judicial revisions of the Constitution as ratification of a judicial power to rewrite it runs counter to still another requirement: ratification requires complete disclosure. In order to bind a principal, ratification must be "with a full knowledge of all the material facts. If the material facts be either suppressed or unknown, the ratification is treated as invalid."[16] The people are told that when the Court speaks, it is the voice of the Constitution; that it is the Constitution, not the Court, that requires a given decision.[17] That cannot be converted into ratification of progressive judicial violation of its limits. Moreover, the people could rely on Hamilton's rejection in Federalist No. 78 of the possibility that "the courts on the pretense of a repugnancy, may substitute their own pleasure

[14] In 1864 a Senate Select Committee stated in Sen. Rept. No.24 (February 29, 1864) at 5: "There is no chemistry in time to transmute wrong into right. . . . The cases of misinterpretation are of no value. Such was the noble declaration of Charles James Fox in the British Parliament. . . . 'Whenever any usage appeared subversive of the Constitution, if it had lasted for one or two hundred years, *it was not a precedent, but a usurpation*'." Reprinted in A. Avins, *The Reconstruction Amendments' Debates* 44 (1967).

Congressman George Meader commented on similar claims: "Forbearance does not make law. The fact that Congress, in instances where the President has refused to comply with a congressional request for information, took no action does not prove that there was any executive privilege. It proves nothing at all except that Congress chose not to assert its authority or test its powers." 104 *Cong. Rec.* 3849 (March 10, 1958).

[15] Federalist No. 78 at 509.

[16] Owings v. Hull, 34 U.S. (9 Pet.) 606, 628 (1835), per Justice Story. See also Benneke v. Insurance Co., 105 U.S. 355, 360 (1881).

[17] Infra, text accompanying notes 32 and 43.

to the constitutional intention of the legislature," on his representation that the judges had no warrant to depart from the Constitution.[18] As Louis Lusky put it, the people expect the Justices to view the Constitution as expressing "the will of those who made it" and "to ascertain their will."[19] Until the Court candidly discloses—as Justice Jackson vainly urged in the desegregation case—that it is "making new law for a new day,"[20] the people hardly can be held to acquiesce in what they have not been told.

A number of other considerations argue powerfully against allowing judicial "practices" to supplant the Constitution. Notable "contemporary constructions" are contrary to the modern practice. Hamilton, as we have seen, rejected the notion that the Court may depart from the Constitution; and in *Marbury v. Madison* Chief Justice Marshall declared that Congress may not alter the Constitution,[21] later explaining that the Court may also not "change that instrument."[22] Justice Story emphasized that "we are not at liberty to add one jot of power to the national government beyond what the people have granted in the Constitution."[23] The Court "has repeatedly laid down the principle that a contemporaneous legislative exposition of the Constitution when the Found-

[18] Federalist No. 78 at 507, 509.
[19] Louis Lusky, *By What Right?* 31–32 (1975).
[20] Richard Kluger, *Simple Justice* 681 (1976).
[21] 5 U.S. (1 Cranch) 137, 177 (1803).
[22] *John Marshall's Defense of McCulloch v. Maryland* 209 (G. Gunther ed. 1969).
[23] Houston v. Moore, 18 U.S. (5 Wheat.) 1, 48 (1820), dissenting opinion. In 1 *Commentaries on the Constitution of the United States* §426 at 325, Story wrote that if a constitutional restriction "be mischievous, the power of redressing the evil lies with the people by an exercise of the power of amendment. If they choose not to apply the remedy, it may fairly be presumed that the mischief is less than would arise from a further extension of the power, or that it is the least of two evils."

ers of our Government and framers of the Constitution were actively participating in public affairs, long acquiesced in, fixcs the construction to be given its provisions." [24]

The very concept of federalism, A. V. Dicey observed, posits "an immutable Constitution." [25] President Madison stated in his Veto Message of May 3, 1817 that the integrity of the Constitution depends on the permanent partition between the State and federal jurisdictions. [26] For the States did not insist on safeguarding their sovereignty only to place themselves at the mercy of an untrammeled Court. [27] That is likewise the lesson of a written Constitution. The Founders, Chief Justice Marshall explained, resorted to a written Constitution in order that delegated powers be defined and limited. [28] Constitutions, said Justice William Paterson, who had been a leading Framer, were "reduced to written exactitude and precision. . . . The Constitution is certain and fixed; it contains the permanent will of the people." [29] That

[24] Hampton & Co. v. United States, 276 U.S. 394, 412 (1928). Justice William Johnson early referred to the "presumption that the contemporaries of the constitution have the greatest claim to our deference . . . because they had the best opportunities of informing themselves of the framers of the constitution, and of the sense put upon it by the people when it was adopted by them." Ogden v. Saunders, 25 U.S. (12 Wheat.) 213, 270, 290 (1827). See also Stuart v. Laird, 5 U.S. (1 Cranch) 299, 309 (1803); Prigg v. Pennsylvania, 41 U.S. (16 Pet.) 539, 621 (1842).

[25] A. V. Dicey, *Introduction to the Study of the Constitution* 142 (7th ed. 1903) "Acton in writing to General Lee after the ending of the War between the States in America, had described the preservation of States rights as 'the redemption of democracy'." Robert Speaight, *Life of Hillaire Belloc* 132 (1957).

[26] 1 James Richardson, *Messages and Papers of the Presidents* 585 (1896).

[27] For example, Article V provides that "no State shall be deprived of equal suffrage in the Senate."

[28] Marbury v. Madison, 5 U.S. (1 Cranch) 137, 176 (1803).

[29] Van Horne's Lessee v. Dorrance, 2 U.S. (2 Dall.) 303, 308 (C.C.D. Pa. 1795).

was a basic presupposition of the Founders.[30] As Marshall asked, "To what purpose are powers limited . . . if those limits may, at any time be passed by those intended to be restrained."[31]

It is a striking fact that the Court itself has never iterated the "acquiescence" argument academicians have made on its behalf. To the contrary, as Robert Bork commented, "The Supreme Court regularly insists that its results . . . do not spring from the mere will of the Justices . . . but are supported, indeed compelled, by a proper understanding of the Constitution. . . . Value choices are attributed to the Founding Fathers, not to the Court."[32] With Charles Warren, I

---

[30] Philip Kurland wrote:

The concept of the written constitution is that it defines the authority of government and its limits, that government is the creature of the constitution and cannot do what it does not authorize. . . . *A priori,* such a constitution could only have a fixed and unchanging meaning, if it were to fulfill its function. For changed conditions, the instrument itself made provision for amendment which, in accordance with the concept of a written constitution, was expected to be the only form of change.

P. Kurland, *Watergate and the Constitution* 7 (1978).

In South Carolina v. United States, 199 U.S. 437, 448–449 (1905), the Court declared, "The Constitution is a written instrument. As such its meaning does not alter. That which it meant when adopted, it means now. . . . Any other rule of construction would abrogate the judicial character of this court, and make it the mere reflex of the popular opinion and passion of the day." (quoting Chief Justice Taney). See also Hawke v. Smith, 253 U.S. 221, 227 (1920); Thomas Cooley, *Constitutional Limitations* 54 (1st ed. 1868).

[31] Marbury v. Madison, 5 U.S. (1 Cranch) 137, 176 (1803).

[32] R. Bork, "Neutral Principles and Some First Amendment Problems," 47 Ind. L.J. 1, 3–4 (1971). Earlier Professor Felix Frankfurter advised President Franklin Roosevelt that "People have been taught to believe that when the Supreme Court speaks it is not they who speak but the Constitution, whereas, of course, it is *they* who speak and *not* the Constitution. And I verily believe that is what the country needs most to

would maintain that "however the Court may interpret the provisions of the Constitution, it is still the Constitution which is the law, not the decisions of the Court."[33] Justices as different as Chief Justice Burger and Justices Douglas and Frankfurter have insisted upon looking to the Constitution itself rather than to what their predecessors have said about it.[34] For usurpation is no more legitimated by repetition than larceny; the last infraction stands no higher than the first. It is a superb irony that activists should preach adherence to "practice" while consigning a host of long-standing precedents, canons of construction, and constitutional interpretations to the scrap heap.

This monograph, I have been told, is a quixotic undertaking because the Court is little likely to overrule its decisional course. That in nowise discredits the historical inquiry. The whole historical enterprise rests on man's age-old efforts to reconstruct his past, his need to know, whether or not it may serve some present-day purpose. Although I do not anticipate that the historical facts will lead the Court to mend its ways—those who enjoy the exercise of uncurbed power are unlikely to surrender it merely because it has been usurped—the fact remains that in due course academic studies have influenced the Court.[35] Then too, the Court

---

understand." *Roosevelt and Frankfurter: Their Correspondence 1928–1945* 383 (M. Freedman ed. 1967).

[33] 3 Charles Warren, *The Supreme Court in United States History* 470 (1922).

[34] Supra Chapter 1 note 7.

[35] "More and more we are looking to the scholar in his study, to the jurist rather than to the judge or lawyer, for inspiration and for evidence." Benjamin Cardozo, *Growth of the Law* 11 (1924). Just now, Judge Robert Bork has noted, scholars "encourage the courts to yet more daring adventures in constitution-making." R. Bork, Foreword, to Gary McDowell, *The Constitution and Contemporary Constitutional Theory* viii (1985). Nevertheless, Felix Frankfurter considered that "exposure of the Court's abuse

itself, in *Erie Railway Co. v. Tompkins* (1938), condemned
its own century-old *Swift v. Tyson* doctrine as unconstitutional.[36] It is to be hoped, at least, that the historical facts

of its powers will bring about a shift in the Court's viewpoint." J. P. Lash,
From the Diaries of Felix Frankfurter 54 (1975). Cf. Learned Hand, "Have
the Bench and Bar Anything to Contribute to the Teaching of Law?" 24
Mich. L. Rev. 466, 480 (1924); C. E. Hughes, "Dedication of Myron
Taylor Hall," 18 Cornell L.Q. 1 (1932); Nathan Glazer, "Lawyers, The New
Class and the Constitution," 2 Const. Commentary 27, 38 (1985).

[36] Supra notes 4 and 5.
The recent "sodomy" case, Bowers v. Hardwick, 54 U.S.L.W. 4919
(June 30, 1986), is a gleam on the horizon. There Justice White observed
that despite the procedural implications of the due process clause language, the Court has read substantive restrictions into due process and
recognized "rights that have little or no textual support in the constitutional language," id. at 4921, and in fact are precluded by the history of
the Constitution. The Court "refused to discover new fundamental rights
embedded in the Due Process Clause," explaining that "The Court is
most vulnerable and comes nearest to illegitimacy when it deals with
judge-made constitutional law having little or no cognizable roots in the
language or design of the Constitution." Id. Otherwise, White stated,
"the Judiciary necessarily takes to itself further authority to govern the
country without express constitutional authority." Id. at 4922.
Dissenting, Justice Blackmun jumped off from Justice Holmes' statement that "it is revolting to have no better reason for a rule of law than
that so it was laid down at the time of Henry IV," particularly if "the rule
simply persists from blind imitation of the past." Id. at 4923. Blackmun
overlooked that this was uttered in the context of the common law,
whereunder Parliament had permitted courts to fashion private law, for
example, torts and contracts, subject to revision or rejection by Parliament. Very different is the judicial role in interpreting the Constitution
which limits judicial power, and confines it to interpreting, not legislating. From Francis Bacon on it has been said, as the Court itself has reiterated, that it is not for the Courts to make law, still less to revise the
Constitution. For citations see R. Berger, "The Activist Legacy of the
New Deal," 59 Wash. L. Rev. 751, 785 (1984). The power of amendment
was reserved to the people by Article V, as Chief Justice Marshall recognized: the judicial power "cannot be the assertion of a right to change
that instrument." *John Marshall's Defense of Maryland v. McCulloch* 209
(G. Gunther ed. 1969).

may lead the court to curtail its increasing intrusion into the States' internal affairs. For the moment that hope was disappointed by the Court's 5-to-4 decision in *Garcia v. San Antonio Metropolitan Transit Authority,* holding that Congress' control of municipal transportation is not judicially reviewable.[37] That amounts to a blank check to Congress. Justice Powell's vigorous dissent justly charges that the decision constitutes "an outright rejection of . . . the intention of the Framers of the Constitution."[38] The Massachusetts Constitution of 1780, paralleled by five other early State constitutions, declared that "A frequent recurrence to the fundamental principles of the Constitution . . . [is] absolutely necessary to reserve the advantages of liberty and to maintain a free government."[39] Those principles may not be divorced from the Founders' own explanations of what they intended to accomplish. Otherwise we shall have a document that means only what a changing body of Justices chooses at any given moment to have it mean[40]—a flimsy bulwark of our liberties.

[37] Supra Chapter 8. Justice Rehnquist is "confident" that the minority view will "in time again command the support of a majority of the Court." 53 U.S.L.W. 4135, 4149 (February 19, 1985). Only one or two appointments by President Reagan could tip the scales. He urges return of many functions to the States.

[38] Id. 4148.

[39] Article XVIII, 1 Poore 959. Similar provisions are contained in the constitutions of New Hampshire (1784), Article XXXVIII, 2 Poore 1283; North Carolina (1776), Article XXI, 2 Poore 1410; Pennsylvania (1776), Article XIV, 2 Poore 1542; Vermont (1777), Article XIV, 2 Poore 1860.

[40] "American constitutional law," Leonard Levy wrote, "exists in the collective eye of those who happen at any time to dominate the Court." L. Levy, *Against the Law* 25 (1974). But "there still remains a distinction between a constitution which . . . provides that the law shall be whatever the supreme court thinks fit, and the actual constitution of the United States. . . . 'The constitution . . . is whatever the judges say it is,' if interpreted as denying this distinction, is false." H. L. A. Hart, *The Concept of Law* 141 (1961).

Finally, if the Constitution stands in need of revision, let the people amend it in accordance with Article V. Nowhere are the Justices authorized to amend the Constitution; in fact, the Article V machinery for amendment by the people is under established principles *exclusive,* barring other means of amendment.[41] Judicial revision is the less defensible because the Justices are not elected; they are not accountable to the people; and they are all but irremovable.[42] It therefore

---

The notion that the Constitution is what the judges say it is, is far removed from the thinking of the Founders. Jefferson explained, "It is jealousy, and not confidence which prescribed limited Constitutions to *bind down* those whom we are obliged to trust with power"; they should be bound "down from mischief by the chain of the Constitution." 4 Elliot 543. See also Marshall, supra text accompanying note 31.

[41] See Hamilton, supra text accompanying note 15. In the Virginia Convention, Judge Edmund Pendleton said, "the system itself points out [in Article V] an easy mode of removing any errors which shall have been experienced." 3 Elliot 303. Elbridge Gerry, one of the framers, said in the First Congress that the people have directed a "particular mode of making amendments which we are not at liberty to depart from." 1 *Annals of Congress* 503 (1789). In his Farewell Address, President Washington said, "If in the opinion of the People, the distribution or modification of the Constitutional powers be in any particular wrong, let it be corrected by amendment in the way in which the Constitution designates. But let there be no change by usurpation; for though this, in one instance may be the instrument of good, it is the customary weapon by which free governments are destroyed." 35 George Washington, *Writings* 228–229 (J. Fitzpatrick ed. 1940). Justice Black stated in Bell v. Maryland, 378 U.S. 226, 342 (1964), "The Founders gave no such amending power to this Court." See also Hawke v. Smith, 253 U.S. 221, 227 (1920): "It is not the function of courts . . . to alter the method for change which the Constitution has fixed." McPherson v. Blacker, 146 U.S. 1, 36 (1892): the Constitution may not be "amended by judicial decision without action by the designated organs in the mode by which alone amendments can be made." See also supra Chapter 1, note 32.

[42] Michael Perry observed that "the principle of electorally accountable policymaking is axiomatic; it is judicial review, not that principle, that requires justification." Perry, supra note 1 at 262–263. More recently he urged activists "to get on with the task of elaborating a defensible non-originalist conception of constitutional text interpretation and judicial

deprives the people of the right of self-government—for example, the bulk of the American people demand death
penalties but are encumbered by the Court's death penalty
decisions.[43] Judicial erosion of the Constitution threatens
constitutional guarantees, which are then made to turn on
the accidents of political appointments with the concomi-
tant vagaries of personal predilections.[44]

In their zeal to ameliorate social injustice, academicians
undermine the constitutionalism that undergirds our democratic system.[45] Their defense of the Justices' substitution of

---

role." M. Perry, "The Authority of Text, Tradition, and Reason: A Theory
of Judicial 'Interpretation'," 58 S. Calif. L. Rev. 551, 602 (1985). For Paul
Brest's disappointment with seven activist attempts to frame such a theory, see P. Brest, "The Fundamental Rights Controversy: The Essential
Contradictions of Normative Scholarship," 90 Yale L.J. 1063, 1067–1089
(1981). He considers that "no defensible criteria exist" whereby to assess
"value-oriented constitutional adjudications." Id. 1065; and he pleads
with academe "simply to acknowledge that most of our writings [about
judicial review] are not political theory but advocacy scholarship—ami-
cus briefs ultimately designed to persuade the Court to adopt our various
notions of the public good." Id. at 1109.

[43] Raoul Berger, *Death Penalties: The Supreme Court's Obstacle Course*
(1982).

[44] "The authority of nine unelected jurists to strike down laws would
be unacceptable in a democratic polity, one that is supposed to be 'a government of laws, not of men', unless judicial review were believed to be a
faithful attempt to interpret the Constitution, the highest law of the land.
Consequently to support their opinions, the Justices will ignore or even
wilfuly misrepresent the text and history of the Constitution, rather than
admit they are revising it." John Burleigh, "The Supreme Court and the
Constitution," 50 *Public Interest* 151 (Winter 1978).

[45] "The two fundamental correlative elements of constitutionalism for
which all lovers of liberty must yet fight are the legal limits to arbitrary
power and a complete responsibility of government to the governed."
Charles McIlwain, *Constitutionalism: Ancient and Modern* 146 (rev. ed.
1946). Sidney Hook observed that "whoever places emphasis upon the
product rather than the process, upon an all-sanctifying end rather than
upon the means of achieving it, is opening the doors to anarchy." Sidney
Hook, *Philosophy and Politics* 36 (1980).

their own meaning for that of the Founders displaces the choices of the people in conventions that ratified the Constitution, and it violates the basic principle of government by consent of the governed. The people, said Justice James Iredell, one of the ablest of the Ratifiers, "have chosen to be governed under such and such principles. They have not chosen to be governed or promised to submit upon any other."[46] When the Court does for the people "what they have not chosen to do for themselves," said Justice Story, "it is usurping the function of a legislator,"[47] and even worse, it is acting as a constitutional convention. Thereby, Justice Harlan declared, "it has violated the constitutional structure which it is its highest duty to protect."[48]

Academe has forgotten Cardozo's wise caution: the judges' "individual sense of justice . . . might result in a benevolent despotism if the judges were benevolent men. It would put an end to the rule of law."[49] That rule requires that we "be governed by the same preestablished rules and not by the whim of those charged with executing those rules."[50] The manifest will of the Framers, as disclosed by *their* explanations of the terms they employed, constitutes those "preestablished rules, designed to limit all delegations of power."[51] "[W]e have not yet found a better way to pre-

[46] Supra Chapter 1, note 34.

[47] 1 Story, §426 at 325.

[48] Oregon v. Mitchell, 400 U.S. 112, 203 (1970).

[49] Benjamin N. Cardozo, *The Nature of the Judicial Process* 136 (1921).

[50] Philip Kurland, "Curia Regis: Some Comments on the Divine Right of Kings and Courts 'To Say What the Law Is'," 23 Ariz. L. Rev. 581, 582 (1981). To "engage in result-oriented adjudication" is to leave "far behind the rule of law enforced by impartial and impersonal judges." Leonard Levy, *Against the Law: The Nixon Court and Criminal Justice* 438 (1974).

[51] See Chief Justice Marshall, supra Chapter 1, note 37. "To implement real limits on government the judges must have reference to standards which are external to, and prior to, the matter to be decided. The con-

serve freedom," the Court recently stated, "than by making
the exercise of power subject to the carefully crafted restraints spelled out in the Constitution."[52] Although this
salutary pronouncement often has been more honored in
the breach than in the observance, it is no less solidly rooted
for that. Academe's apologies for judicial disregard of constitutional restraints[53] may yet come back to haunt it.[54] Mil-
lennia ago, Confucius warned that "he who thinks old em-
bankments useless and destroys them, is sure to suffer the
desolation caused by overflowing water."[55]

tents of those standards are set at their creation. Recourse to 'the intention of the framers' in judicial review, therefore can be considered as indispensable to realizing the ideas of government limited by law." Richard
Kay, "Book Review," 10 Conn. L. Rev. 801, 805–806 (1978).

[52] Immigration & Naturalization Service v. Chadha, 103 S. Ct. 2764,
2788 (1983).

[53] See, e.g., supra, Chapter 1, note 65.

[54] Shifting political winds prompted Alan Dershowitz of Harvard
Law School, a prominent activist, to say, "'at least for the rest of this century the Supreme Court and the lower federal courts will be archenemies
of civil rights, the Bill of Rights, civil liberties and civil decencies'. . . .
He decried the fact that while formerly liberals called for judicial activism
and conservatives for judicial restraint, the stances have been switched."
Susan Smith, "'Inquiries' Explores Utility of Legal Education," 79 Harv.
L. Record 11 (September 21, 1984). The Warren Court overturned precedents in droves; see Kurland, supra note 9. Why should the successor
Court feel bound by those decisions rather than by the older precedents
that are faithful to the intention of the Framers? The name of the game is
"Two Can Play."

[55] Will Durant, *Our Oriental Heritage* 673(1954). "[N]othing can destroy a government more quickly than its failure to observe its own laws
or worse, its disregard of the charter of its existence." Mapp v. Ohio, 367
U.S. 433, 459 (1961). Washington had warned in his Farewell Address, "let
there be no change by usurpation; for though this, in one instance, may
be the instrument of good, it is the customary weapon by which free governments are destroyed." 35 G. Washington, *Writings*, 229 (J. Fitzpatrick
ed. 1940).

APPENDIX

"Original Intention" in Historical Perspective

THE ongoing debate about the role the original intention of the Founders should play in constitutional construction has neglected the historical roots of the doctrine. A recent attempt to show that it has no roots in the common law[1] prompted me to study the sources for myself.[2] Here I shall set forth a compressed version of my findings.

A Discourse Upon . . . Statutes,[3] probably written prior to 1567,[4] recounted,

> yt is knowne of themselves & by theire lyvinge voice as Frowycke saieth that upon the Statute of Westminster 2,ca.1 [1285] it was demaunded of the statute makers whether a warrantie with assettz shulde be a barre, & they answered that it shulde. And so, in our own dayes, have those that were the penners & devisors of statutes bene the grettest lighte for exposicion of statutes. If they have not given anie declaracion of theire myndes, then it is to be sene howe the statute hathe bene put in use, & theire au-

[1] H. J. Powell, "The Original Understanding of Original Intent," 98 Harv. L. Rev. 885 (1985).

[2] Raoul Berger, "'Original Intention' in Historical Perspective," 54 Geo. Wash. L. Rev. 101 (1986).

[3] *A Discourse Upon the Exposicion and Understandings of Statutes* (Samuel Thorne ed. 1942).

[4] Id. 10–11.

thoritye must persuade us that were mooste neerest the statute, and that we do see muche receyved & leaned unto in bookes.[5]

Thus, light was first to be sought from the makers' "declaracion of their myndes," and in the absence of such a declaration, from those that "were mooste neerest the statute." Respect for the latter was expressed by Chief Justice Prisot in 1454: "The judges who gave these decisions in ancient times were nearer to the statute than we now are, and had more acquaintance with it."[6] It remains the rule under the heading of "contemporaneous construction" because, as our Justice William Johnson explained, contemporaries of the Constitution "had the best opportunity of informing themselves of the understanding of the framers . . . and of the sense put upon it by the people when it was adopted by them."[7] It is difficult to conclude that judges who deferred to the "understanding of the framers" when it was received at second hand would have rejected the drafters' own explanation of their intentions. Indeed, S. B. Chrimes concluded that "the rule of reference to the intention of the legislators . . . was certainly established by the second half of the fifteenth century."[8]

In *Throckmerton v. Tracy* (1555),[9] the associate justices honored the intent of the makers of a statute, emphasizing that words must give way to intent. To begin with the argument of Serjeant Dyer, before long to be Chief Justice of Common Pleas,

[5] Id. 151, 152. See also Theodore Plucknett, *Statutes and Their Interpretation in the First Half of the Fourteenth* Century 149–155 (1927).

[6] C. K. Allen, *Law in the Making* 193 (6th ed. 1958) (quoting Windham v. Felbridge, Y.B. Mich. 33 Hen. 6, f.38, 41, pl. 17 (1454).

[7] Ogden v. Saunders, 25 U.S. (12 Wheat.) 213, 290 (1827).

[8] S. R. Chrimes, *English Constitutional Ideas in the Fifteenth Century* 293 (1966).

[9] 1 Plowden 145, 75 Eng. Rep. 222 (C.P. 1555).

to call upon the propriety of words, when the intent of the parties appears, is not commendable, nor had it been practiced by the Judges in former times, but on the contrary they have applied the words to fulfill the intent, rather than have destroyed the intent by reason of the insufficiency of the words.[10]

In some cases, he said, "the words have been taken out of their proper signification, in order to perform that intent, and in others the intent has supplied the deficiency of the words."[11] Dyer carried the day. Citing Bracton, Justice Staunford stated, "the words shall be construed according to the intent of the parties, and not otherwise."[12] Justice Saunder said, "to cavil about words in subversion of the plain intent of the parties," was by Tully "accounted meer injury and injustice. And such interpretation of the law he has admonished men to avoid, and to observe and follow the intent of the words."[13] Justice Humphrey Brown's views were "to the same purpose."[14] Edmund Plowden, a contemporary lawyer "of singular ability,"[15] wrote in his *Commentaries*, "everything that is within the intent of the makers of the act, although it be not within the letter, is as strongly within the Act as that which is within the letter and intent also."[16] Centuries later, our own Supreme Court observed that "Without going back to the famous [medieval] case of the drawing of blood in the streets of Bologna, the books

[10] 1 Plowden at 159, 75 Eng. Rep. at 246.

[11] 1 Plowden at 160, 75 Eng. Rep. 246.

[12] 1 Plowden at 160, 75 Eng. Rep. at 247.

[13] 1 Plowden at 161, 75 Eng. Rep. 249.

[14] 1 Plowden at 162, 75 Eng. Rep. 75 Eng. Rep. at 250. Chief Justice Brook dissented.

[15] Max Radin, *Handbook of Anglo-American Legal History* §183 at 317 (1936).

[16] Quoted in Thorne, supra note 3 at 60. "[W]hen it is declared that such is the true intent of the Makers of the Act, then it is not contrary to the Text, but a right Interpretation of the Letter thereof." Stradling v.

FEDERALISM: THE FOUNDERS' DESIGN

196

are full of authorities to the effect that the intention of the law-making power will prevail even against the letter of the statute."[17]

In *Magdalen College Case* (1615) Edward Coke, revered expositor of the common law, said "in acts of Parliament which are to be construed according to the intent and meaning of the makers of them, the original intent and meaning is to be observed."[18] Chief Justice Fleming explained in 1611 that "touching construction of words, they shall be taken according to the . . . intent of the parties."[19] Writing in 1677, Lord Chancellor Hatton declared, "when the intent is proved, that must be followed . . . but whensoever there is a departure from the words to the intent that must be well proved that there is such meaning."[20] Thus, Hatton postulated that resort must be had to the intention, but stressed that it must be "well proved." John Selden, a preeminent seventeenth-century scholar, stated, "A Man's Writing has but one true Sense, which is that which the Author meant when he writ it."[21] And a leading legal historian of our

Morgan, Plowden 199, 205, 75 E. R. 305, 314 (Exch.1559). "Judicial expositions have always been founded upon the intent of the Legislature, which they have collected sometimes by considering the cause and necessity of making the Act . . . sometimes by foreign circumstances." Plowden 205, 75 Eng. Rep. 315.

[17] Hawaii v. Mankichi, 190 U.S. 197, 212 (1903).

[18] 11 Co. Rep. 66, 73, 77 Eng. Rep. at 1245 (1615).

[19] Hewit v. Painter, 1 Bulstrode 174, 175, 80 Eng. Rep. 864, 865 (K.B. 1611). The Earl of Clanrickard's Case, Hobart 273, 277, 80 Eng. Rep. 413, 423 (C. P. 1613) was led to "exceedingly commend the Judges that are curious and almost subtil . . . to invent reasons and means to make Acts, according to the just intent of the parties."

[20] Christopher Hatton, *A Treatise Concerning Statutes or Acts of Parliament: and the Exposition Thereof* 14–15 (1677). "[W]hen the words express not the intent of the Makers the Statute must be further extended than the bare words." Id. 28.

[21] John Selden, *Table Talk: Being the Discourses of John Selden, Esq.* 10 (1696).

time, Samuel Thorne, concluded that "Actual intent . . . is
controlling from Hengham's day to that of Lord Notting-
ham (1678)."[22] Such statements were epitomized in Matthew Bacon's Abridgment (1736):

> Such a Construction ought to be put upon a Statute, as may
> best answer the Intention which the Makers had in view. . . .
> Every Thing which is within the Intention of the Makers of a
> statute is, although it be not within the Letter thereof, as much
> within the Statute as that which is within the Letter. . . . [T]hat
> which is within the Letter of a Statute is not within such Stat-
> ute, if it be not within the Intention of the Makers thereof.[23]

In 1756, Thomas Rutherforth, assimilating the interpretation of statutes to that of wills, wrote that "The end which
interpreters aims at, is to find out what was the intention of
the writer, to clear up the meaning of his words,"[24] as Selden had indicated 100 years earlier. When Blackstone set out
to state the common law in 1765 he likewise wrote that a
construction must be "as near to the minds and apparent intent of the parties, as the rule of law will permit. For the
maxims of the law are that *verba intentioni et non contra de-
bent inservire* [words ought to wait upon the intention, not
the reverse]." And he continued, "where the intention is
clear, too minute a stress be not laid on the strict and precise
application of words."[25]

These statements are fortified by a number of cognate
rules. A frequently cited common law rule of construction is
that statutes are to be so construed "as shall suppress the
mischief, and advance the remedy."[26] One way to ascertain

[22] Thorne, supra note 3 at 60 note 126.
[23] 4 Matthew Bacon, *A New Abridgment of the Law* 647–648 (3d ed.
1768).
[24] 2 Thomas Rutherford, *Institutes of Natural Law* 309 (1756).
[25] 2 William Blackstone, *Commentaries on the Law of England* 379
(1765).
[26] Heydon's Case, 3 Co. Rep. 7b, 76 Eng. Rep. 637, 638 (1584).

the mischief was to consult the preamble of the statute; as said by Chief Justice Dyer, the preamble is "a key to open the minds of the makers of the act, and the mischiefs which they intended to redress."[27] Another way in medieval days was to learn from the "lyving voices" of the makers; and still another, as we have seen, was to follow in the footsteps of contemporaries of the statute. There was no resort to legislative history in the early common law for the simple reason that there was none until Thomas Hansard "began in 1803 to print the Parliamentary Debates, which were not at first independent reports but were taken from the newspapers."[28] Given that old words are permitted to embrace new applications—"commerce" applies equally to transportation by airplane as by oxcart—the word "intent" no less applies to contemporarily recorded evidence of the legislative intent when such evidence became available. It offends common sense to conclude that if such unmistakable evidence of the makers' intention to cure a certain mischief was at hand that it would be rejected because, for instance, it was not a "contemporaneous construction" that itself carried weight only because it was thought to reflect that intention. As Chief Justice Marshall remarked, "Where the mind labors to discover the design of the legislature, it seizes everything from which aid can be derived."[29] No wonder that he remarked he could cite from the common law "the most com-

[27] Quoted Herbert Broom, *A Selection of Legal Maxims* 439 (rev. ed. 1848).

[28] 11 *Encyclopaedia Britannica* 162 (14th ed. 1929). In his early days, when accounts of the debates surreptitiously crept into the newspapers, Samuel Johnson composed "the speeches entirely out of his own head. . . . To John Nichols he confessed that some of the speeches were 'the mere coinage of his own imagination'." Joseph Krutch, *Samuel Johnson* 48 (1944).

[29] United States v. Fisher, 6 U.S. (2 Cranch) 358, 386 (1805).

plete evidence that the intention is the most sacred rule of interpretation."[30]

Judge Bork noted that the original intent of the Framers serves to constrain the judges' authority.[31] That responds to the Founders' fear of illimitable authority,[32] which results when judges are allowed, in the words of Chancellor Kent, "a dangerous discretion to roam at large in the trackless field of their own imaginations."[33] Even an apologist for an activist Court, Mark Tushnet, acknowledges that the originalist view—"we are indeed better off being bound by the dead hand of the past than being subjected to the whims of willful judges trying to make the Constitution live"—is "fairly powerful."[34]

There is no need to trace the course of original intent after adoption of the Constitution because a vigorous critic of "intentionalism," H. J. Powell, concedes that it has been the prevailing doctrine. He locates its roots in the Virginia

[30] *John Marshall's Defense of McCulloch v. Maryland* 167 (G. Gunther ed. 1969).

[31] Robert Bork, "Original Intent and the Constitution," 7 *Humanities Magazine* 22, 23 (1986). "Recourse to 'the intention of the framers' in judicial review, therefore, can be considered as indispensable to realizing the ideas of government limited by law." Richard Kay, "Book Review," 10 Conn. L. Rev. 801, 805–806 (1978).

[32] Chief Justice Marshall declared, "The powers of the legislature are defined and limited; and that those limits may not be mistaken or forgotten, the constitution is written. To what purpose are powers limited, and to what purpose is that limitation committed to writing, if those limits may, at any time, be passed by those intended to be restrained?" "If the Constitution is alterable at the pleasure of the legislature (or the courts)," he continued, "then written Constitutions are absurd attempts on the part of the people, to limit a power in its nature illimitable." Marbury v. Madison, 5 U.S. (1 Cranch) 137, 178 (1803).

[33] 1 James Kent, *Commentaries on American Law* 373 (9th ed. 1858).

[34] Mark Tushnet, "Following the Rules Laid Down: A Critique of Interpretivism and Neutral Principles," 96 Harv. L. Rev. 781, 787 (1983).

and Kentucky Resolutions, and though he sharply differs with their analysis, he observes that "The rhetoric of 'original intent' has endured, and indeed flourished, long after the universal rejection of most of its accompanying complex of ideas."[35] The "victors viewed the 'revolution of 1800' [the election of Jefferson] as the people's endorsement of the approach to constitutional interpretation embodied in the 'doctrines of 1798'."[36] "By the outbreak of the Civil War," he concludes, "intentionalism in the modern sense reigned supreme in the rhetoric of constitutional interpretation."[37]

A few citations to confirmatory evidence will suffice. In 1838 the Supreme Court stated that construction

> must necessarily depend on the words of the Constitution; the meaning and intention of the conventions which framed and proposed it for adoption and ratification to the Conventions . . . in the several states . . . to which this Court has always resorted in construing the Constitution.[38]

In the 39th Congress, the framer of the Fourteenth Amendment, Senator Charles Sumner, stated, "Every Constitution embodies the principles of its framers. It is a transcript of their minds. If its meaning in any place is open to doubt . . . we cannot err if we turn to its framers."[39] To this may be added a unanimous January, 1872 Report of the Senate Judiciary Committee respecting a plea for a statutory grant of women's suffrage:

> In construing the Constitution we are compelled to give it such interpretation as will secure the result intended to be accomplished by those who framed it and the people who adopted it. . . . A construction which would give the phrase . . . a

[35] Powell, supra note 1 at 926–927.
[36] Id. 934.
[37] Id. 946.
[38] Rhode Island v. Massachusetts, 37 U.S. (12 Pet.) 657, 721 (1838).
[39] *Cong. Globe,* 39th Cong. 1st Sess. 677 (1866).

meaning differing from the sense in which it was understood and employed by the people when they adopted the Constitution, would be as unconstitutional as a departure from the plain and express language of the Constitution.[40]

It remains to be said that Jacobus tenBroek, writing in 1939, said that the Court "has insisted with almost uninterrupted regularity, that the end and object of constitutional construction is the discovery of the intention of those persons who formulated the instrument."[41]

[40] S. Rep. No. 21, 42d Cong. 2d Sess. 2 (1872), *reprinted in* Alfred Avins, *The Reconstruction Amendments' Debates* 571 (1967).

[41] Jacobus tenBroek, "Use by the Supreme Court of Extrinsic Aids in Constitutional Construction: The Intent Theory of Constitutional Construction," 27 Calif. L. Rev. 399 (1939).

Bibliography

Books

Allen, C. K. *Law in the Making* (6th ed., Oxford, Clarendon Press, 1958).

Avins, Alfred. *The Reconstruction Amendments' Debates* (Richmond, Va., Virginia Commission on Constitutional Government, 1967).

Bacon, Francis. *Selected Writings* (New York, Random House, 1955).

Bacon, Matthew. *A New Abridgement of the Law* (3d ed. London, 1768).

Bailyn, Bernard. *The Ideological Origins of the American Revolution* (Cambridge, Mass., Harvard University Press, 1967).

Beloff, Max. *The American Federal Government* (London, Oxford University Press, 1959).

Berger, Raoul. *Death Penalties: The Supreme Court's Obstacle Course* (Cambridge, Mass., Harvard University Press, 1982).

———. *Government by Judiciary: The Transformation of the Fourteenth Amendment* (Cambridge, Mass., Harvard University Press, 1977).

Blackstone, William. *Commentaries on the Laws of England* (London, 1765–1769).

Broom, Herbert. *A Selection of Legal Maxims* (rev. ed London, 1848).

Burke, Edmund. *Reflections on the Revolution in France* (New York, Collier, Harvard Classics, 1909).

Cahn, Edmond, ed. *Supreme Court and Supreme Law* (New York, Simon & Schuster, 1954).

Cardozo, Benjamin N. *Growth of the Law* (New Haven, Yale University Press, 1924).

———. *The Nature of the Judicial Process* (New Haven, Yale University Press, 1921).

Carroll, Lewis. *Through the Looking Glass* (Norton ed. 1971).

Chafee, Zecheriah. *Three Human rights in the Constitution of 1787* (Lawrence, Kan., University of Kansas Press, 1956).

Chrimes, S. B. *English Constitutional Ideas in the Fourteenth Century* (Cambridge, Cambridge University Press, 1966).

Cooley, Thomas. *Constitutional Limitations* (Boston, Little Brown, 1886).

———. *A Treatise on the Law of Taxation* (Boston, Little Brown, 1886).

Corwin, Edward S. *The Commerce Power Versus States' Rights* (Princeton, N.J., Princeton University Press, 1936).

———. *Constitutional Theory* (New Haven, Yale University Press, 1934).

———. *The Doctrine of Judicial Review* (Princeton, N.J., Princeton University Press, 1914).

———. *The Twilight of the Supreme Court: A History of Our Constitutional Theory* (New Haven, Yale University Press, 1934).

Durant, Will. *Our Oriental Heritage* (New York, Simon & Schuster, 1954).

Elliot, Jonathan. *Debates in the Several State Conventions on the Adoption of the Federal Constitution* (2d ed. Washington, D.C., 1836).

Farrand, Max. *The Records of the Federal Convention 1787* (New Haven, Yale University Press, 1911).

Flack, Harry. *The Adoption of the Fourteenth Amendment* (Baltimore, Johns Hopkins University Press, 1908).

Frankfurter, Felix. *The Commerce Clause* (Chapel Hill, University of North Carolina Press, 1937).

Gay, Peter, and Cavanaugh, G. J., *Historians at Work* (New York, Harper & Row, 1972).

Graham, Howard J. *Everyman's Constitution* (New York, Norton, 1968).

Graubard, S. R. *Burke, Disraeli and Churchill* (Cambridge, Mass., Harvard University Press, 1961).

Gunther, Gerald, ed. *John Marshall's Defense of McCullough v. Maryland* (Stanford, Cal., Stanford University Press, 1969).

Hamilton Alexander. *The Papers of Alexander Hamilton*. H. Syrett and J. Cooke, eds. (New York, Columbia University Press, 1962).

Hart, H. L. A. *The Concept of Law* (Oxford, Clarendon Press, 1961).

Hatton, Christopher. *A Treatise Concerning Statutes and Acts of Parliament: and the Exposition Thereof* (London, 1677).

Holmes, O. H. *Collected Legal Papers* (New York, Harcourt Brace 1920).

Howe, M. de W. *Justice Oliver Wendell Holmes: The Shaping Years* (Cambridge, Mass., Harvard University Press, 1963).

Hughes, C. E. *The Supreme Court of the United States* (New York, Columbia University Press, 1928).

Hyman, H. M. *A More Perfect Union* (New York, Knopf, 1973).

Jensen, Merrill. *The Articles of Confederation* (Madison, Wis., University of Wisconsin Press, 1940).

Kenyon, Cecelia, ed. *The Antifederalists* (Indianapolis, Bobbs-Merrill, 1966).

Kent, James. *Commentaries on American Law* (9th ed. Boston, Little Brown, 1858).

Kluger, Richard. *Simple Justice* (New York, Knopf, 1976).

Krutch, Joseph. *Samuel Johnson* (New York, Henry Holt, 1944).

Kurland, Philip B. *Politics, the Constitution and the Warren Court* (Chicago, University of Chicago Press, 1970).

———. *Watergate and the Constitution* (Chicago, University of Chicago Press, 1978).

Lash, J. P. *From the Diaries of Felix Frankfurter* (New York, W. Norton, 1975).

Lusky, Louis. *By What Right* (Charlottesville, Michie Co., 1975).

McClellan, James. *Joseph Story and the American Constitution* (Norman, University of Oklahoma Press, 1971).

McIlwain, Charles H. *Constitutionalism: Ancient and Modern* (Ithaca, Cornell University Press, 1947).

———. *The American Revolution: A Constitutional Interpretation* (New York, Macmillan, 1924).

———. *The High Court of Parliament and Its Supremacy* (Hamden, Conn., Archon Press, 1962).

McMaster, J. B., and Stone, F., *Pennsylvania and the Federal Consitution 1787–1788* (Lancaster, Pa., Inquirer Printing, 1888).

McRee, G. J. *Life and Correspondence of James Iredell* (New York, Appleton, 1857–1858).

Madison, James. *Writings*. G. Hunt, ed. (New York, Putnam, 1900–1910).

Main, J. T. *The Antifederalists: Critics of the Constitution* (Chapel Hill, University of Carolina Press, 1961).

Mason, A. T. *The States Rights Debate: Antifederalism and the Constitution* (Englewood Cliffs, N. J., Prentice Hall, 1964).

Montesquieu, Charles de. *The Spirit of the Laws*. Translated by M. de Secondat (Philadelphia, 1802).

Morison, S. E. *The Oxford History of the American People* (Oxford, Oxford University Press, 1965).

———, and Commager, H. S. *The Growth of the American Republic* (New York, Oxford Press, 1952).

Murphy, W. T. *The Triumph of Nationalism: State Sovereignty, the Founding Fathers, and the Making of the Constitution* (Chicago, Quadrangle Books, 1967).

Padover, S. K. *Jefferson* (New York, Harcourt Brace, 1942).

Paludan, P. A. *A Covenant With Death* (Urbana, University of Illinois Press, 1975).

Perry, Michael. *The Constitution, the Courts, and Human Rights* (New Haven, Yale University Press, 1982).

Plucknett, Theodore. *Statutes and Their Interpretation in the Fourteenth Century* (Cambridge, Cambridge University Press, 1960).

Radin, Max. *Handbook of Anglo-American Legal History* (Saint Paul, West Publishing Co., 1936).

Rakove, J. N. *The Beginnings of National Politics* (New York, Knopf, 1979).

Richardson, J. O. *Messages and Papers of the Presidents 1789–1897* (Washington, D.C., Government Printing Office, 1897).

Rossiter, Clinton. *Alexander Hamilton and the Constitution* (New York, Harcourt Brace, 1964).

Rutherford, Thomas. *Institutes of Natural Law* (Cambridge, J. Bentham, 1754–1756).

Rutland, Robert. *The Ordeal of the Constitution: The Antifederalist Ratification Struggle of 1787–1788* (Norman, University of Oklahoma Press, 1965).

Selden, John. *Table Talk: Being the Discourses of John Selden, Esq.* (London, 1696).

Smith, Homer. *Man and His Gods* (Boston, Little Brown, 1953).

Speaight, Robert. *Life of Hillaire Belloc* (New York, Farrar Strauss, 1957).

Storing, Herbert, ed. *The Complete Anti-Federalist* (Chicago, University of Chicago Press, 1981).

Story, Joseph. *Commentaries on the Constitution of the United States* (5th ed. Boston, Little Brown, 1905).

Sullivan, W. N. *The Limitations of Science* (New York, New American Library, 1949).

Taine, Hippolyte A. *History of English Literature* (New York, Frederic H. Ungar, 1965).

Thorne, S. E., ed. *A Discourse Upon the Exposicion and Understandinge of Statutes* (San Marino, Cal., Huntington Library, 1942).

Van Doren, Carl. *The Great Rehearsal: The Story of the Making and Ratifying of the Constitution of the United States* (New York, Viking Press, 1948).

Warren, Charles. *The Supreme Court in United States History* (Boston, Little Brown, 1926).

White, L. P. *The States and the Nation* (Baton Rouge, Louisiana State University Press, 1953).

Wills, Garry. *The Federalist Papers by Alexander Hamilton, James Madison and John Jay* (New York, Bantam Books, 1982).

———. *Cincinnatus: George Washington and the Enlightenment* (New York, Doubleday, 1984).

Wilson, Edmund, ed. *The Shock of Recognition* (New York, Modern Library, 1943).

Wilson, James. *Works*. R. McCloskey, ed. (Cambridge, Mass., Harvard University Press, 1969).

Wood, G. S. *The Creation of the American Republic 1776–1787* (Chapel Hill, University of North Carolina Press, 1969).

Wolfe, Christopher. *The Rise of Modern Judicial Review* (New York, Basic Books, 1986).

Wright, B. F. *Consensus and Continuity 1776–1787* (Boston, Boston University Press, 1958).

ARTICLES

Abraham, Henry. "Book Review," 6 Hastings Constitutional Law Quarterly 467 (1978).

Bator, Paul. "Some Thoughts on Applied Federalism," 6 Harvard Journal of Law and Public Policy 54 (1982).

Berger, Raoul. "Constructive Contempt: A Post-Mortem," 9 University of Chicago Law Review 601 (1942).

———. "Insulation of Judicial Usurpation: A Comment on Lawrence Sager's Court-Stripping Polemic," 44 Ohio State Law Journal 611 (1983).

———. "The Fourteenth Amendment: Light From the Fifteenth," 74 Northwestern University Law Review 331 (1979).

———. "Michael Perry's Functional Justification of Judicial Activism," 8 University of Dayton Law Review 465 (1983).

Berns, Walter. "The Meaning of the Tenth Amendment," in R. A. Goldwin, ed., *A Nation of States* 126 (1961).

———, ed. "Teaching the Founding of the United States," 13 Teaching Political Science 5 (1985).

Bork, Robert. Foreword to Gary McDowell, *The Constitution and Contemporary Constitutional Theory* (Cumberland, Va., Center for Judicial Studies, 1985).

———. "Neutral Principles and Some First Amendment Problems," 47 Indiana Law Journal 1 (1971).

———. "Original Intent and the Constitution," 7 Humanities Magazine 22 (1986).

Brest, Paul. "The Misconceived Quest for the Original Understanding," 60 Boston University Law Review 204 (1980).

Bridwell, Randall. "The Scope of Judicial Review: A Dirge for the Theorists of Majority Rule?" 31 South Carolina Law Review 617 (1980).

Burleigh, John. "The Supreme Court v. the Constitution," 50 *Public Interest* 151 (Winter, 1978).

Choper, Jesse. "Federalism," in R. Collins, ed. *Constitutional Government in American History* 373 (1981).

Corwin, Edward S. "The Passing of Dual Federalism," 36 Virginia Law Review 1 (1950).

Cover, Robert. "Book Review," *New Republic* 26 (January 14, 1978).

Cox, Archibald. "Federalism and Individual Rights Under the Burger Court," 73 Northwestern University Law Review 1 (1978).

Diamond, Martin. "What the Framers Meant by Federalism," in R. A. Goldwin, ed. *A Nation of States* 24 (1961).

Douglas, William O. "Stare Decisis," 49 Columbia Law Review 375 (1949).

Ely, John H. "Constitutional Interpretivism: Its Allure and Impossibility," 53 Indiana Law Journal 399 (1978).

Epstein, Richard A. "Common Law, Labor Law and Reality," 92 Yale Law Journal 1435 (1983).

Fairlie, H. S. "Constitutionally Legitimate Judicial Review and Death Penalties: Some Lessons From Abroad," 6 Supreme Court Review 467 (Canada, 1984).

Fairman, Charles. "Does the Fourteenth Amendment Incorporate the Bill of Rights?" 2 Stanford Law Review 5 (1949).

Frankfurter, Felix. "Can the Supreme Court Guarantee Toleration?" 43 *New Republic* 85 (1925).

Gangi, William. "Judicial Expansionism: An Evaluation of the Ongoing Debate," 8 Ohio Northern University Law Review 1 (1981).

Gardner, Howard. "Book Review," New York Times Book Review Section, July 22, 1984, § 3.

Grey, Thomas. "Do We Have an Unwritten Constitution?" 27 Stanford Law Review 703 (1975).

Hand, Learned. "Have the Bench and Bar Anything to Contribute to the Teaching of Law?", 24 Michigan Law Review 466 (1924).

Horwitz, M. J. "The Emergence of an Instrumental Conception of American Law, 1780–1820," in 5 *Perspectives in American History* 287 (1971).

Howard, A. E. D. "*Garcia* and the Values of Federalism: On the Need for a Recurrence to Fundamental Principles," 19 Georgia Law Review 789 (1985).

Hughes, Charles E. "Dedication of Myron Taylor Hall," 18 Cornell Law Quarterly 1 (1932).

Jackson, R. H. "Back to the Constitution," 25 American Bar Association Journal 745 (1939).

James, Henry. "Hawthorne," reprinted in Edmund Wilson, ed. *The Shock of Recognition* 560 (1955).

Kay, Richard. "Book Review," 10 Connecticut Law Review 801 (1978).

Kirk, Russell. "The Prospects for Territorial Democracy in America," in R. A. Goldwin, ed. *A Nation of States* 42 (1961).

Kurland, P. B. "Some Comments on the Divine Right of Kings and Courts 'To Say What the Law Is'," 23 Arizona Law Review 581 (1981).

Levinson, Sanford. "Book Review," *The Nation* 243 (February 26, 1983).

Lofgren, C. A. "The Origins of the Tenth Amendment, History, Sovereignty, and the Problems of Constitutional Intention," in R. Collins, ed. *Constitutional Government in America* 331 (1981).

Lusky, Louis. "Book Review," 6 Hastings Constitutional Law Quarterly 403 (1979).

Lynch, Gerald. "Book Review," 63 Cornell Law Review 1091 (1978).

Mason, A. T. "The Bill of Rights: An Almost Forgotten Appendage," in S. C. Halpern, ed. *The Future of Our Liberties: Perspectives on the Bill of Rights* 39 (1932).

Mendelson, Wallace. "Book Review," 6 Hastings Constitutional Law Quarterly 437 (1978).

Miller, A. R. "Interview," 77 Harvard Law Record 2 (December, 1983).

Miller, A. S. "Book Review," Washington Post, November 13, 1977, § E at 5.

Monaghan, Henry. "The Constitution Goes to Harvard," 17 Harvard Civil Rights–Civil Liberties Law Review 117 (1978).

Morris, Richard. "We The People of the United States: The Bicentennial of a People's Revolution," 82 American Historical Review 1 (1977).

Oaks, D. H. "Judicial Activism," 7 Harvard Journal of Law & Public Policy 1 (1982).

Perry, Michael. "Book Review," 78 Columbia Law Review 685 (1978).

———. "Interpretivism, Freedom of Expression and Equal Protection," 43 Ohio State Law Journal 261 (1981).

Posner, R. A. "Toward an Economic Theory of Federal Jurisdiction," 6 Harvard Journal of Law & Public Policy 41 (1982).

Richardson, H. G. & Sayles, G. O. "Parliament and Great Councils in Medieval History," 77 Law Quarterly Review 212 (1961).

Shapiro, Martin. "American Federalism," in R. Collins, ed. *Constitutional Government in America* 359 (1981).

Storing, Herbert. "The 'Other' Federalist Papers: A Preliminary Sketch," 6 Political Science Reviewer 215 (1976).

———. "The Problems of Big Government," in R. A. Goldwin, ed. *A Nation of States* 65 (1961).

Ten Broek, Jacobus. "Use by the Supreme Court of Extrinsic Aids in Constitutional Construction: The Intent Theory of Constitutional Construction," 27 California Law Review 399 (1939).

Tucker, H. St. George. "The General Welfare," 8 Virginia Law Review 167 (1922).

Tushnet, Mark. "Book Review," 57 *Texas Law Review* 1295 (1979).

———. "Following the Rules Laid Down: A Critique of Interpretivism and Neutral Principles," 96 Harvard Law Review 781 (1983).

Van Alstyne, William. "The Second Death of Federalism," 89 Michigan Law Review 1709 (1985).

Van Tyne, C. J. "Sovereignty in the American Revolution: An Historical Sketch," 12 American Historical Review 529 (1907).

Wechsler, Herbert. "The Political Safeguards of Federalism: The Role of the States in the Composition and Selection of the National Government," 54 Columbia Law Review 543 (1954).

Miscellaneous

1 *Annals of Congress* (1798) (Washington, Gales & Seaton, 1834; print with running title "History of Congress").

2 *Annals of Congress* (1791) (Washington, Gales & Seaton, 1834).

Bacon, Matthew, *A New Abridgment of the Laws of England,* 8 vols. (London, 3d ed., 1768).

Barrett, E. L., Bruton, P. W., & Honnold, J. *Constitutional Law: Cases and Materials* (Brooklyn, Foundation Press, 2d ed., 1963).

Documentary History of the Constitution, 5 vols. (Washington, Department of State, 1901–1905).

Johnson, Samuel. *Dictionary of the English Language,* 2 vols. (London, 1765).

Journals of the Continental Congress. (Washington, Government Printing Office, 1904–1933).

Smith, P. H., ed. *Letters of the Delegates to Congress, 1774–1791,* 6 vols. (Washington, D.C., Government Printing Office, 1980).

Index of Cases

Trustees of Dartmouth College v. Woodward, 17 U.S. (4 Wheat.) 517 (1819): 130

Ullman v. United States, 350 U.S. 422 (1956): 11
United States v. Butler, 297 U.S. 1 (1936): 117
United States v. Champlin Refining Co., 341 U.S. 290 (1951): 128
United States v. Classic, 313 U.S. 299 (1941): 87, 106
United States v. Curtiss-Wright Export Corp., 299 U.S. 304 (1936): 44, 96
United States v. Darby, 312 U.S. 100 (1941): 77, 147
United States v. Dewitt, 76 U.S. (9 Wall.) 41 (1869): 144
United States v. Fisher, 6 U.S. (2 Cranch) 358 (1805): 198
United States v. E. C. Knight Co., 156 U.S. 1 (1895): 142, 153
United States v. Kahriger, 345 U.S. 22 (1953): 148
United States v. Pink, 315 U.S. 203 (1942): 44
United States v. Popper, 98 Fed. 423 (D.N.D. Cal. 1899): 146
United States v. Wheeler, 254 U.S. 281 (1920): 105

Van Horne's Lessee v. Dorrance, 2 U.S. (2 Dall.) 304 (C.C.D. Pa. 1795): 11, 184
Veazie v. Moore, 55 U.S. (14 How.) 568 (1852): 153

Ware v. Hylton, 3 U.S. (3 Dall.) 199 (1796): 25, 33, 45
Wayman v. Southard, 23 U.S. (10 Wheat.) 1 (1825): 13
Wickard v. Filburn, 317 U.S. 11 (1942): 148–50
Woodruff v. Parham, 75 U.S. (8 Wall.) 123 (1869): 136–37

Index